ENCOUNTERS WITH ANCIENT EGYPT

Ancient Egypt in Africa

D1527449

UCL

PRESS

Institute of Archaeology

Encounters with
Ancient
Egypt

Titles in the series

Ancient Egypt in Africa

Edited by

David O'Connor and Andrew Reid

PRESS

Institute of Archaeology

First published in Great Britain 2003 by UCL Press,
an imprint of Cavendish Publishing Limited, The Glass House,
Wharton Street, London WC1X 9PX, United Kingdom
Telephone: + 44 (0)20 7278 8000   Facsimile: + 44 (0)20 7278 8080
Email: info@uclpress.com
Website: www.uclpress.com

Published in the United States by Cavendish Publishing
c/o International Specialized Book Services,
5824 NE Hassalo Street, Portland,
Oregon 97213-3644, USA

Published in Australia by Cavendish Publishing (Australia) Pty Ltd
45 Beach Street, Coogee, NSW 2034, Australia
Telephone: + 61 (2)9664 0909   Facsimile: + 61 (2)9664 5420

© Institute of Archaeology, University College London   2003

British Library Cataloguing in Publication Data
O'Connor, D.
Ancient Egypt in Africa – (Encounters with ancient Egypt)
1 Egypt – Civilization 2 Africa – Civilization – Egyptian influences
3 Egypt – Relations – Africa 4 Africa – Relations – Egypt
I Title II Reid, A.
932

Library of Congress Cataloguing in Publication Data
Data available

ISBN 1-84472-000-4

1 3 5 7 9 10 8 6 4 2

Designed and typeset by Style Photosetting, Mayfield, East Sussex
Email: style@pavilion.co.uk

Printed and bound in Great Britain

Cover illustration: Left: eighteenth(?) Dynasty (1569–1315 BC) sandstone head of an Egyptian official. Provenance unknown (ht. ca. 15 cm; © Petrie Museum of Egyptian Archaeology, UC14640). Right: Terracotta head (ca. 13th century AD) said to have been kept at the Oni's palace, Ife, Nigeria (ht. ca. 25 cm; © Museum of Ife Antiquities, 2020 (79.R.10)).

Series Editor's Foreword

This series of eight books derives from the proceedings of a conference entitled 'Encounters with Ancient Egypt', held at the Institute of Archaeology, University College London (UCL) in December 2000. Since then, many new chapters have been especially commissioned for publication, and those papers originally provided for the conference and now selected for publication have been extensively revised and rewritten.

There are many noteworthy features of the books. One is the overall attempt to move the study of Ancient Egypt into the mainstream of recent advances in archaeological and anthropological practice and interpretation. This is a natural outcome of London University's Institute of Archaeology, one of the largest archaeology departments in the world, being the academic host. Drawing on the Institute's and other related resources within UCL, the volumes in the series reflect an extraordinary degree of collaboration between the series editor, individual volume editors, contributors and colleagues. The wide range of approaches to the study of the past, pursued in such a vibrant scholarly environment as UCL's, has encouraged the scholars writing in these volumes to consider their disciplinary interests from new perspectives. All the chapters presented here have benefited from wide-ranging discussion between experts from diverse academic disciplines, including art history, papyrology, anthropology, archaeology and Egyptology, and subsequent revision.

Egyptology has been rightly criticized for often being insular; the methodologies and conclusions of the discipline have been seen by others as having developed with little awareness of archaeologies elsewhere. The place and role of Ancient Egypt within African history, for example, has rarely been considered jointly by Egyptologists and Africanists. This collaboration provides a stimulating review of key issues and may well influence future ways of studying Egypt. Until now, questions have rarely been asked about the way Egyptians thought of their own past or about non-Egyptian peoples and places. Nor has the discipline of Egyptology explored, in any depth, the nature of its evidence, or the way contemporary cultures regarded Ancient Egypt. The books in this series address such topics.

Another exceptional feature of this series is the way that the books have been designed to interrelate with, inform and illuminate one another. Thus, the evidence of changing appropriations of Ancient Egypt over time, from the classical period to the modern Afrocentrist movement, features in several volumes. One volume explores the actual sources of knowledge about Ancient Egypt before the advent of 'scientific' archaeology, while another explores knowledge of Ancient Egypt after Napoleon Bonaparte's expeditions and the unearthing of Tutankhamun's tomb. The question asked throughout these volumes, however, is how far fascination and knowledge about Ancient Egypt have been based on sources of evidence rather than extraneous political or commercial concerns and interests.

As a result of this series, the study of Ancient Egypt will be significantly enriched and deepened. The importance of the Egypt of several thousands of years ago reaches far beyond the existence of its architectural monuments and extends to its unique role in the history of all human knowledge. Furthermore, the civilization of Ancient Egypt speaks to us with particular force in our own present and has an abiding place in the modern psyche.

As the first paragraph of this Foreword explains, the final stage of this venture began with the receipt and editing of some extensively revised, and in many cases new, chapters – some 95 in all – to be published simultaneously in eight volumes. What it does not mention is the speed with which the venture has been completed: the current UCL Press was officially launched in April 2003. That this series of books has been published to such a high standard of design, professional accuracy and attractiveness only four months later is incredible.

This alone speaks eloquently for the excellence of the staff of UCL Press – from its senior management to its typesetters and designers. Ruth Phillips (Marketing Director) stands out for her youthful and innovative marketing ideas and implementation of them, but most significant of all, at least from the Institute's perspective, is the contribution of Ruth Massey (Editor), who oversaw and supervized all details of the layout and production of the books, and also brought her critical mind to bear on the writing styles, and even the meaning, of their contents.

Individual chapter authors and academic volume editors, both from within UCL and in other institutions, added this demanding project to otherwise full workloads. Although it is somewhat invidious to single out particular individuals, Professor David O'Connor stands out as co-editor of two volumes and contributor of chapters to three despite his being based overseas. He, together with Professor John Tait – also an editor and multiple chapter author in these books – was one of the first to recognize my vision of the original conference as having the potential to inspire a uniquely important publishing project.

Within UCL's Institute of Archaeology, a long list of dedicated staff, academic, administrative and clerical, took over tasks for the Director and Kelly Vincent, his assistant as they wrestled with the preparation of this series. All of these staff, as well as several members of the student body, really deserve individual mention by name, but space does not allow this. However, the books could not have appeared without the particular support of five individuals: Lisa Daniel, who tirelessly secured copyright for over 500 images; Jo Dullaghan, who turned her hand to anything at any time to help out, from re-typing manuscripts to chasing overdue authors; Andrew Gardner, who tracked down obscure and incomplete references, and who took on the complex job of securing and producing correctly scanned images; Stuart Laidlaw, who not only miraculously produced publishable images of a pair of outdoor cats now in Holland and Jamaica, but in a number of cases created light where submitted images revealed only darkness; and Kelly Vincent, who did all of the above twice over, and more – and who is the main reason that publisher and Institute staff remained on excellent terms throughout.

Finally, a personal note, if I may. Never, ever contemplate producing eight complex, highly illustrated books within a four month period. If you *really must*, then make sure you have the above team behind you. Essentially, ensure that you have a partner such as Jane Hubert, who may well consider you to be mad but never questions the essential worth of the undertaking.

Peter Ucko
Institute of Archaeology
University College London
27 July 2003

Contents

Note: No attempt has been made to impose a standard chronology on authors; all dates before 712 BC are approximate. However, names of places, and royal and private names have been standardized.

Contributors

Bruce Bennett is Senior Lecturer in History at the University of Botswana. He has researched and published on two main areas: British political and church history in the 19th and 20th centuries, and the history of southern Africa, examining the interactions between missionaries, administrators and southern African populations in colonial encounters. He received his PhD from the University of Cambridge.

Martin Bernal is Professor Emeritus in the Department of Government and Near Eastern Studies at Cornell University. He works on the comparative politics of East Asia. He is best known as the author of *Black Athena* (1987), which re-examined the construction of the roots of classical civilisation. He received his PhD from the University of Cambridge.

David Edwards has held research and teaching posts at the University of Leicester where he is an Honorary Visiting Fellow. He has written extensively on the archaeology and history of the Sudan and Sudanic Africa. His publications include *The Archaeology of the Meroitic State: new perspectives on its social and political organisation* (1996), and he has just completed *The Nubian Past: an archaeology of the Sudan* (2003). He received his PhD from the University of Cambridge.

Bayo Folorunso is Reader in the Department of Archaeology and Anthropology, University of Ibadan, Nigeria. His publications include studies on comparative archaeology (ethnography and archaeology) in the historical period, on cultural resource management, and on agriculture and settlement among the Tiv of Nigeria (with S. O. Ogundele). He gained his PhD from the University of Paris-Sorbonne, France.

Dorian Fuller is Lecturer in Archaeobotany at the Institute of Archaeology, University College London. His recent field research has included surveys in Central Sudan, as well as excavations in India, Pakistan and Morocco, and he is now co-directing excavations near the Nile Fourth Cataract. Dorian is currently preparing for publication archaeological evidence from Lower Nubia, recovered by the Pennsylvania-Yale Expedition (1961–1963). He has already published several significant articles on archaeobotany. He received his PhD from the University of Cambridge.

Kevin MacDonald is Senior Lecturer in African Archaeology at the Institute of Archaeology, University College London. He has carried out major excavations in Mali and Mauritania, and his most recent book is *The Origins and Development of African Livestock* (2000, with Roger Blench). His research interests include the origins of complex societies in the Sahara, and the fate of the Holocene hunter-gatherers of West Africa. He received his PhD from the University of Cambridge.

Robert Morkot works as an independent scholar, combining teaching, principally for the University of Exeter, with writing and museum work. His publications include *The Black Pharaohs: Egypt's Nubian rulers* (2000), and 'Egypt and Nubia' (in Susan Alcock *et al.*, *Empires: perspectives from archaeology and history*, 2001). His postdoctorate studies were undertaken at the Humboldt University, Berlin and at University College London, where he received his PhD.

John North has been Professor of History at University College London since 1992. His research is on the pagan religion of Romans in the pre-Christian period and on the religious history of the Roman Empire. Published work includes *Pagan Priests* (1990, ed. with Mary Beard), *The Religions of Rome* (1998, with Mary Beard and Simon Price), and *Roman Religion* (2000). He is currently working on conceptions of polytheism and monotheism in relation to the Greco-Roman pagan tradition and to the competition between pagans and Christians. He received his D Phil from the University of Oxford.

David O'Connor is Lila Acheson Wallace Professor in Ancient Egyptian Art and Archaeology at the Institute of Fine Arts of New York University, Professor Emeritus of the University of Pennsylvania, and Curator Emeritus of the Egyptian Section of its Museum of Archaeology and Anthropology. He has excavated extensively in Nubia and at Malkata, Thebes and at Abydos in southern Egypt since 1967. His publications include *Ancient Egypt: a social history* (1983), *Ancient Nubia: Egypt's rival in Africa* (1993), *Ancient Egyptian Kingship* (1995, with David Silverman), and *Amenhotep III: perspectives on his reign* (1998, with Eric Cline). He received his PhD from the University of Cambridge.

Andrew Reid is Lecturer in East African Archaeology at the Institute of Archaeology, University College London. He has conducted research in Botswana, Tanzania and Uganda and has published extensively on complex societies in eastern and southern Africa, focusing particularly on the role of cattle. Recent publications include *Ditswa Mmung: the archaeology of Botswana* (1998, ed. with Paul Lane and Alinah Segobye). His current research is on the archaeology of the Buganda Kingdom. He received his PhD from the University of Cambridge.

Michael Rowlands is Professor of Material Culture in the Department of Anthropology, University College London. His recent publications include *Social Transformations in Archaeology* (1998, with Kristian Kristiansen) and 'Remembering to Forget: sublimation as sacrifice in war memorials' (1999, in Adrian Forty and Susanne Küchler, *The Art of Forgetting*). His current research includes a comparison of cultural heritage and national identities in Mali and Cameroon, and the study of innovation and change in general. He received his PhD from the University of London.

David Wengrow is a Junior Research Fellow at Christ Church, University of Oxford. His research addresses the nature of early social transformations in Egypt and Iraq, and the role of the remote past in the formation of modern political identities. Recent publications include 'The Evolution of Simplicity: aesthetic labour and social change in the Neolithic Near East' (*World Archaeology* 33, 2001) and 'Forgetting the *Ancien Régime*: republican values and the study of the ancient Orient' (in D. Jeffreys, *Views of Ancient Egypt since Napoleon Bonaparte: imperialism, colonialism and modern appropriations*, 2003, in the *Encounters with Ancient Egypt* series, UCL Press). He received his D Phil from the University of Oxford.

List of Figures

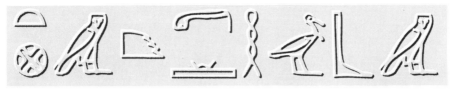

INTRODUCTION – LOCATING ANCIENT EGYPT IN AFRICA: MODERN THEORIES, PAST REALITIES

David O'Connor and Andrew Reid

This book moves the theme of Ancient Egypt in Africa back to where it belongs, amongst the leading challenges and opportunities facing the historians and archaeologists of Africa today. By the end of the 20th century most researchers had lost interest in a once much discussed issue – whether there had been significant interaction between Ancient Egypt and the rest of Africa – because expanding archaeological knowledge was revealing how important independent internal dynamics had been in the shaping of Africa's varied cultures and civilizations. The chapters in this book comprise a major contribution to the intellectual history of archaeology by demonstrating in detail how earlier theories about Ancient Egypt in Africa were shaped and distorted by racial prejudice, colonial and imperial interests and now out-moded scholarly ideas. But these same chapters re-affirm that at the heart of the debate were questions of genuinely great interest and significance, which deserve to be the focus of renewed and detailed research.

To state these questions in an extreme, almost simplistic form: was Ancient Egypt to some, or even much, of Africa the source of sophisticated culture as Greece was to much of Europe, or, did Egyptian civilization incorporate fundamental African concepts markedly different from those dominant in the ancient Near East and the Mediterranean lands? In the course of this volume contributors note that there is material, both recovered and recoverable, that could well provide answers to these questions.

Re-opening the debate about Ancient Egypt in Africa in ways embracing all Africanists, instead of already committed groups of scholars such as the Afrocentrists, would also be a powerful contribution to lessening the parochialism affecting the study of early Africa. North Africa is typically studied with little reference to sub-Saharan Africa, and vice versa; within the former, Egypt is typically discussed with little reference to other North African cultures, including those with contacts extending deep into the Sahara and beyond, while within sub-Saharan Africa there is a natural tendency to focus on the demanding study of specific (often in themselves vast) regions without reference to 'commonalities' in thought, symbol and action that might link them together. However, as Rowlands (Chapter 4) and others show, much can be done along these lines.

This book is also an absorbing sociological study in documenting the widely ranging attitudes modern Africans have to Ancient Egypt. Interest is strong in some communities, but many African Christians and Muslims consider Ancient Egypt in very negative terms; in the Bible and the Quran "Egypt of the pharaohs" is the epitome of tyranny and obdurate paganism. In contrast, empathy with the Israelites, and similar early Near Eastern societies, can be strong for reasons well beyond religious affiliation. As Bennett (Chapter 8: 109) wryly observes, southern African peoples "recognized in the world of the early Old Testament a pastoral society more familiar and comprehensible to them than to the missionaries" who had introduced them to it in the first place!

In order to provide an introduction to the common fundamental themes that underlie the extraordinarily rich and diverse chapters comprising the book, the co-editors have divided this introduction into two. The first section explores the ideological, political and economic dimensions of the debates about Ancient Egypt in Africa carried on by European, American and African scholars and others in the 19th and 20th centuries, and shows how they were very much a part of the modern history of Africa itself. This demonstrates that the many archaeologies of Africa today are independent ones, reflecting the internal ideological and societal dynamics of the varied cultures that produced them; but that the question of contacts with and perhaps influence from Ancient Egypt is one that should remain open and challenging.

The second section focuses upon what we know about Egypt's early contacts and influence in other parts of Africa; the potential for further research; and the extent to which one can characterize Egyptian civilization itself as in some significant way African.

It is hoped that the net effect of this introductory chapter is to persuade readers, and especially those developing careers in both Egyptology and African archaeology, anthropology and history, that the topic of Ancient Egypt in Africa provides opportunities for exciting and innovative research in the field, library and laboratory. This book (excepting biological issues) is the most comprehensive introduction to Ancient Egypt in Africa that can be provided today; 25 years from now, a book on the same topic should belong to an unbelievably richer world of both knowledge and theory.

Modern theories

In addressing the issue of Ancient Egypt in Africa this book has adopted what may seem a rather unusual structure of first tackling 19th and 20th century production of knowledge before examining the actual evidence for ancient Egyptian presence. This structure emphasizes the manner in which preconception and assumption have consistently led evidence towards particular conclusions. The concern of this book is essentially to consider the location of Ancient Egypt within broader cultural worlds. On the face of it this appears to be a rather simple issue to resolve: geographically Egypt is indisputably situated in Africa. Yet this statement immediately throws up the question, What exactly is Africa? and the logical corollary, What is African? The geographical division of the world into continents is a consequence of European geographical traditions and its fixation with categorization. Mazrui (1986) for instance presents a provocative case for redrawing the continent's boundaries to include the Arabian peninsula. On the other hand many people, from Africa and beyond, consider Africa properly to equate with 'black' or sub-Saharan Africa. Not surprisingly, the definition of what is African, and what it is to be African, is still more complex. As Mudimbe (1988) has discussed at length, these are constructs which have been generated by European discourse and their definition serves the function of helping to define European worlds in contradistinction to Africa and the other continents. 'African' has been important in western terminology because it helps to define the opposite of 'European', with implicit notions of civilization and sophistication equally important to this definition. This dichotomy will be seen to have been central to the very different issues of locating Ancient Egypt and of locating Africa (see Wengrow, Chapter 9). Hence, the dominant perception of Ancient Egypt, particularly in western thought, has long been '*in* Africa, but not *of* Africa'. In this volume, unless otherwise stated, the term 'African' will be used to refer to people and objects directly from the African continent (as conventionally defined) with Egypt forming the north-eastern border.

Popular interest in Ancient Egypt's relationship with Africa has grown since the late 1980s, and is particularly associated with the growth of Afrocentrism in the USA. This growth was in part related to the publishing of Bernal's *Black Athena* (1987; and see Chapter 2), which further encouraged scholars in a number of disciplines to reconsider the academic production of knowledge as an element of western imperialism. African archaeologists, especially those working outside the north-eastern corner of the continent, have been reluctant to re-awaken interest in Ancient Egypt. This is largely because the topic, as many of the chapters of this book demonstrate, has an embarrassing history of supposition and invention which African archaeologists, rather ironically, considered to be safely buried, having been suitably dealt with in the past. In this volume re-excavation and examination of these old theories has been a difficult but ultimately enlightening experience.

Almost no archaeological evidence is currently considered to indicate ancient Egyptian contact with the rest of the African continent, excepting the Middle Nile. This rather bald statement does not mean that researchers should not try to look for shared features or 'commonalities' between Ancient Egypt and the rest of Africa; as this introduction and Rowlands (Chapter 4) encouragingly show, there are ways in which links may be seen. Potential connections are unlikely to be represented in material culture, but rather may be looked for in shared ideas and beliefs. Before moving on to such innovations, it is first important to discuss why the notion of ancient Egyptian contacts with the rest of Africa proved so popular in the past, despite the lack of material evidence. Ultimately, in the absence of solid evidence, ideology, or more correctly, ideologies, have served to provide the mortar which holds many of these theories together. Ideologies, it should be noted, can be positive as well as negative and Rowlands calls for the adoption of positive ideologies in generating dialogues towards meaningful contemporary African development, an outcome upon which all of the contributors can readily agree.

Locating Ancient Egypt has therefore been an exercise in ideological definition, for the most part serving less to understand Ancient Egypt itself and more to define the position of the commentator. It is in this very important context that Bernal's and North's contributions (Chapters 2 and 3), which may at first glance seem unrelated to the theme of Ancient Egypt in Africa, become central to the rest of the book. These chapters ably demonstrate that in defining Ancient Egypt's cultural location in relation to European civilization, via Ancient Greece, an implicit assumption was being made regarding Ancient Egypt's relationship with the rest of Africa. These purported relationships therefore served, and indeed in contemporary ideologies continue to serve, the purpose of constructing and ordering the world. Hence, for Europeans colonizing the African continent, locating Ancient Egypt somewhere in the Near East ordered their own relationship with Africans. Equally for Afrocentrists, locating Ancient Egypt firmly within Africa cements their belief in the significance of the African continent.

For obvious reasons, European perceptions of Ancient Egypt have had a profound influence on the African continent. As several of the chapters in this book demonstrate (Reid, Chapter 5; Folorunso, Chapter 6; Bennett, Chapter 8; Wengrow, Chapter 9), European explorers, missionaries and administrators across the length and breadth of the continent used Ancient Egypt as a counterpoint to African societies in rationalizing and legitimizing their own position of dominance. This ideological perspective was not honed in the heat of colonial expansion, but was founded on centuries of European exploitation of African slaves. Whilst Christian-based perspectives, reliant on the single human origin laid out in the Book of Genesis, saw Africans as peoples who had strayed and lost their belief in God, suffering as a direct result, secular opinions developed during the 18th century increasingly argued for separate human origins, effectively making African populations sub-human or non-human (Sanders 1969). This dichotomy helps to explain some of the differences in opinion expressed by secular and religious European observers in the late 19th century. In particular, Bennett (Chapter 8) has noted Livingstone's persistent recognition of African intellectual capabilities. Unfortunately, such views were very much in the minority. Instead most writers held viewpoints based on the subdivision of the world's populations into races and the social evolutionary ranking of these races into an order of sophistication. This is graphically depicted in Figure 1:1, an early 20th century manifestation of these ideas.

These ideologies helped to rationalize the European acquisition of the African continent. Europeans felt that they had a moral imperative to take control of populations who were believed to be incapable of improvement by themselves. Evidence of this was found in archaeological material across the continent. In late 19th century Africa, the vast majority of Europeans simply could not believe that Africans were capable of socio-political and cultural innovation, and drew support for this from the various archaeological manifestations they encountered on the African continent, which 'proved' the presence of non-African civilizations and emphasized the deterioration in society since these civilizations passed into the hands of Africans: at Great Zimbabwe, the proposed later African phase was referred to as "Bantu degeneracy" and "the Age of Decadence" (Hall 1905). These theories of past non-African civilizations were equally important in generating precedents for colonialism

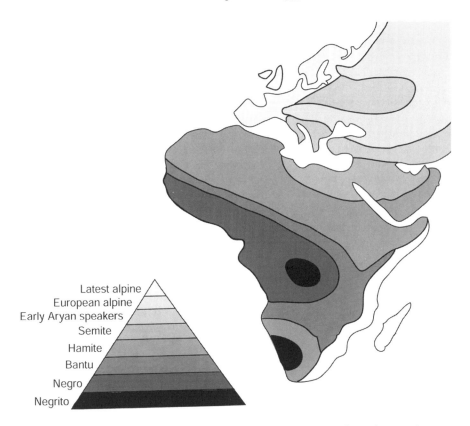

Figure 1:1 Detail of Taylor's racial stratification based on physical anthropology and environment (after Taylor 1927: 211).

on the African continent, most infamously prosecuted in the case of Great Zimbabwe in what was then Rhodesia (Garlake 1982; Hall 1990, 1995; Mahachi and Ndoro 1997).

It is important to understand the nature of the early contacts between Europeans and Africans and their ideological underpinnings because they frame much of the subsequent development of ideas. In these encounters Ancient Egypt was by no means the only 'non-African' civilization which was pictured developing colonies on the African continent, rather it was seen as one of several Mediterranean and Near Eastern societies which had left their imprint. However, the significant developments and discoveries of Egyptology, made in the 19th century, together with its direct biblical connections, served to make Ancient Egypt a popular and well-known reference point for European writers. Although archaeologists realized at an early stage that there was virtually no evidence for Ancient Egypt in the greater part of the African continent, popular ideas persevered and Ancient Egypt continued to dominate academic understanding of the archaeological record. Archaeologists interpreted their material in relation to Ancient Egypt and other non-African civilizations, their interpretations clearly dominated by Egypt's presence. Thus, long after it was recognized that there was no evidence of direct contact with Ancient

Egypt, it was still thought that most elements of innovation, such as pottery, metallurgy, domesticated plants and animals and systems of kingship, had spread up the Nile Valley (see Reid, Chapter 5 and Folorunso, Chapter 6). Diffusion was of course an extremely important explanation in late 19th and early 20th century archaeology and in broader thought. In the absence of evidence for migrations, diffusion was to many the obvious means by which Africa had been encultured. In Europe, much of the dating prior to the advent of the radiocarbon dating technique was ultimately reliant on proving claims of cultural connections to Egypt with its pharaonic chronologies. Diffusion can often become a much less precise concept than migration and evidence for diffusion can concomitantly be more ambiguous.

The generation of European historical knowledge of Africa was an important element in the construction and maintenance of European authority and power over Africa, processes which have also been noted in other parts of the world (e.g. Mudimbe 1988; Said 1978). As Zachernuk (1994: 430) puts it, "because Europeans claimed to understand the world they could claim the world". However, as a number of the chapters in this volume demonstrate, there was not a single dominant European viewpoint, and there was also significant African development of the discourse, albeit contributions that were more often than not ignored by Europeans. Furthermore, there was not a simple European–African dichotomy, but there were European and African traditions which by no means necessarily related to conventional unitary notions of oppressor and oppressed. On the European side the difference in perspective between missionary and secular opinion on African origins has already been noted (see also Reid, Chapter 5 and Bennett, Chapter 8). A further example of discord was the intervention of the British Association for the Advancement of Science into the debate on the origins of Great Zimbabwe, sending first Randall-MacIver and then Caton-Thompson to investigate. Their research was a result of the general scepticism held in British academic circles of the southern African colonial insistence on the exotic origins of Great Zimbabwe. Both archaeologists argued for an African origin. Caton-Thompson's public presentation in Pretoria in 1929, in which she concluded that Great Zimbabwe was quite clearly built entirely by Africans, ended in uproar; she was roundly denounced by public and academics alike. Raymond Dart, respected for his studious work on australopithecines, stormed from the room, having "delivered remarks in a tone of awe-inspiring violence" and "curiously unscientific indignation" (*Cape Times*, 3 August 1929, quoted by Hall 1990: 63). Despite Caton-Thompson's conclusion, generally southern African colonists rejected the idea of the African origins of Great Zimbabwe (Hall 1995), a rejection which can still be found in Zimbabwe today (Mahachi and Ndoro 1997). These various positions indicate differences of opinion and demonstrate aspects of the gulf which rapidly developed between mother state and colony.

African responses to the notion of exotic origins varied. Whilst the contributors to this volume have generally been concerned to dismiss such ideas, African populations were clearly able to make positive use of exotic origins as an ideological tool. Within the relative confines of southern Nigerian history, Zachernuk (1994) has highlighted four separate initiatives in which the 'Hamitic Hypothesis' was positively used to advance group interests. Rather than colonial dupes, apeing their superiors, Zachernuk argues that these were groups pursuing their goals by using the available colonial and intellectual structures to further their own interests. For this Nigerian colonial intelligentsia, resorting to the concept of exotic origins was not only an effective means of disarming European cultural power, it was also an important means of establishing an elite history which strengthened their position as against other African actors, such as colonial chiefs.

A further example of the adoption of colonial ideologies has structured the conflict in Rwanda. The Tusi pastoralist minority, who were politically advantaged at the time of European takeover, were regarded as remnants of a Hamitic population which had migrated into the Great Lakes (see Reid 2001). Having dominated the precolonial system and with this purported link with superior migrant populations, colonial policies of indirect rule (German and Belgian) led to the isolation and non-inclusion of the Hutu agricultural majority. Before the Hutu insurrection in the early 1960s, Tusi used their association with the 'Hamitic Hypothesis' to claim legitimacy as what Kopytoff (1987: 52–61) has termed "latecomers". The notion of latecomers was a widespread political tool in precolonial Africa, used to invert the more traditional hierarchies, based on "firstcomers", and undermine their ritual and political claims regarding the ownership of land and resources.

In showing how eurocentric perspectives endowed the term with negative values, the above discussion of ideologies indicates the significance of the term 'African'. As a consequence all things and all people 'African' were invested with these negative values in western thought. Elements of the process by which this was done, and in particular the significance which was given to archaeology and culture in this process, is touched upon by a number of chapters in this volume. Hence the importance of examining African origins and authorship is to expose these past cultural impositions, and, more importantly, to endow people of African origin with positive images of their own heritage and its significance.

The most obvious development addressing these ideological imbalances, which also happens to be an example of people of African origin drawing positively from major influxes of supposedly superior populations, is Afrocentrism. Afrocentrism is an approach that explicitly sets out to redress the negative images which have often been developed of Africans and to promote positive constructions of African heritage. Under these very broad objectives, there are a number of different forms of Afrocentrism. Of most relevance to discussions here is what Adams (1993) has called "Nile-Valley Afrocentrism", particularly concerned with Egyptian and to a lesser extent Nubian civilization. Of course, in Afrocentric accounts migrants from Egypt were not seen as exotic, being themselves African and coming from the black civilization of Egypt (e.g. Diop 1974, 1987). This movement has drawn considerable strength from the writings of Cheikh Anta Diop (MacDonald, Chapter 7). As already mentioned, the growth of Afrocentrism in America in the 1980s probably played a major role in inspiring and even demanding the kinds of critique that are attempted in this volume. Afrocentrism has helped to focus public attention on the manner in which knowledge has been constructed and to reconsider the basis upon which key assumptions have been made. In particular this focus has ensured that active African contributions have not been overlooked through ideologically inspired oversight, or outright hostility towards Africans and their intellectual capabilities. A number of the contributions in the following pages demonstrate how Europeans, especially from the late 19th century onwards, actively used eurocentric concepts of the relative location of Ancient Egypt, on the one hand, and Africa, on the other, to deny Africans any link to Egyptian civilization. Afrocentrism has also endeavoured to promote a renewed sense of cultural pride within education, particularly in Afro-American communities, initiatives which have been a good deal more effective than more conventional academic disciplines, but often at the expense of ignoring all African developments other than Ancient Egypt.

Afrocentrism does, however, have its weaknesses, one of which is the maturity to develop self-critique (Roth 2001). Many of the sources upon which writers such as Diop relied were at least out of date and at worst downright inappropriate even by the 1950s, Frobenius being a notable example (Folorunso, Chapter 6; Howe 1998). This may in part explain the hyper-diffusionism inherent in Afrocentric approaches, in the most extreme cases arguing that all global cultural forms are the result of direct diffusion from a black Egypt. To a great extent, Diop's understanding of the development of sub-Saharan Africa retained the migratory paradigm but simply changed the colour of the migrants. Whilst this has the very positive outcome of connecting Africans with Ancient Egypt, it still serves to argue that, subsequent to the influx of Egyptian-derived innovation, sub-Saharan Africa has been without history, unable to change and indeed culturally stagnating. It is very important to recognize that Diop himself did not access much of the startling research that had recently emerged concerning the later archaeology of the African continent. In West Africa, which most closely preoccupied Diop, innovative new research emphasizing independent West African initiatives only really emerges in the 1970s (Grébenart 1988; McIntosh and McIntosh 1980, 1993; Roset 1987; Shaw 1977). Perhaps this absence of archaeological detail on the part of Afrocentrists, together with the absence of an explicit critique of eurocentric approaches on the part of African archaeologists, explains why so little common ground has been found between the two. For African archaeologists, the need to promote African esteem by emphasizing connections with Egypt does not arise because, albeit only in recent decades, African archaeology has been able to demonstrate a bewildering range of independent political developments across the length and breadth of the continent (e.g. Connah 1987, 1998; McIntosh 1999a; Shaw *et al.* 1993). It is in part due to these developments that the new and rapidly increasing number of archaeologists of African descent emerging on the continent have largely avoided Afrocentrism and any notion of exotic origins for regional precolonial political and technological developments. Instead they are beginning to develop an understanding of independent regional processes of political development and cultural change (e.g. Abungu 1998; Andah 1987; Kusimba 1999; Oyelaran 1998; Pikirayi 1993; Pwiti 1996; Togola 1996).

This development of Africans generating their own archaeology and history is entirely appropriate and wholeheartedly supported by the contributors to this volume. A consequence of the focus on independent processes of innovation and of the development of archaeological infrastructures in African nations is, however, the emergence of nationalist archaeologies. This development is encouraged by the desire to promote national unity in many countries. It is also a consequence of archaeologists developing their discipline within the separate confines of each state, which means that peer review is effectively restricted to the small number of archaeologists in each country. Hence, a potential problem which may develop in the future is that archaeologies of precolonial societies will begin to replicate national boundaries, which were arbitrarily imposed on Africa by the Treaty of Berlin in 1885 and which bear no resemblance to actual cultural boundaries. Rowlands (Chapter 4) considers that processes of localization were already instigated during the colonial era by colonial ethnographies, histories and archaeologies, which focused on 'differences' and the isolation of 'ethnic groups'. The legacy of these colonial studies is still evident. Recent anthropology has ably demonstrated the artificial and largely eurocentric nature of these constructs and their role in defining and regulating colonial society. Despite significant instances of ethnoarchaeology (e.g. Hodder 1982) agreeing with this, the anthropological critique has had little impact on African archaeology and, more worryingly, upon general society. Hence 'tribal' models of local government are based on colonial policies of indirect rule (Mamdani 1996). Additionally, legislatures in many African countries are based on three sources: National Law, developed since Independence and therefore still very restricted in scope; Colonial Law, based in turn on the statutes of the mother state; and Tribal or Traditional Law, being based almost entirely on colonial and neocolonial ethnographies (see for example the S. M. Otieno case in Kenya – Cohen and Odhiambo 1992). It is in the context of a self-critically aware discipline, conscious of its previous inappropriate manipulation of the past, and of its responsibilities towards the development of the African continent in the future, that Rowlands explores the possibility of 'commonalities' across the African continent incorporating and including Ancient Egypt. This innovative endeavour, it should be stressed, does not look back to the blighted historiographical past but instead looks to the future development of disciplines concerned with the African past from the position of a critically aware and mature understanding of the context and significance of the generation of knowledge. It is from this perspective that Rowlands' intriguing chapter should be judged. This approach enables a re-inspection of some of the themes drawn on by writers such as Frobenius and Frankfort without being infected by the open or implicit racism within their writing.

In essence, then, this volume, in locating Ancient Egypt in Africa, is clearing away the encumbrances and false connections of the past which were perceived to link Ancient Egypt with Africa, and paves the way for future research to re-explore potential links and associations, and indeed disassociations. This is done most boldly by Rowlands (Chapter 4), but new directions are also suggested by Wengrow (Chapter 9), Edwards (Chapter 10), Morkot (Chapter 11) and Fuller (Chapter 12) in establishing a more mature understanding of the politics of the Middle Nile, heavily influenced by Ancient Egypt (whoever the Ancient Egyptians were): culturally independent, but actively incorporating ancient Egyptian items into their own distinct political and cultural forms.

It is also important to recognize that there have been other African interest groups besides archaeologists who have been concerned to disassociate Africa from Ancient Egypt. It is intriguing that certain contemporary Christian preachers in West Africa (Folorunso, Chapter 6) and in southern Africa (Bennett, Chapter 8), with their very different histories of development, should both castigate their congregations with the warning against sin: 'Do not go back to Egypt.' Clearly, for many Christian populations Ancient Egypt is not an object of admiration but a warning against sin, greed and tyranny. The persecution of the Israelites and the identification many African populations have felt with their suffering, not to mention their status as chosen people, means that for many Africans Ancient Egypt remains an unlikely source of admiration or inspiration.

It is also worth considering one final African viewpoint on Ancient Egypt, which may caution the broader investigation of Ancient Egypt in Africa. Julius Nyerere, first president of Tanzania, and widely acknowledged as one of Africa's leading statesmen, used Ancient Egypt as a metaphor for inappropriate social development in creating his vision of a socialist future. Nyerere's *Ujamaa* villagization policy, in which Tanzanians were to recreate a perceived precolonial golden age where egalitarian villages made communal decisions and took community action, failed not least because many Tanzanian societies had never lived in sedentary villages. For Nyerere (1973: 59–60):

> the pyramids of Egypt, and the Roman roads of Europe, were material developments which still excite our amazement. But because they were only buildings, and the people of these times were not developed, the empires, and the cultures, of which they were a part have long ago collapsed. The Egyptian culture of those days – with all the knowledge and wisdom which it possessed – was quickly overthrown by foreign invasion, because it was a culture of a few; the masses were slaves who simply suffered.

While this version of Egyptian history may be somewhat dubious and may ultimately have its roots in missionary education, Nyerere's next point is one which archaeologists, historians and others must note: "it is doubtful whether either the Egyptian pyramids or the Roman roads have made the slightest difference to the histories of the countries concerned, or the lives of their peoples" (Nyerere 1973: 60). If the direction of the present volume is ultimately to prove successful, academics must find more appropriate means of communicating the significance of their work, beyond the confines of their own disciplines, to enhance life in broader society.

Ancient realities

In the world of post-modernism, to speak of any kind of 'realities' is perhaps dangerous; but the archaeological and textual evidence relevant to ancient civilizations and the contacts between them has a materiality that provides the bedrock of any discussion. Equally important, however, is that it be recognized that this evidence often has an inherent ambiguity, a capacity to support two or more alternative interpretations of more or less equal plausibility. This particular reality is one often not sufficiently allowed for in discussions about Ancient Egypt in Africa. This in turn can obscure the possibility that the ambiguity can sometimes be avoided or removed by a more sustained analysis of the evidence itself, by comparison with other data, or by the recovery of new evidence that confirms one of the several possible interpretations.

The focus here is twofold. First, to review and evaluate available evidence on prehistoric (5000–3000 BC) and historic (3000 BC–500 AD) Egypt's contacts with, and influence upon, other parts of Africa. Second, to consider whether some of the characteristic concepts, practices and material products of the Ancient Egyptians might display a 'commonality' with those current in other African regions, whether in the past, or in recent and even contemporary times. In other words, did Ancient Egypt have an African dimension – major cultural features or forms which it shared with other parts of Africa, and which were distinct from the primary cultural features and forms of the early Near Eastern, Mediterranean and European worlds?

This discussion of Egypt's African dimension does not include consideration as to whether Ancient Egyptians were "black" or, to be more accurate, African in their genetic composition. It seems very likely, however, that the majority of the Ancient Egyptians will eventually be shown to be genetically closely related to some populations in other parts of Africa. Geographically, Egypt is part of Africa; genetically different groups can and do occupy different, and even the same, parts of any continent, but geographical propinquity often does promote a high degree of genetic similarity over quite vast areas.

Bernal (Chapter 2) and North (Chapter 3) debate the issue of Egypt's influence upon the development of Greek civilization. Bernal argues for influences of fundamental importance from Egypt, the Levant and the Balkans, along with equally important factors internal to Greek society; and considers Egyptian influence already very strong from ca. 2000 BC onwards. North welcomes healthy and even radical challenges to accepted ways of thinking about ancient history, but also argues that Bernal's fundamental proposition – "we should look to see the balance of inherited belief about the past and take that as the best available indication of the truth" – "is the precise opposite of the methods by which the past is studied today". Bernal (2001: 29) also attributes colour to the Ancient Egyptians, remarking that, for example, they would not have been 'white' by the standards of 19th and 20th century Britain or America, prompting North to point out that while this links them to "modern groups who seek to confirm their status through the association" it also involves the un-historical concept that origins alone define and determine all subsequent developments.

This ongoing debate about Egypt and Greece is of interest in itself, but also has relevance to the overall theme of this book. First, insofar as ancient Egyptian civilization is African to a significant degree, *and* had a substantial influence on Greek culture, then Africa can be said to have played a part (as yet, not fully defined) in the development of European civilization in general. Whether that influence occurred as early as Bernal argues, or belongs to a period of intensified relations after 700 BC, Egyptian influence upon Greek sculpture, architecture and, in less clear ways, politics and religion is a generally recognized phenomenon. Not all, however, would agree: Sarah Morris, for example, has raised serious doubts on the art-historical side (Bernal 2001: 300–301; and see Tanner 2003).

Second, Bernal's (and others') ideas about the influence of Egypt on Greece provide a revealing methodological complement to theories about the spread of ancient Egyptian influence, and even of Ancient Egyptians, into sub-Saharan Africa. An important example of the latter is provided by Cheikh Anta Diop (MacDonald, Chapter 7). In fact, the approaches are similar, and could be combined into a grand theory with Ancient Egypt central (although not necessarily uniquely so) to civilization in both Greece and Africa. However, there is another significant similarity. While Greece and Egypt were certainly in contact before 700 BC (Minoans and Mycenaeans were visiting Egypt by 1500 BC), the historical, archaeological and linguistic evidence cited by Bernal for a *formative* impact of Egypt on Greece in the second millennium BC is considered by many scholars to be much too thin to support the thesis (e.g. Lefkowitz and Rogers 1996; Bernal's response 2001). Similarly, as the chapters by Reid (Chapter 5), Folorunso (Chapter 6) and MacDonald (Chapter 7) make clear, the evidence used to affirm Egyptian influence on Africa, at least after 4000 BC, is so insubstantial as to be negligible; yet all three urge renewed, if more self-critical, attention to the issue of Ancient Egypt in Africa. And indeed the case of Bernal's provocative theories indicates that fresh thinking can be stimulated. For example, Yurco (1996: 73, 83) does not accept Bernal's more extreme ideas; however, he thinks Bernal rightly identifies an Egyptian Levantine 'empire' in the twelfth Dynasty (dated to 1938–1755 BC), although others would still disagree with this. Yurco also provides a historically based rationalization (on a different tack from Bernal's) as to why Herodotus found the Colchians (east of the Black Sea) similar in appearance and custom to the Egyptians.

Turning now to the extent of Egypt's contacts with other parts of Africa, the focus is first on the historic period (3000 BC–500 AD), because prehistoric contacts involve a different set of issues, which are best treated separately. Egypt's principal African contacts were with Nubia, Punt and Libya. The locations of Punt and Libya are not yet established, so they and their inhabitants are therefore known only from Egyptian textual and art-historical sources (O'Connor and Quirke 2003a, b). However, Nubia's location and its archaeology are richly, if still very incompletely, documented (Adams 1977; O'Connor 1993; Trigger 1976a), and culturally distinctive burials of Nubians have been found in Egypt (Bietak 1968; Friedman 2001; Junker 1920). Moreover, a Nubian Dynasty (the twenty-fifth) controlled both countries from 715 to 657 BC, its presence in Egypt well attested by monuments and inscriptions (Welsby 1996). From early times, Egypt called Nubia *Ta Nehesy* ("Land of the Nubian") or *Ta Zety* ("Land of the Bow", a favourite Nubian weapon). Later, it was also called Kush.

The Libyans (Hölscher 1937; Leahy 1985, 1990) were originally called the Tjehenu and Tjemehu, appellations surviving into Roman times (Snape 2003). After 1500 BC, other groups of Libyans are named, including the Rebu or Libu, from whom the Greek and modern name of Libya is derived. Cyrenaica was most likely the Libyans' homeland, supporting the nomadic lifestyle which, according to Egyptian sources, characterized them. However, despite much archaeological work on neolithic and Greco-Roman remains, the material culture of the Bronze Age and early Iron Age Libyans (3000 BC–500 BC) has never been identified. Libyans also settled in Egypt's western Delta during the earlier first millennium BC (Kitchen 1973: 345–347, 366–368, 371–372, 376–377), but their presumably (to some degree) distinctive remains have never been found in this archaeologically poorly explored region.

Punt, like Nubia and Libya, was known to Egypt in the Old Kingdom (2575–2150 BC) and even before. Earlier scholars located it in Somalia (a minority have always preferred Arabia), but Kitchen's case (1971, 1973) for a location along the coast from roughly Port Sudan to northern Eritrea is now accepted by most (although see Meeks 2003; O'Connor and Quirke 2003b). A few still argue for Somalia, for the rhinoceros and giraffe (Meeks 2003: Figures 4:2, 4:3) apparently found in Punt (Naville n.d.: 11 ff, pls. 69 ff) would not be found near the coast further north. However, Kitchen (1993: 604) has suggested that Punt extended far inland, to the necessary savannah lands, as far as "Kassala, and Er-Roseires southward"; but he may have mistakenly identified a depiction of Irem, an inland Nubian region, as Punt (O'Connor 1987).

Despite the relatively precise locations suggested, Punt has not been located on the ground. We can have some confidence that it will be discovered, however, because Egyptian expeditions left inscriptions and even structures there (Kitchen 1993: 596), remains of which are likely to have survived. An archaeological culture of 2300–1700 BC at Mahal Taglinos on the Gash River (eastern Sudan) has been identified with "the inland gateway to the Land of Punt" (Fattovich 1991: 46), but this remains unverified.

Numerous representations of Nubians, Puntites and Libyans occur in Egyptian art (Meeks 2003; O'Connor and Quirke 2003b), but only in the Nubian case can they be cross-checked against an indigenous archaeology. Such representations become standardized and stereotypical, and it is never certain when they represent contemporary reality. However, significant changes in representation are introduced over time and, at least initially, they might be thought to have been based on direct observation. Three types of African are consistently differentiated from each other – and from Egyptians – in skin colour, treatment of the hair (and sometimes beard), and costume and ornamentation. Puntite and Egyptian males are assigned similarly reddish skins, but Nubians typically have darker ones, and Libyans at most periods have light coloured, yellowish skin. Initially (ca. 2400 BC), Nubians and Puntites may have been shown as fairly similar in appearance and dress (short linen kilts – Borchardt 1913), but by ca. 1400 BC they are distinctly different.

By 2000 BC Nubians wore loincloths of leather, sometimes decorated with beadwork patterns attested in contemporary Nubian graves as well. Subsequently, in the New Kingdom (1539–1075 BC) many continued to be similarly dressed, but others wore linen kilts or even fully representative Egyptian dress; in both cases, skin colours and hair treatment remain distinctively Nubian (O'Connor and Quirke 2003b). The distinction, as can be seen in Figure 1:2, may be between the by now heavily Egyptianized Nubians of northern and central Nubia (archaeologically attested; see e.g. Säve-Söderbergh and Troy 1991), and opponents, prisoners of war and 'tribute-bearers' from still independent southern Nubia (O'Connor 1993: 65–66). During the same period, Puntites display hairstyles different from the Nubian: most wore long hair, with a head band and fillet; other Puntite hair is cap-like and perhaps a mark of elite status. Short linen kilts appear typical, and some, possibly elite, wore shirts as well (see Säve-Söderbergh 1946: 8–30).

Libyans are from the outset more flamboyant in appearance. In the Old Kingdom, males are largely nude, but with long, flowing hair, decorated leather bands crossing on the chest, a necklet with long pendant, and a 'phallus sheath', an uncertain identification since some women wear it also, outside a tight kilt (Borchardt 1913; Ucko 1969: 48). By the New Kingdom, significant change is evident. Libyans wear their hair shorter and with side-locks, and most males wear a leather cloak, knotted over one shoulder and open in front (O'Connor and Quirke 2003b). Many Libyans still have the 'phallus sheath', and others wear kilts (O'Connor 1990: 47–55). Archaic features (crossed chest bands, long hair) are rare and associated with rulers. Perhaps this was conscious archaism by Egyptian artists or by Libyan rulers, deliberately reviving an iconographically early form of appearance as a mark of prestige (O'Connor 1990: 68–74; Tait 2003b: 4).

The geographical circumstances, strategic significance and economic value of Nubia, Punt and Libya varied substantially and so, as a result, did Egyptian policies

Figure 1:2 Nubians from independent southern Nubia (upper register) and Egyptianized Nubians (lower register) depicted in the eighteenth Dynasty tomb of Huy, Thebes (Davies 1926: pl. XXX).

towards them. Nubia, relatively easily accessible along the Nile, attracted Egyptian expansion. Its mixed economy (crop growing and cattle herding) and its role as a trade corridor for desirable goods (e.g. ebony, ivory and gold) flowing from further south to Egypt supported indigenous social and political systems militarily threatening to Egypt (O'Connor 1986, 1987, 1991a). For millennia (with interruptions) Egypt dominated northern Nubia and after 1500 BC central Nubia as well. However, by 1000

BC all of Nubia was independent, and remained so, to ultimately become the long-lived Napatan Meroitic Kingdom of 800 BC–300 AD (Welsby 1996).

Relations with Punt and Libya were very different. The former, the source of a much-desired incense and other products (Figure 1:3), was remote and difficult to get to; Egyptians normally reached it by ships along the Red Sea coast, although there was also a (very difficult) land route (see discussion in Meeks 2003). Not surprisingly, Egypt and Punt seem always more or less equal trading partners until, after 300 BC, the situation was changed by the foundation of Ptolemaic harbour towns and coastal bases (about 270 in all!) along the Red Sea coast as far south as the Bab el Mendab, and development of seaborne trade with India (Hölbl 2001: 55–58).

As for Libya, Cyrenaica's limited, largely pastoral resources did not attract Egyptian colonization or even trade. Instead, a long history of conflict was caused by repeated Libyan harassment of the western Delta and is reflected in Egyptian art (Figure 1:4). By ca. 1250 BC, Libyan incursions took on the more serious form of actual invasions, prompted perhaps by the formation of an aggressive 'nomadic state' (O'Connor 1990: 89–108) in Cyrenaica itself. Nevertheless, although it fortified the coastal road to Libya as far west as Zawiyet Umm el-Rakham, pre-Ptolemaic Egypt never seriously attempted control of Cyrenaica (Snape 2003). On the contrary, the descendants of Libyan prisoners of war integrated into the Egyptian army, rose to

Figure 1:3   Tribute of the Puntites (both registers) depicted in the eighteenth Dynasty tomb of Rekhmira, Thebes (Davies 1943: pl. XVII).

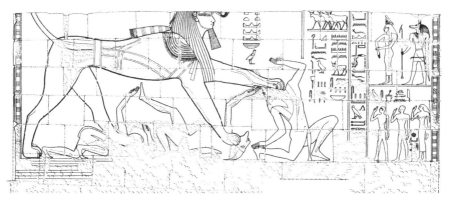

Figure 1:4   King Taharqo (twenty-fifth Dynasty), in the form of an Old Kingdom royal sphinx, tramples Libyan enemies (after Macadam 1955: pl. IX).

power and founded Dynasties which ruled over much of Egypt (the twenty-second, twenty-third and twenty-fourth, 945–715 BC – Kitchen 1973). Finally, coastal Cyrenaica (colonized earlier by the Greeks) came under Ptolemaic control (Hölbl 2001: index under Cyrenaica), but whether this led to any serious Egyptianization – the Ptolemies were largely Hellenic in culture – or impacted significantly upon the indigenous Libyans is unknown.

It is now important to consider how the peoples and cultures of Nubia, Punt and Libya responded to the long if varied contacts with Egypt. For reasons already given, only Nubia can provide an answer to this question on account of its extant indigenous archaeology and, latterly, its texts (after 800 BC and in Egyptian or, later, Meroitic). Despite much contact, Nubia was relatively culturally distinct from Egypt until 1700 BC. Thereafter, intensifying Egyptianization set in, to the extent that Napatan-Meroitic culture (715 BC–300 AD) is in important ways Egyptian in form and content. For example, many Egyptian deities and myths are incorporated into Nubian religion, and art and temple architecture was very similar to Egypt's. How Egyptianization occurred, however, and interacted with indigenous Nubian culture is still very much an open question. As Morkot's (Chapter 11) case-history shows, scholars' ideas on this topic are often overly simplistic and have led to proposals that were improbable, yet surprisingly enduring. As he shows, the notion that Theban priests fleeing a troubled Egypt brought Egyptian culture to the barbarian predecessors of the twenty-fifth Dynasty is unlikely. The larger context suggests a regional chiefdom in close contact with Egypt via trade, and expanding militarily to ensure its monopoly (Morkot 2000: 138–144).

In any event, Napatan-Meroitic civilization, despite Egyptianization, remained distinctive in fundamental ways. As Edwards (Chapter 10) and Fuller (Chapter 12) demonstrate, Nubia was then probably organized as a Sudanic segmentary state, not a more centralized and bureaucratic kingdom like Egypt's. At other levels, its 'food and culinary culture' differed from Egypt's, and was more akin to the Sudanic world's (Edwards, Chapter 10). Moreover, its northern burial customs and monuments seem to mirror the "social relations and local networks" characteristic of a segmentary state (Fuller, Chapter 12).

Moving to Egyptian contact with Africa beyond these three regions, there are opportunities for new and significant research, involving extensive fieldwork in North East Africa. For example, there survive on New Kingdom temple walls extensive lists of toponyms in the Levant and Near East, and in Africa (Meeks 2003: 56–57; O'Connor and Quirke 2003b). Although used for iconographic purposes, the lists are based on actual knowledge; the Levantine/Near Eastern lists include many country, place and tribal names identifiable in other sources and seem to combine a 'world map' with specific itineraries tracing out routes significant for trade, military expeditions and diplomatic contacts (Redford 1982). *A priori*, this should also be true of the African lists, but only very few of the toponyms can be geographically located at present (O'Connor 1982: 925–940). However, their very existence indicates that Egyptian contacts and knowledge were quite extensive, although not necessarily extending very deeply into sub-Saharan Africa. A suggestion by Topozada (1988: 162) that by 1345 BC Egyptian armies were campaigning as far south as the Gezirah between the Blue and White Niles seems implausible on present evidence. Only further research, combined with fieldwork, will be able to reveal more about these African lists.

A second, potentially major source of Egyptian influence upon sub-Saharan Africa is Nubia, especially in its highly Egyptianized Napatan-Meroitic phase. While the distinctively Nubian and even Sudanic aspects of this period have justifiably been emphasized in recent discussions (Edwards, Chapter 10; Fuller, Chapter 12), its strongly Egyptian aspects are also a historical reality, and likely to have had some effects on other African groups in close contact with the Napatan-Meroitic state. Who those contacts were, and how far in turn they passed aspects of, ultimately, Egyptian culture to communities more remote from Nubia and its immediate neighbours is a matter for further thorough research.

Finally, some intriguing aspects of Egyptian 'outreach' during the first millennium BC and later should not be overlooked. The possible significance of the Ptolemaic foundations along the Red Sea coast as mediators transmitting some aspects of traditional, i.e. non-Hellenic, Egyptian culture to parts of East Africa has already been noted. An earlier expression of Egyptian interest in parts of Africa relatively remote from Egypt was the circumnavigation of Africa carried out by Phoenicians commissioned to do so by a native Egyptian pharaoh, Necho II (610–595 BC), which is generally accepted as a historical event (Drioton 1962: 584; Gardiner 1961: 357). Since we know nothing of its causes or results, this episode is little discussed, but it indicates a strong Egyptian interest in Africa at the time, as do the sometimes aggressive policies followed in the twenty-sixth Dynasty (664–525 BC), to which Necho II belonged, in the Red Sea and Nubia, as well as Libya (Gardiner 1961: 352–364; Lloyd 2000: 369–383).

The preceding review shows that historic Egypt was in contact with a wide range of areas in Africa, even if we do not know – apart from Nubia – what the effects of these contacts might have been. However, they were clearly all structured by a fundamental climatic reality, the extreme aridity of the Sahara for most of the historic period (Grove 1993). As a result, while Egyptian contact with various regions in North East Africa looks like a potentially rich source of information, this seems unlikely for West and Central Africa, except insofar as Egyptian influence was mediated via

Nubia. Certainly, an inscription of Queen Hatshepsut (1473–1458 BC – see Breasted 2001: 134–135) refers to a tribute of ivory (700 tusks?) from the Tjemehu (i.e. the Libyans), which has reminded scholars of the trans-Saharan caravan trade between West Africa and the North African littoral in more recent times (Hayward 1990: 107).

Prehistoric Saharan climates, however, differed significantly from the historic. Prior to the latter, the Sahara fluctuated between periods of aridity and others, more moist, that supported widespread, mobile populations. As MacDonald shows (Chapter 7), linguistic and archaeological evidence indicates that a relatively well-populated Sahara emptied – in a variety of directions – during a long hyper-arid phase (18000–10000 BC), only to be repopulated, from a variety of points including Egypt, from 10000 to 5000 BC. Thus, at various times, direct and indirect contacts probably extended across Saharan Africa, although these were increasingly qualified by linguistic differentiation. Moreover, the Afro-Asiatic speaking ancestors of the ancient Egyptians were not deeply involved in developments in the Sahara, but rather entered and colonized the lower Nile (Egypt and northern/central Nubia) from the south-western Sudan during the period 5000–4000 BC. MacDonald notes that ancient Egyptian indicates "minimal interaction of early Egyptian with speakers of 'inner African' language phyla", speakers of which may have been displaced or acculturated along the lower Nile.

The last observations dovetail with Wengrow's views (Chapter 9), in which he demonstrates that the neolithic pastoral cultures (fifth millennium BC) of Middle Egypt (the Badarian) and of Central Sudan (Khartoum Neolithic) are so similar in fundamental ways that one can envisage such communities extending from Middle Egypt to modern Khartoum. Not only was there "a coherent and widely disseminated body of beliefs and practices", at least in the mortuary realm, over this vast area, but recent analogy shows that this pastoral society had the potential for the political developments that led ultimately to the pharaonic state, and its distinctive characteristics. This 'African' model of social evolution fits the circumstances better than others based primarily on the archaeological record of South West Asia.

Wengrow's chapter also leads to the possibility that Ancient Egypt displays substantial 'commonalities' with other African cultures, suggesting an African origin for major aspects of its civilization, arising from the prehistoric circumstances described above. Wengrow himself notes that Egyptian royal ceremonies focused on the king's body and displaying "his active role in binding the inhabited land to an ordered image of the cosmos" are consonant with current scholarly understanding of African political forms. A seminal figure in this debate, as Wengrow indicates, was Henri Frankfort, while important new lines of potential discussion are being opened up by Michael Rowlands (Chapter 4).

Frankfort (1948: 70) believed that Egyptian culture arose from "a North and East African substratum". In this, he was to an extent influenced by now outmoded ideas and preconceptions (Ray 1991; Bennett, Chapter 8; Reid, Chapter 5; Wengrow, Chapter 9), but his frequent citations from African ethnography – over 60 are listed in the index – demonstrate that there is a powerful resonance between recent African concepts and practice on the one hand, and ancient Egyptian kingship and religion on the other. Frankfort's ideas were taken a stage further in a West African context in Meyerowitz's (1960) thorough comparison of Akan and ancient Egyptian kingship.

Rowlands (Chapter 4) provides much additional evidence suggesting that "sub-Saharan Africa and Ancient Egypt share certain commonalities in substantive images and ideas, yet whose cultural forms display differences consistent with perhaps millennia of historical divergence and institutionalization". Frankfort (1948: 34) emphasized two points. First, kingship in Egypt was "the channel through which the powers of nature flowed into the body politic to bring human endeavor to fruition" and was thus closely analogous to the widespread African belief that "chieftains entertain closer relationship with the powers in nature than other men" (Frankfort 1948: 33, ch. 2). Second, the Egyptian king's metaphorical identification as an all powerful bull who tramples his enemies and inseminates his cow-mother to achieve regeneration was derived from Egyptian ideas and beliefs about cattle for which best parallels can be found in some, but not all, recent African societies (Frankfort 1948, ch. 14, 'Egypt in Africa').

Specialists in Egypt or the Near East have rarely analyzed Egypt's potential African dimension as Frankfort did (but cf. Autuori 1998); not surprisingly, his observations need to be qualified. In particular, Frankfort's belief in the absolute divinity of the Egyptian king was mistaken, although perhaps only to a degree (Posener 1960; on Egyptian kingship in general – Bonhême and Forgeau 1988; O'Connor and Silverman 1995). Moreover, his impression that Egyptians were free of a pervasive anxiety was overly optimistic; in reality, they experienced individual and societal anxiety in a cosmos which, although ordered, was surrounded by, and interpenetrated with, an aggressive and negative chaotic force, called 'Isfet' (Allen 1988: 20, 24–25; Assmann 1989a; Baines 1991; Cline and O'Connor 2003: 127, 129).

Rowlands' approach (Chapter 4) is different from Frankfort's and focuses primarily upon the African, rather than Egyptian evidence. His discussion, however, ought to suggest to Egyptologists many striking relationships to the Egyptian case. Analyzing a complex set of conceptual relationships which form an internally varied 'commonality' through much of sub-Saharan Africa, Rowlands begins with the belief that containers can be ritually empowered to hold spirits capable of both benefiting and harming a community or kin group. He then goes on to show that this notion of containment pervades some sub-Saharan societies at many levels. The human body is treated as "a container of powerful substances and can be manipulated to attract external forces to come and inhabit it", but the concept also expands outward to form a "schemata of envelopes" involving kin groups, communities and chiefdoms. Operative here are principles of exclusion and inclusion, involving "rituals of closure concerned with enclosing the means of transmitting life and defending these against loss or diminishment due to the hostility of others" (Rowlands, Chapter 4: 46, 47).

Rowlands' argument ultimately leads him to chiefs and kings, whose bodies are ritually empowered containers for "ancestral and material substances … dispersed to subjects for them to absorb", and thus be maintained; but chiefs are also highly ambiguous and threatening in emanating both benevolence and menace. They unify in themselves "two contradictory principles" normally kept separate, in that they "combine life giving forces with the power to kill" (Rowlands, Chapter 4: 52).

To examine Egyptian kingship from the perspective provided by Rowlands is instructive, especially if we follow Frankfort's emphasis (in Wengrow's words, Chapter 9: 125) "upon the concrete dimensions of experience and activity through which royal power was expressed in Egypt". Egyptian sources present the king as both supremely benevolent and terrifyingly menacing. As the son and delegate of the deities, the king conveys life and order (in Egyptian, 'Maat' – Assmann 1989b) to his people and to the world. However, the king also embodies the overwhelming aggression of divine force. Ritually, he joins the deities in defending cosmos against chaos or Isfet. Literally, he defends the terrestrial realm; the king brutally crushes Egypt's foreign foes (axiomatically chaotic) and equally ruthlessly – via burning, impalement and other means (Lorton 1976) – punishes Egyptians who transgress Maat through ritual error, criminality or rebellion. Like the chiefs discussed by Rowlands, the king combines "life giving forces with the power to kill" (Rowlands, Chapter 4: 52). Overall, this Egyptian concept of kingship, so akin to African models, seems very different to that held in the ancient Near East (Frankfort 1948; Postgate 1995).

Egyptian royal ceremonies and activities, structured around the concept of containment and the principles of inclusion and exclusion, vividly convey the king's roles. Through these ceremonies, divine powers of benevolence and aggression are repeatedly revealed as inherent in the king, while at the same time the king's person and powers are protected and made effective against Isfet or chaotic force at the many levels – supernatural and human – at which it operates. Involved are not only special ceremonies, such as the coronation, and the rites of renewal or the heb-sed festival, but also the routine ceremonies of the private and official life of the king. Via these, the king's body – "a container for powerful substances" – is situated in a series of ritually empowered, additional containers which both manifest and protect his powers. The king's body is washed, anointed and cosmeticized; the significance of these acts is made specific by a royal shower-bath, the wall decoration of which endlessly repeats the hieroglyphs for "life" and "dominion" (Fisher 1917; O'Connor 1991b: 177) which, in temple scenes, are literally poured over the king by gods! This first container is followed by another, a layer of crowns, regalia and ceremonial dress. Further activities involve containing and enfolding performative ceremonies (enthronement, audience, processions), most taking place within the palace, which itself forms a series of expressive and protective containers or 'envelopes'. These display and protect the king's powers and at the same time symbolically represent the 'schemata of envelopes' formed by state, world and cosmos.

These last points are manifested by the New Kingdom palace, major structures rarely referred to in detail in discussions of Egyptian kingship (O'Connor 1989, 1991b, 1995). The palace's equivalence to cosmos is evident, with ceilings decorated as the sky, sundisks placed above doorway lintels, and floors painted to represent the earth and the natural world. This cosmological context imparts several levels of meaning to the king's routinized activities. The latter included rest, refreshment, cleansing and adornment in a residential suite at the extreme rear; formal enthronement in a rear-lying throne hall, symbolically protected by other chambers completely surrounding it; and ceremonial progress through a reception hall, across an open court and exiting through an elevated façade into the outside world of the royal city and its inhabitants. The palatial context makes it clear that these events are to be equated with the successive manifestations of the creator god as he brings into being, and vitalizes, cosmos; and with the sun god's similarly structured revitalization of that cosmos every day.

Foreigners are depicted prostrate on palace floors, and as helpless before a smiting pharaoh on doorway jambs, columns, and palace façades in order to evoke the king's aggressive aspect; but this is more evocatively expressed in scenes of royal victories on the external walls of temples (Smith 1998: ch. 19). However, two monumental gateways into the royal mortuary temple complex of Ramesses III (1187–1156 BC) uniquely contrast and correlate the benevolent and aggressive manifestations of the Egyptian kingship. Their interior rooms celebrate the king's sexual potency, as related to his *nefrut* or maidens, emblematic of the fertility of Egypt itself. Their external faces, however, display the king smiting foreign male foes and displaying them as prisoners, scenes which inscriptions elsewhere in the complex make clear incorporate the idea that such male enemies, terrified into helplessness, become feminized and metaphorically subject to rape by the pharaoh (O'Connor forthcoming).

In conclusion, there is a relative abundance of ancient materials relevant to contact and influence, as well as striking correlations between ancient Egyptian civilization and the ethnography of recent and current sub-Saharan communities, chiefdoms and states. There are considerable theoretical problems in comparing the two, not least those imposed by chronology. There is clearly a historical disjuncture between Ancient Egypt and many of the significant African societies considered here, particularly those encountered in 19th and 20th century ethnographies. By the time of the Ptolemaic period in Egypt around 300 BC, many African societies were only just beginning to practice farming and, on the basis of present evidence, a number of regions towards the south of the continent were still awaiting domesticated plants and animals. Therefore, it is important to recognize not only the chronological disjuncture, which mitigates against direct contact or influence, but also the very different economies and scales of social organization of the societies being considered here. Perhaps the fact that commonalities do exist suggests that, *because* of the great time depth and different organization, these commonalities may result from inherently African processes. The scope of the topic is vast; the range of expertise required very wide; and the need for additional, predominantly archaeological, fieldwork is great. Research into Ancient Egypt in Africa, approached either from the Egyptian or from the African perspective, is therefore extraordinarily challenging – but that should make it all the more attractive!

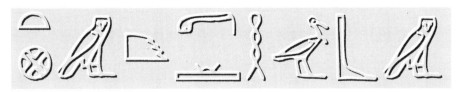

CHAPTER 2

AFROCENTRISM AND HISTORICAL MODELS FOR THE FOUNDATION OF ANCIENT GREECE

Martin Bernal

This chapter deals with two distinct versions of the early history of Greece, which I have called the Ancient and the Aryan Models. The difference between the two Models turns, in part, upon Egypt's geographical location on the African continent and European preconceptions regarding the capabilities of African populations. According to the Aryan Model, which is still generally dominant today, Classical Greek civilization was the result of a conquest of present-day Greece from the north by the 'Hellenes'. These were Indo-European speakers, or 'Aryans'. The indigenous population of the Aegean, whom they conquered, are simply labelled by modern scholars as 'Pre-Hellenes'. All that proponents of the Aryan Model 'know' about the 'Pre-Hellenes' is that they were Caucasian – definitely not Semitic speakers or Egyptians – and they did not speak an Indo-European language. This last point is necessary because less than 40 per cent of the Greek vocabulary and very few Greek proper names can be explained in terms of other members of the Indo-European linguistic family.

The Aryan Model was only developed in the 1830s and 1840s. Until the beginning of the 19th century, scholars had accepted the ideas of writers of the Classical, Hellenistic and Roman periods (500 BC–250 AD) on Greece's distant past. This overall view, which I call the 'Ancient Model', was that the ancestors of the Greeks had lived in idyllic simplicity until the arrival of Egyptian and Phoenician leaders. These had acquired cities and introduced the arts of civilization, specifically 'Greek' religion, irrigation, various types of weapons and the alphabet. Ancient writers maintained that Greeks had continued to learn from the Egyptians, through study in Egypt, and that many, if not most, of the greatest Greek statesmen, philosophers and scientists had visited the Nile Valley.

I have two concerns here. The first of these – to which *Black Athena Volume 1* (Bernal 1987) is devoted – is historiographical; that is to say, it is concerned with the writing and philosophy of history. The second is historical, setting out what I believe to be the least unlikely picture of what actually happened in the past.

The focus of my historiographical work has been on the shift from the Ancient to the Aryan Model, between 1780 and 1840. I am convinced that the first stage of this process, the abandonment of the Ancient Model, was not the result of scholarly developments, or 'internalist' factors. Rather, it was caused by changes in the general intellectual atmosphere, or for 'externalist' reasons. To put it crudely, I see four major forces as having effected the change. These were: (1) the establishment of the paradigm of progress; (2) the triumph of Romanticism; (3) the revival of Christianity after the French Revolution; and more important than all the others, (4) the application of racism to considerations of the relationship between Ancient Egypt and Ancient Greece.

No one has ever doubted that Ancient Egypt was much older than Ancient Greece. In Classical Antiquity and the Middle Ages the long-term passage of time was generally seen to be one of decline. Therefore, the Egyptians were not only seen as the teachers of the Greeks but as their moral and intellectual superiors. This image was reversed with the onset of the idea of progress which became dominant in Europe in the late 17th century. The historical process was now seen as one of improvement. Accordingly, the later Greeks had the advantage over the earlier Egyptians.

Romanticism, which also grew up in the 18th century, is essentially a view of the inadequacy of reason and the need to take sentiment or feeling into account. Romantics longed for small, dynamic communities with their inhabitants bonded by emotion. Therefore, they preferred the squabbling Greek city states to stable, long-lasting empires ostensibly ruled by reason, including Rome, China and Egypt, that were admired by the thinkers of the Enlightenment.

There was a great Christian revival throughout Europe and North America after the French Revolution and the defeat of Napoleon in 1815. Many in the newly Christian upper classes hated Freemasonry. Freemasonry was seen not only as the ultimate conspiracy within the Enlightenment, but also as having been behind the French Revolution itself. They also developed a loathing of Ancient Egypt, which they saw as being a central foundation of Freemasonry (but see Hamill and Mollier 2003).

Racism became an obsession in northern Europe by the end of the 17th century, with the establishment of racial slavery in America. As Europeans were treating Africans inhumanely, they tried to dehumanize them both actually and conceptually. Thus, Central and West Africans were portrayed by northern Europeans as animals or devils and as the epitome of barbarism. The role of Egypt as the foundation of western civilization was difficult to fit into this picture as Egypt was inconveniently situated on the African continent. There were two solutions: one, that of the Enlightenment and the Freemasons in particular, that Egypt was civilized and white (Hamill and Mollier 2003); the second, that of the Romantics, was to hold that it was uncivilized and black. However, there was also a third view.

The Ancient Egyptians as blacks and as the founders of western civilization

At the end of the 18th century, this third vision began to be advocated. According to this the Ancient Egyptians were both African and the founders of western civilization. The probable – and improbable – beginning of this intellectual trend came from the works of the intrepid Scottish traveller James Bruce. In the 1760s and 1770s Bruce travelled through Egypt and spent several years in Ethiopia (Bruce 1790). He was a conservative and at times advocated the beneficial effects of slavery. At the same time, however, he saw connections between the civilizations of Ethiopia and Egypt, and believed that the Ethiopian form was the older. For Bruce, the source of the (Blue) Nile was the source of civilization. Bruce finally published the descriptions of his travels in 1790. Fifteen years before that, however, he had many meetings with notables in both England and France on the eve of the French Revolution. It was in the heady atmosphere of this period that the idea that the ancient Egyptians were both civilized and black Africans took shape.

The two men who established this concept were Charles François Dupuis and Constantine Chasseboeuf dit Volney. Dupuis was an erudite scholar of antiquity and a brilliant inventor. He was also a supporter of the Revolution and an organizer of the anti-Christian 'Religion of Reason' promoted by Jacobin leaders of the Revolution, which incidentally used many Egyptian symbols. Dupuis argued that Egyptian astronomy, which he believed to be the fundamental science, came to Egypt from the south (Dupuis [1795] 1822: 73). It was a conversation with Dupuis that inspired the younger Volney to write his mysterious and immensely popular prose poem *The Ruins of Empires*, first published in 1792. This included, near its beginning, the famous passage,

> There a people, now forgotten, discovered, while others were still barbarians, the elements of the arts and sciences. A race of men now rejected from society for their *sable skin and frizzled hair*, founded on the study of the laws of nature, those civil and religious systems which still govern the universe.

(Volney [1804] 1991: 16–17; emphasis added)

Volney's explicit linkage of 'Negroes' to the origin of western civilization provided a powerful weapon for abolitionists. In France the great abolitionist, Reverend Grégoire, in his book *An Enquiry Concerning the Intellectual and Moral Faculties, and Literature of Negroes*, devoted the first chapter to Volney's arguments, emphasizing that the Ancient Egyptians were 'Negroes' and concluding, "Without ascribing to Egypt the greatest degree of human knowledge, all antiquity decides in favour of those who consider it as a celebrated school, from which proceeded many of the venerable and learned men of Greece" (Grégoire [1810] 1997: 25).

Grégoire's work, published in 1808, was translated into English in Brooklyn in 1810, and as early as 1814 it was giving more confidence to educated African Americans (Hodges 1997: xix–xx). The theme that Black Egyptians had founded civilization was taken up in two powerful pamphlets published in 1829. One, *The Ethiopian Manifesto, Issued in Defence of the Black Man's Rights in the Scale of Universal Freedom* was by Robert Alexander Young. The other, which was still more influential, was Walker's *Appeal to the Coloured Citizens of the World*. Walker argued that Egyptian enslavement of the Israelites had been far less onerous and demeaning than that of Africans in the United States (Walker [1829] 1993: 27–30, 39). Despite this attempt at reconciliation, there was a tension among African Americans between identification with the glories of Ancient Egypt and empathy with the Israelites, suffering under, then escaping from, Egyptian slavery (Champion: 167–168). The late St Clair Drake plausibly drew a distinction between 'Free Negroes' especially in the north, who emphasized their descent from the Egyptian civilization, and those under slavery in the south, among whom an identification with enslaved Israel was predominant (Drake 1987: 130–131).

The rise of the Aryan Model

There is no reason to suppose that the European scholars who created the new field of *Altertumswissenschaft* (the Science of Classical Antiquity) knew of such writings. They were acutely aware, however, of Dupuis, Volney and Grégoire. Volney's *Ruins* was first translated into German by Georg Forster, the German Jacobin. Forster was the son-in-law of Christian Gottlob Heyne, who dominated ancient studies at Göttingen for the 50 years (1760–1810) in which *Altertumswissenschaft* was developed at that university.

Connop Thirlwall, the first writer – in either English or German – of a history of Greece in the 'new' mode, wrote of the Ancient Model in the 1830s,

> It required no little boldness to venture even to throw out a doubt as to the truth of an opinion [the Ancient Model] sanctioned by such authority and by the prescription of such a long and undisputed possession of the public mind, and perhaps it might never have been questioned, if *the inferences drawn* from it had not provoked a jealous enquiry into the grounds on which it rests.
>
> (Thirlwall 1835: 63; emphasis added)

The major inference here would seem to be the idea that the Egyptians were black and that therefore blacks had been the originators of 'white' civilization. This was not only distressing, but for 'progressive' European intellectuals it was 'unscientific'. In the 19th century, racial 'science' made it clear not merely that 'whites' were now better than 'blacks', but also, according to the idea of permanent racial essences, that they had always been so. Therefore Greek historians must have been mistaken and suffering from the mysterious diseases of 'barbarophilia' or 'Egyptomania' when they stated that 'Semitic' Phoenicians and African Egyptians had civilized Greece.

Karl Otfried Müller (1820–1824), one of the first products of Humboldt's new educational system, made the first attack on the Ancient Model. The first volume of his *Geschichten Hellenischer Stämme und Städte* (History of Hellenic Tribes and Towns) was published in 1820. In it Müller argued that the legends upon which the model was based were inconsistent and that there was no *proof* that any Egyptian or Phoenician colonizations had taken place. I am convinced that it is useless to expect proof in such areas and that, in any event, it is strange to demand it of those who maintain the ancient tradition, while waiving the requirement of proof for those who challenge it. Nevertheless, Müller was remarkably successful both because of the new ideological conditions outlined above and because his book on the subject was published in 1820 on the eve of the Greek War of Independence. This war became the one liberal cause it was possible to support in an age of extreme reaction. The Philhellenes who went to Greece were only the tip of the iceberg of a mass student movement for whom Hellas became an object of veneration.

German scholars very quickly denied the role of the Egyptians in the formation of Greece, and French and British scholars fell into line in the following decades. It is sometimes argued that it was the great 19th century advances in knowledge of ancient languages and archaeology that led to this change. However, the Egyptian half of the Ancient Model was destroyed before the languages of Mesopotamia, written in cuneiform, were understood, and well before Heinrich Schliemann discovered Mycenaean material culture. While it is true that Champollion deciphered hieroglyphics in the 1820s, his results were not accepted by German classicists for another 30 years, after Lepsius had substantially improved the decipherment. Thus, Champollion's breakthrough cannot have played a role in the destruction of the Ancient Model. Therefore, the only way in which one can explain the abandonment of the Ancient Model is through the general ideological changes described above.

By contrast, there was an important internalist cause behind the establishment of the Aryan Model. This was the working out of the Indo-European language family and the establishment of Greek as a member of it. If, as seems reasonable, one supposes that there was once a single people who spoke the ancestral language, or Proto-Indo-European, and that this people lived somewhere to the north and east of the Balkans, one must postulate that the Aegean basin received some substantial influence from the north. This could have taken a number of different forms, but given the ethnic predispositions of the mid-19th century, it was immediately seen as a conquest by a master race of Hellenes, whose vigour had been steeled by ethnic formation in the cold of Central Asia or the Steppe.

For several decades, the new image of Greek origins co-existed uneasily with the traditional belief that Phoenicians – though not the Egyptians – had played a significant role. This view was attacked in the 1890s but survived until the 1920s. Following Astour (1967) and others, I associate this historiographic downplaying of the Phoenicians – who were seen as the Jews of Antiquity – with the rise of racial, as opposed to religious, anti-Semitism at the end of the 19th century. This reached a paroxysm after 1917 with the perceived and actual association of Jews with Bolsheviks in the Russian Revolution. Conversely, I attribute the revival of interest in the Phoenicians to increasing Jewish self-confidence after the foundation of the State of Israel. Since the 1960s, Jewish scholars have led the gradual rehabilitation of the Phoenicians' central role in the formation of Greek civilization. The restoration of the Egyptian facet of the Ancient Model has been slower. The leading champions of the Ancient Egyptians have been black Americans, who have been much further from the academic establishment than Jewish professionals.

Sustaining the Ancient Model

To return to the impact of Dupuis, Volney and Grégoire, both black and white abolitionists continued to use their arguments after academics were abandoning the Ancient Model. For instance, John Stuart Mill (1850: 29–30) wrote:

> It is curious withal, that the earliest known civilization was, we have the strongest reason to believe, a negro civilization. The original Egyptians are inferred, from the evidence of their sculptures, to have been a negro race: it was from negroes, therefore, that the Greeks learnt their first lessons in civilization; and to the records and traditions of these negroes did the Greek philosophers to the very end of their career resort (I do not say with much fruit) as a treasury of mysterious wisdom.

This was a response to Thomas Carlyle's notorious article, 'On the Nigger Question' (see Bernal 2001: 457 n. 76). The purity of Mill's position on this issue is somewhat tarnished by his own commercial interests. Mill held a position as a high official in the East India Company, a long-term foe of its rival, the slave-owning West Indian planters.

Such views favouring the Ancient Model faded among people of European descent after the abolition of slavery in the United States in 1865. They continued, however, among African Americans. Intellectuals such as Frederick Douglass and scholars such as W. E. B. Dubois and St Clair Drake were uncertain about the 'Blackness' or 'negro physiognomy' of the Ancient Egyptians but they had no doubts about the 'Africanity' of Ancient Egypt or the size of the Egyptian contribution to Greek civilization (Drake 1987; Dubois 1975: 40–42, 1976: 120–147).

Among the group now known as 'Afrocentrists' there is little or no doubt about black African origins of European civilization. It should be emphasized that, as many of the leading writers in this group write for a popular audience and are without the resources available to academics, they make many mistakes in detail. In their main concern, the 'blackness' or 'Africanity' of Ancient Egypt, they belong to a scholarly tradition going back to the 1770s. The Afrocentrists continue the late 18th century 'black' version of the Ancient Model described above, although they are in general less interested in the contributions of Egyptian civilization to Greece. It is the academic establishment and European champions of the Aryan Model, not the Afrocentrists, who have made a fundamental break with tradition.

Until recently, the ideas of the black scholars have been unknown to non-blacks. Even today, their views tend to be seen as 'special pleading' or 'therapy rather than history'. This is indeed an important aspect of black 'vindicationalist' scholarship and it can certainly distort their conclusions. Nevertheless, I am convinced that it is not helpful to view Afrocentric writers on these topics merely in terms of socio-pathology, as is frequently done (Appiah 1993; Howe 1998). Indeed, it is totally inappropriate for European and Euro-American scholars to do so when the Aryan Model itself serves the same therapeutic function for many Europeans and Euro-Americans.

Attempting revision

Even though I see the Aryan Model as having been 'conceived in sin or even error', I do not believe that this in itself invalidates it as a useful historical tool. However, despite heavy criticism (as highlighted in Lefkowitz and Rogers 1996), the collation of studies in archaeology, Bronze Age documents and mythology, published in *Black Athena Volume II* (Bernal 1991), lead me to conclude that the ancients were right when they emphasized the centrality of Egyptian and Levantine cultures in the formation of Ancient Greece. I maintain that 40–45 per cent of Greek words and a higher proportion of proper names can be shown to have Egyptian or Semitic etymologies. Thus, there is no need for a substantial 'Pre-Hellenic' substratum to explain the non-European bulk of the Greek vocabulary.

The fact that these sources support the Ancient Model does not, however, mean rejecting all work carried out within the framework of the Aryan Model, or a complete return to the Ancient Model. There is no doubt that some crucial new factors, most notably the knowledge that Greek is fundamentally an Indo-European language, must be taken into account. Thus, I argue for the establishment of a 'Revised Ancient Model'. According to this, Greece has received repeated outside influences both from the east Mediterranean and from the Balkans. It is this extravagant mixture that has produced this attractive and fruitful culture and the glory that *is* Greece.

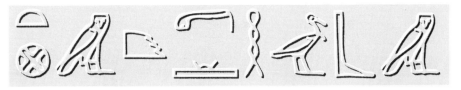

CHAPTER 3

ATTRIBUTING COLOUR TO THE ANCIENT EGYPTIANS: REFLECTIONS ON *BLACK ATHENA*

John A. North

Professional ancient historians have had a serious problem with Bernal's *Black Athena* (Bernal 1987, 1991, 2001; and see Chapter 2, this volume). They could hardly fail to see that its publication was an important event for the subject, attracting far more widespread interest and discussion than any other recent ancient history publication. The attention it has received from them has often, though not invariably, been highly critical and some of it quite ferociously so (Lefkowitz 1997; Lefkowitz and Rogers 1996). The author himself had, as he said later, predicted that there would be scepticism about his work, though what he predicted was not so much overt hostility as silent indifference. He thought he would be ignored, just as the work of those (e.g. Astour 1967) on whom he looked back as forerunners of his efforts had been ignored, or so he said (on all this, see Bernal in van Binsbergen 1996/7: 5–8). But it is hard not to think that he had some idea of the passionate reactions that his work would provoke. The very title, *Black Athena*, whether his or his publisher's choice, leaves little doubt that the work was intended to be a bold and provocative challenge to established assumptions and to attract all the attention it could. The title itself places the contention that Egyptians were black Africans, and that the Greeks were culturally indebted to them, at the very heart of the debate Bernal was trying to evoke.

Much of the problem for the ancient historian lies in the fact that, despite the courting of controversy, *Black Athena* is in many ways a great deal less original in its propositions and claims than it seems to be or has often been supposed to be. This particular controversy is not simply a question of a radical disagreement between new ideas and established positions: most ancient historians would find much of the main argument of *Black Athena I* perfectly acceptable to them, since, despite what an uninformed reader might infer from the book itself, there is in fact a great deal of common ground between Bernal's views and the work of many earlier ancient historians writing in the years since World War II.

The central proposition of *Black Athena* is that the role of the Greeks in creating modern civilization has been exaggerated in the past by the elimination from learned debate of a great many outside influences on their cultural development, particularly those of Egyptians and Phoenicians, which had been fully recognized in earlier centuries. The plain implication of this case is that up to the 1990s, i.e. through most of the last century, there was no serious research into outside influences on Greek cultural development. But this is simply not true: there was a great deal of work, widely known and disseminated, dealing both with the influence of Egypt and with that of the early Western Asiatic civilizations. There is no need to look further than the work of Burkert (1984), one of the most admired and widely imitated classical scholars of the post-war classical period, to see how partial a view is being presented by Bernal. Even a brief, but brilliant, introduction to early Greek history published in the Fontana series (Murray 1980: 80–99) has a chapter examining oriental influences in the eighth and seventh centuries BC. Of course, Bernal is making different use of the material he considers and he is looking in different directions from those emphasized in much of the earlier work. He focuses wholly on the Greek debt to Egyptians and to Phoenicians and has little to say about the debt to the civilizations of Mesopotamia (by way of contrast, see West 1997). But the basic contention of *Black Athena* is not some great intellectual revolution; rather it is moving in the same direction as had much other work in the post-war period. I return later to the question of the original contribution of *Black Athena I*, which is by no means negligible when seen in proportion.

Here, as elsewhere in this discussion, however, the right answer depends on finding the right question. It may or may not be fair to argue that the supreme contribution of the Greeks, their unique historic achievement, was already contested long before the publication of *Black Athena I*. It would be much harder to argue that such arguments had had much impact on generally received ideas about the Greek historic achievement outside the tiny (all too tiny) group of professional ancient historians. It was, and still is, a very widely accepted proposition that the Greeks originated almost all the great cultural achievements of 'the West', to use a thoroughly misleading term: history-writing, philosophy, art in the forms we know it, political debate, democracy, drama, mathematics, natural science, scholarship in general; this list could be extended a great deal without difficulty and frequently is. Textbooks galore start their story from the Greek foundations of modern culture; university courses, not least 'Western Civilization' courses, begin with the Greek City, its cultural and political activities and the writings of its citizens; television programmes pick up on the same theme, without any suggestion that this attribution of credit is at all contested or problematic. The Greek miracle seems beyond challenge.

Like it or not, however, all this derives from an intellectual construction that attributed the primary responsibility for European and American culture to this particular ancient ethnic/linguistic group, perceived as co-members of the Indo-European race. In that sense, a great deal of 19th century scholarship must be seen as working towards this conclusion. It needs to be accepted: (1) that this was in some sense a racial construction, emphasizing the role of those perceived as co-race-members and eliminating the apparent influence of those who were not; and (2) that the fact of the construction cannot be separated from the process through which European nations were simultaneously establishing imperial domination over other parts of the world.

The proposition being put forward was, therefore, that the very civilization that Europeans claimed to be spreading to the rest of the world was the invention exclusively of their own ancestors, their own representatives in the ancient world, and therefore owed little or nothing to the peoples of Africa or Asia that they were so successfully seeking to subordinate. In other words, the notion of a classical inheritance descending through Greeks and Romans, renewed by the Renaissance and descending to the European nations and thence to America has been, and in some ways still is, a cultural tool of the greatest possible value to the project of western imperialism.

A postcolonial version of Bernal's work along these lines raises very serious issues indeed, issues that would question much of the traditional understanding of classical learning and its influence in the 19th and 20th centuries. Even if classical historians take the strongest exception to this view of their discipline and its history, they can hardly deny that the question itself is a valid one and that it calls for a serious answer. But in fact these are not the particular issues that Bernal himself has emphasized in his work so far. His work may have the implications that are sketched in above, as I believe it does; but that is not the direction in which Bernal himself has shown any wish to push his arguments.

It seems to me that the fundamental challenge to ancient historians implicit in Bernal's thesis lies elsewhere, and that the challenge has less to do with his substantive conclusions than with the issues of methodology that he raises. What irritates ancient historians more than anything else, and not surprisingly so, is the total rejection of their method and its validity. The three models propounded by Bernal, 'Ancient', 'Aryan' and 'Revised Ancient', which provide the core of his view, provide a clear example of Bernal's mode of exposition of these issues. He asserts in effect that before the early 19th century the ancient model went virtually unchallenged; from the time of the Greeks themselves – indeed from the time of their myths – it was universally accepted that the Egyptian civilization had been far older than the Greek and that the Greeks had a substantial debt to the Egyptians and to their ancient cultural traditions. Against this universal agreement of mankind, nobody rebelled until the 19th century. It seems perfectly clear that readers at this point are supposed to be thinking: 'How could these learned 19th century eccentrics possibly have rejected a truth so universally accepted by previous generations?' This extraordinary refusal to see the truth before their eyes turns out to have a suitably spectacular explanation: the scholars in question were all blinded by racial or political prejudices. Having realized this, we of today must now return from these wild shores of 19th century speculation to the safe ground of handing on the truth as successive earlier generations have preserved it for us. Of course, this is an exaggeration of Bernal's position on these matters; but this is the underlying rhetorical strength of what he says: he seeks artfully to create the impression that departing from the norm of the beliefs held by earlier generations requires some special and probably sinister explanation. From an ancient (or modern) historian's point of view, however, departing from the views of the past held by earlier generations is the very foundation of their activity.

Bernal's critique cannot be limited to the particular area dealt with in his book. Greek relations with Egypt and with the Phoenicians provide only one example of a far more widespread phenomenon in the development of Ancient History and Archaeology in the 19th century. What applies in this case in fact applies more or less to every other period of ancient history as well. In many areas, the ideas about the Greeks and Romans had rested on an extensive knowledge of their own writings and although these had been read, studied and compared for centuries, work on them until the modern period had largely not been based on any challenge, at least not to the broad lines of the inherited tradition. The founding idea of the modern discipline of Ancient History is exactly that the historian's job today is to test and challenge older views, however long-established, by a process of identifying and analyzing the evidence on which they are supposed to rest. She or he formulates new hypotheses about the period; seeks by all possible means new evidence that might throw light on the situation; expresses scepticism or at least doubt about whatever cannot be proved. This process can of course be very fallible and there is plenty of room for judgments on these matters to be influenced by prejudices of all kinds, including racial ones.

All the same, it follows that, not just in the case of the so-called Ancient Model, but in all parallel cases as well, the tradition of debate that begins in Germany from Niebuhr and his followers treats older ideas as needing to be tested and assessed, not blindly followed. To take a famous example, the accounts of the Roman historians of early Rome as an important centre of power were broadly believed by everybody, including the Romans themselves, until a radical challenge to it was brought up in the 18th century and elaborated by some 19th and 20th century scholars. It has now become clear enough that in some respects this scepticism went too far; the archaeology of the area in the sixth century BC has revealed a major city in contact with other Mediterranean powers and probably dominating a good deal of its area. But in the process of this debate it has become painfully clear how sceptical it is necessary to be about Livy the historian and his methods and how limited was the reliable information available to him; some do indeed still put their trust in the main lines of Livy's accounts, but nobody doubts that these sources are not to be trusted too much when it comes to their report of any complex or detailed transactions (Cornell 1995). But if Bernal's methodology were to be applied to this case, then we should presumably have to return to the ancient model of early Rome and never venture to ask the challenging questions.

To put this another way, the nature of Bernal's attack is not just to do with Greeks, Egyptians and Phoenicians, but with the whole method on which historical research currently rests. The contention is that the best guide to the truth is not the closest and most careful examination of the evidence, nor is it the creation of new models of understanding; rather we should seek to identify the balance of inherited belief about the past and take that as the best available indication of the truth. This is the precise opposite of the methods by which the past is studied today, whether the Greco-Roman past or any other.

A second clear example of Bernal's isolation from the way ancient historians think today is his attitude to the inheritance of credit for ancient achievements. This is of course the most sensitive issue in this whole debate. It is not difficult in looking back at the earlier part of the last century to agree that part of what was driving the 'invention of the Greeks' was a conscious or unconscious sense that the Indo-Europeans were a race that had certain definable characteristics and had retained some coherence over very long periods of time. So it did follow logically that as the role of earlier civilizations was less and less recognized, and the Greeks were more and more identified as the originators of all the important characteristics of modern life, this process implied the monopolization of credit for these achievements. So there are two levels of criticism that we can now validly make of what was happening at that time. The first level is that the evidence was being twisted, and firmly established aspects of the development being omitted or neglected, with a clear underlying agenda. The second level is that the whole enterprise of comparing races with one another on the basis of their claimed achievements in past periods had the effect of inventing a completely misconceived competition between the races. What Bernal in fact does is not to reject this racial competition, but rather he takes up the cudgels in exactly the same competition, though now backing the other sides.

By way of an experiment, let us concede to Bernal the main conclusions for which he is arguing and see where his argument leads:

(1) that it was a universal belief of humankind, held from antiquity continuously until the 18th century, that earlier civilizations had made major contributions to the development of the Greeks' achievements;
(2) that the Greeks' achievements themselves were grossly inflated by racist 19th century scholars who sought to appropriate on behalf of their own perceived race-group all the credit for modern scientific civilization, rebutting the claims of all other race-groups in the process;
(3) that in fact the language of the Greeks contains very large elements of borrowed vocabulary from the Egyptian language, implying substantial influence in the form of actual domination of some kind. (It is in this argument, which takes up by far the greatest part of the whole of *Black Athena*, that Bernal departs most radically himself from the ideas that upheld his 'Ancient Model'. The identification of Egyptian words is in itself highly controversial and I have no view to offer on the subject; but it is important to notice that it is on this claimed linguistic influence that the argument of *Black Athena* turns, not, for instance, on any proof of direct borrowing during the archaic period itself);
(4) that the language in question is related to other African languages and that the Egyptians were themselves black people. There is, of course, a crucial question of interpretation raised by this attribution of colour. It is indeed possible, though not provable, that the Egyptians were black (Snowden 1983); but there can be no doubt at all that the establishing of this particular link is critical to what Bernal is seeking to prove.

What do these four propositions, if we accept them as proved, imply for our purposes? The outcome is in one sense thoroughly benign and liberal. Bernal wants to show that we should now correct the racism of the past and share the credit that was once a monopoly of the Indo-Europeans with other racial groups at the same period: that is precisely why the contemporary aspect of his message plays the part it does. The groups who used to be excluded from their share of credit are groups that can still claim back their credit today; the origins of our culture belong not just to one section of the contemporary population, but can be shared out – 33 per cent Caucasians, 33 per cent blacks, 33 per cent Semitic – corresponding respectively to ancient Greeks, ancient Egyptians and ancient Phoenicians. This explains why the attribution of colour is so crucial to the argument. The message here deserves to be called a gospel of peace, intended to resolve permanently the conflict over credit for the origins of civilization. We should not forget, after all, that it is no part of Bernal's purpose to deny the reality or extent of Greek achievements, only to set them into a correct perspective, taking proper account of those of other ancient groups, previously neglected or eliminated from the reckoning.

The trouble with this resolution is clear enough. What I have been calling 'the competition' in the past was played out under certain rules and it was these rules that delivered the results that are under consideration. One main feature of the competition was a belief that the races of the world were real groups of people moving through huge periods of time with their characteristics of speech and culture retaining a great measure of consistency over centuries or even over millennia. The Indo-Europeans were a race identified entirely on the basis of their languages, without the benefit of any archaeological evidence that would pin them down to any specific location in time or space. But they were being presented as some kind of biological unity with characteristics, including intellectual capacities, traceable over centuries. This whole idea of race in this sense now seems quite unsustainable and unrealistic; it is certainly in deep conflict with the way we think about social change and the functioning of social groups.

In some ways, though not in all, an interesting foil to Bernal's work is provided by the research of Georges Dumézil from the 1930s onwards. Dumézil worked entirely within what he saw as the Indo-European group of peoples, looking for common patterns in their inherited traditions (Dumézil 1941–1945, 1968). One sharp similarity concerns the Greeks themselves. Bernal argues that they are exceptional among the Indo-European groups because their language was more heavily affected by non Indo-European linguistic influences. Dumézil found that he could not absorb them into his theoretical structures and explained this as resulting from their greater creativity, their rejection of older traditions of behaviour often retained by more conservative groups. Dumézil was not, at least overtly, at all interested in the transmission of credit and it is not clear in his work that he accepted the racist theories that were so influential when he started work, though it has sometimes been suspected that he must have done (Belier 1991; Momigliano 1984; Scheid 1983).

What interested Dumézil were patterns of myth and of theology which, he argued, at least in his early work, were reflections at many removes from the original social structure of the society in which Indo-European was first spoken and from which all the later Indo-European languages are supposed to have developed. Indo-Europeans organized themselves, either in reality or at least in ideology, into three groups: the ruler/lawyers; the warrior band; the producer/peasants. This triple structure is then expressed in myths, in ritual programmes and in the structure of different families of gods. These corresponding structures can be identified in different contexts over wide variations of time and space, from remote antiquity to the Middle Ages and from the Celtic West to Iran and north India. Dumézil was a master analyst of texts and rituals and it is very difficult to deny the reality of some of the connections he makes or the intellectual creativity of the ideas he explores. The same range of problems comes up here in thinking about the racial 'competition' discussed above: whether the structures Dumézil postulates can be carried from generation to generation over many centuries amongst peoples living under quite different economic, social and political conditions. Modern notions of race seem to make even Dumézil's postulated transmissions seem inconceivable, unless they can be seen as somehow implicit in the linguistic structures of the group of languages, an idea that raises difficulties of its own and was not apparently the author's own way of arguing his points. In the meantime, Dumézil's complex structures raise very much the same problems of understanding as the notion of cultural credits for particular racial descent groups.

Bernal's real problem, then, is that he seems to be trapped in this racist competition, not admittedly of his own making. What he might have said, but has not said, is that there were two quite different objections that could be made against the elimination of outside influences from the assessment of Greek achievements: first, that it twisted the historical record by eliminating highly relevant data from consideration; second, that it rested on the strange idea that credit for cultural achievements can be transmitted to future generations by some kind of racial inheritance. He cannot make the point himself, if he is, as it seems, still engaged in essentially the same competition.

It is important to note how illegitimate the change of attitude being described here must seem to the losers in the competition as it was originally conceived. From an Afrocentrist point of view, what has happened must seem quite simple: the rules of the competition were made up by a group of Indo-European scholars, who subsequently went on to declare themselves the outright winners. Later on, it looked as though the competition was about to be opened up, so that more of the prizes were to be shared out on a new basis; whereupon the original winners announced in reply that the rules had now changed. It is no longer acceptable that the competitors should be able to claim credit from the efforts of their remote ancestors. It is hardly surprising if they cry 'foul' to this manoeuvre.

There is another still more striking point to be noticed here, one that Bernal (in van Binsbergen 1996/7) himself observed with considerable force. The idea that Egypt was the source of an important African influence on the cultural achievements of the Greeks of the classical period was not a new one when Bernal embraced it. It had been argued by black scholars long before the 1980s. But it was only Bernal who attracted any serious attention and he did so at once. Why? He was not a professional in the areas of ancient history or Egyptology, but rather an expert on contemporary China. One of his grandfathers had made Bernal a famous name in science, at least to an earlier generation; the other was an Egyptologist famous, among other things, for his *Grammar* (Gardiner 1957). But these credentials could hardly have been responsible for Martin Bernal's success on their own. The fact is that he is a white, British-originated professor taking up the same theme as several black predecessors. But only he, not they, drew attention, speaking engagements, notoriety, whole volumes of refutation. All of which may make his position more sympathetic, but it does not make his arguments any more convincing.

In many ways, *Black Athena* can be seen as a healthy, radical challenge in itself to established, perhaps too established, ways of thinking about ancient history. It demands a re-thinking, for instance, of the assumptions on which the prestige of the Greeks is based; and of the place that classical culture played in creating the notion of western civilization. Normally, one might say that such challenges can only be beneficial to a subject, even if they stimulate only a more considered or sophisticated re-statement of the status quo. In this case, a mass of critical comment has tried to show that the weaknesses of the argument undermine the whole project and create acute risks of over-simple and misleading conclusions. Much of the criticism is highly effective, both that in much of *Black Athena Revisited* (Lefkowitz and Rogers 1996) and that of Josine Blok, writing at length on a fundamental aspect of *Black Athena I* (Blok in van Binsbergen 1996/7: 173–208; with Bernal's reply 209–216). All this criticism is no more than the projection of political prejudice, cry the other side. Bernal's own position is to give ground with much grace on individual issues (Blok's paper, he says, is exactly the kind of research he had always hoped to provoke), but to claim that his Kuhnian 'paradigm shift' is quite unaffected by such detailed debates.

What matters most of all is that the *Black Athena* controversy, however important in itself, should not monopolize too much of the attention in this area. A major part of the problem in the past has lain in the separation of the study of early Greece from that of the many earlier civilizations that in so many ways anticipated its development. It is this separation of disciplines that allowed the delusion to survive as long as it did – that Greek culture sprang, like Athena, from the head of Zeus, rather than evolving slowly, as all other cultures do, from the influence of contacts with many different societies. A series of major issues emerges from the controversy, far more apparent than they were before. How did the Greeks achieve their reputation as the supreme cultural innovators? And how justified are we in now maintaining this reputation? And if it is true, as it seems to be, that this area of ancient history research was to some extent at least determined by covert racial considerations, how far is this also true of other areas? Notoriously, the characterization of Carthage and Carthaginian society has at times seemed to be largely driven by anti-Semitic stereotypes of cruel and rapacious merchants. It is not difficult, retrospectively, to recognize prejudices at work and the *Black Athena* controversy illustrates all too clearly the power of the emotional appeal of discovering ancestral claims to glory and ancestral wrongs to be righted, even at the distance of two and a half millennia.

We have seen how important proving the blackness of the Egyptians is to the structure of Bernal's argument. The reason why this attribution of colour also serves as an appropriate metaphorical expression for his whole enterprise is because it provides the crucial link between ancient civilizations and modern groups, who seek to confirm their status through association with these past societies. The question that needs to be raised is what validity any such claims can possibly have. It is of course quite certain, without any need for proof, that many different groups, from many directions and at many different times, had their impact on the development of what became Greek culture. But the thesis, as Bernal has argued it, concerns not so much development as origins: the focus throughout the whole of *Black Athena* is on establishing what first determined the character of the culture. This, too, only makes any sense on a quite un-historical set of assumptions. If the identity of later groups is to be established with reference primarily to the contribution that they made to the progress of human civilization and science, and if the contribution which they made is perceived as the starting-point of a long historical process, then it needs to be accepted that the starting-point determines the nature of the whole later process (van Binsbergen 1996/7: 28–38). So the social, political and economic contexts within which cultural developments occur have no interest or importance, because the development has long ago been defined, fixed and determined by the original inputs from which it started. Hence, at least in principle, studying the influence of Egyptian vocabulary on the language spoken by proto-Greeks in the second millennium BC can tell you more about classical Greek culture than studying Sophocles and Plato.

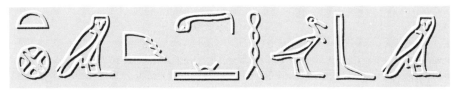

CHAPTER 4

THE UNITY OF AFRICA

Michael Rowlands

> To perpetuate their imperial domination over the people of Africa, the colonizers sought to enslave the African mind and to destroy the African soul. They sought to oblige us to accept that as Africans we had contributed nothing to human civilization except as beasts of burden … The beginning of the rebirth of our continent must be our own rediscovery of our soul, captured and made permanently available in the great works of creativity represented by the pyramids of Egypt, the stone buildings of Axum and the ruins of Carthage and Great Zimbabwe.

(Mbeki 1998: 299)

Since the early 1980s the question of African unity and how this should be conceptualized has taken on both an intellectual and a political salience. South Africa's renaissance discourse, mainly associated with the pronouncements of Thabo Mbeki, has evoked a great deal of emotion about the present fragmented and isolated state of Africa. In part Mbeki's call for a cultural renaissance recalls the post-independence rhetoric of Senghor, Nyerere and Nkrumah, in particular their belief that until a sense of African cultural unity and identity was established, political change and economic development would remain stillborn. The essence of African authenticity would be revived, they argued, only by a return to ancestral heritage to pursue the goal of economic modernity without the alienating materialism of the West. The past would unlock the door to the future, but which past had to be very carefully selected.

The idea of cultural unity across a continent evokes the important questions of what is meant by being 'African' and what we mean by 'origins'. The problems that these questions bring to mind – studies of 'culture areas' and diffusionist arguments – whilst central to the Afrocentrist thesis, are largely ghosts of an unwanted past for most archaeologists, historians and anthropologists. Whilst some may see in this advocacy of cultural interaction a welcome antidote to the autocthonism of processual/post-processual archaeologies, they would not be convinced by the vague language of modified diffusionism, and they require instead a more thorough exploration of the relationship between population movements, linguistic change, and ideas from evolutionary biology as a more rigorous basis for understanding cultural change. The Afrocentrist argument, in particular inspired by the work of the Senegalese philosopher Cheikh Anta Diop (MacDonald Chapter 7, this volume), has not persuaded academics, including many African as well as expatriate archaeologists, to follow a modified diffusionist path. But these scholarly views are incompatible with the spirituality that motivates the African renaissance debate in Africa and African diasporas. Bernal's first paper on the Black Athena project (1985) was published in a special issue of the *Journal of African Civilisations*, the principal journal of the Afrocentrist movement that has been the most ardent supporter of Bernal's general thesis on the Afro-Asiatic roots of 'general civilization'. Any methodological and scholarly objections to the Bernal thesis (see e.g. Foloronso Chapter 6, MacDonald Chapter 7 and North Chapter 3, all this volume) tend to be dismissed by Afrocentrists as the imposition of a false certitude by those academics wielding the hegemony of Western discourse.

In many ways this clash is unfortunate, since the debate could be better informed by paying some attention to how the fragmentation of an African identity has in part been the result of the intellectual work carried out by Western trained academics at work in Africa during the colonial and postcolonial periods. The fact that structural functionalism in anthropology favoured the study of local societies through participant observation, or that art historians discovered tribal art styles, means that we now know Africa academically as 'localized traditions'. The publication of ethnographic monographs committed to the integrated study of one local society, or the Ethnographic Survey of Africa published by the International African Institute, are part of the archive that informs us that Africa is made up of hundreds of discrete peoples and languages. Attempts to discuss the unity of Africa in broader cultural terms have been dismissed as overgeneralized and incapable of dealing with the significant diversity of a continent that anyway was only given a name from the outside (e.g. Maquet 1975, and for a critique see Mudimbe 1988). Some attempts *have* been made to meet the problem at least halfway. Thus, some British anthropologists recognized that history presented a different picture of cultural unity, at least at a regional level (e.g. Murdock 1959). Kuper (1982) has stressed the essential unity of much of southern African forms of kinship, marriage and exchange, and Vansina (1990) talks of long traditions and continuity and change in Equatorial Africa over five millennia.

The challenge remains whether it is possible for academics to discuss a more inclusive notion of Africa that will respond to the perception that a certain unity of cultural form not only exists but has an historical origin. Such a construct could form the basis of a contemporary political revitalization of the continent. For some, such a unity exists in the expansion of Bantu speaking peoples, which gives a linguistic unity on which future political integration can be based. But this is unlikely to satisfy all. It leaves out many of 'first people' status from inclusion as well as the relationship between Egypt and the rest of Africa. The issues are therefore far from trivial ones which can be rejected by scholarly annoyance over the misuse of methodology or by a somewhat patronizing Western display of expert knowledges.

Unfortunately it has been unfashionable for some time to talk about cultural unity, origins or comparison as a means to establish underlying structures. We therefore need to return to some elementary points of classification.

Culture areas or symbolic reservoirs?

Early in the 20th century, the concept of "culture area" was of basic importance to anthropology. The identification of such units in Africa is associated in particular with the work of Frobenius (1898). His work on African culture areas converged with developments in North American anthropology where Holmes (1914) and Wissler (1917) were to introduce culture areas to the study of native North Americans (cf. Harris 1968: 257, 374 ff). The general aim was to identify culture areas composed of extensive and coherent institutionalized cultural complexes reflecting a common historical tradition. The development of a theory of culture areas aimed to answer criticism of diffusionism, which relied on distributions of isolated cultural traits in order to speculate on long range and long-term interaction. Culture history was effectively the study of such regions and their interplay, and the study of diffusion was reduced to the study of interaction.

For Baumann (1955) and Frobenius, culture areas were not intended to equate with continents such as Africa. They were often conceived as forming overlapping sets in which shared characteristics could be as significant as any differences. Frobenius, for example, saw no absolute break between the African and European culture areas but imagined the Mediterranean to be a wedge that had been inserted and driven between the two. He divided Africa into a North Erytheraean (eastern Sudanic) belt and a Southern Erytheraean belt (from Angola to Mozambique), each of them defined as different variants of the institutional complex of sacred kingship and ritual sacrifice. Moreover, both Baumann and Frobenius were concerned to identify sets of material culture components that could be taken to indicate the distribution of a culture area. Ancient Egypt was therefore linked to the North Erytherean area through Nubia. Their shared features included musical instruments, divination and use of oracles, chiefly regalia such as whips, crooks and flails, cattle husbandry as a central source of wealth and the predominance of images of procreation in the cosmology. The overwhelming Egyptocentrism of many works of this period, in particular of Elliot Smith (e.g. 1933) and Perry (1923) (see Champion 2003a), obscured the more central question of whether a shared repertoire of cultural forms can really be identified for sub-Saharan Africa. Seligman (1934), for example, was an early proponent of the idea that ancient Egyptian kingship had a sub-Saharan origin, in particular in some part of prehistoric Nubia, and that in general cultural historical terms, the cultural 'flow' had been south to north. Perhaps the most significant work on the institutional complex of sacred kingship has been by the structuralist de Heusch (1985) who claims that widespread patterns of ritual kingship exist in sub-Saharan Africa (and Ancient Egypt). According to de Heusch, these predate effective state formation as defined politically and economically in any region.

The concept of culture area seems to continue to be useful if it engages in defining the distribution of a coherent institutionalized set of cultural forms that may have a common origin. The concept is less useful when it implies that a region must have boundaries and the interaction between centres may be defined in terms of a language of diffusion. De Heusch uses a 'cultural logic' approach derived from studies in structuralism. Lévi-Strauss, for example, was effectively concerned with demonstrating the essential unity of Amerindian myth by showing that a myth comes into being essentially as the transformation of one myth into another (Lévi-Strauss

1970). Myths are organized into groups that form a series of transformations but each myth in a group contains elements that are also found in other groups. The overall effect is one of overlapping sets which are unified to form a single chain which, in the case of Amerindian myths, link those of Amazonia to the north-west coast of America, as a system of transformations. De Heusch (1985) applies a similar method to the study of ritual in Africa and in particular focuses on the structure of sacrifice as ritual killing, whereby a life is given to form a means of communication with the supernatural. For him the essential issue is the act of giving which, as part of managing the relationship between the living and the supernatural, requires the provision of a life or a surrogate (see Evans-Pritchard's (1956) classic analysis of Nuer sacrifice). For others, ritual killing rather than sacrifice is the essential act (e.g. Girard 1977). It can equally be involved as a means of cleansing or purifying polluted spaces or mediating between the inside and the outside (the sphere of the home and the natural world) without specifying a sacred/profane dichotomy. If we marginalize Egypt and the Egyptocentrist focus as a peripheral development within the wider context of African culture history, we might be able to follow this structuralist path and discover a continent-wide set of transformations in the cosmology of giving and receiving life as part of morally conceived relationships. The essential theme of managing the transfer of life from the natural to the domesticated world could take many different localized transformations without requiring a diffusionist argument of population movements and migration.

Structural functionalism's emphasis on describing the integration of social acts made description itself an unending task and it transformed comparison into a meaningless programme. Structuralism was one escape that would reveal "common structural principles which inform a large number of superficially different social systems" (Kuper 1979: 111), allowing the detail of description (kinship, myth, etc.) to be stripped away in order to reveal a basic structure and its transformations. The analogue is with syntax in language construction where content is unimportant by comparison to seeing how variation is structured through a series of contrasts or a system of differences. Thus content is sacrificed for breadth of comparison in structural analysis. From any particular local ethnographic viewpoint, the structure appears too all encompassing and overgeneralized to be able to deal with available detail. The fact that comparative analysis is a matter of scale is therefore not a surprising conclusion. But scale in what sense is not all that clear.

The problem of recognizing uniformities over large areas, which will also take into account localized differences within them, has been considered within the framework of social knowledge. Barth (1987), for example, accounts for cultural variation in inner New Guinea by showing how many different groups draw from a similar vocabulary, material cultures and social practices. For him, scale is an issue in defining a tradition as an overall pattern in the distribution of knowledge and ideas (Barth 1987: 78), similar to Redfield's (1956) "great tradition" which may be defined as a collective heritage transmitted from past to present. Both recognize that differences occur in the modes of transaction and handling of knowledge over time so that detecting commonalities between Bali and Melanesia can show how different modes of transmission have channelled their development in very different trajectories. In Bali, gurus increase cultural capital by disseminating knowledge widely and by objectifying it in complex temple and court systems to which all have access. In

Melanesia, elders who have been initiated into secret knowledge hoard and control access to it as a means of retaining status. The contrast is in some ways similar to Redfield's (1956) distinction between great and little traditions.

If archaeologists talk of tradition at this general level it is usually with some degree of circumspection. For example, Indo-European has been used to describe a language family (Renfrew 1990) or a tradition that divides society into three functions (Dumézil 1949) or as a form of sacred kingship (e.g. Benevensite 1973). All three aspects may be accounted for by asserting the presence of Indo-European as a foundational model, not supported by written texts, but still in the minds of Indo-European speaking peoples as shared knowledge which may be articulated only in specific contexts of experience and use. A similar attempt to grasp a sense of higher unity shared by particular local traditions can be seen in Tambiah's (1990) writing on Therevada Buddhism in Thailand, Burma and Sri Lanka as a collective tradition that takes different forms or divergent trajectories in these three settings. In other words, Barth and Tambiah both argue that cultural difference occurs as a result of the transmission of knowledge, although this is only possible because they share cultural commonalities. Sterner (1992: 72) uses a similar argument describing the culture history of the Mandara Mountains of north Cameroon as a "symbolic reservoir containing the core of symbols, beliefs, values and ideas upon which cultures are founded". On a more regional scale in Mandara, where there exist many autochthonous peoples speaking related Chadic languages, she observed that a constant splintering and fusing of groups, promoting strong senses of distinction and conflict between them, could do so only because they drew from the same symbolic reservoir which ensured its reproduction over time. This is not far different from Barth's account of traditions of knowledge generating deep differences in form even where similar substantive ideas are embraced. The particular attraction of Barth's approach lies in the recognition of how deep analogues in substantive ideas – in his case between Bali and inner New Guinea – can be combined with comparing the modes by which knowledge is transmitted, adopted and transformed over time (Barth 1990: 640). He suggested that the processes that result from these interactions "generate regional trends over time, but also discontinuous variation and incompatible syntheses in different parts of the same region" (Barth 1987: 80).

A similar impression exists that sub-Saharan Africa and Ancient Egypt share certain commonalities in substantive images and ideas, yet whose cultural forms display differences consistent with perhaps millennia of historical divergence and institutionalization. Whereas Barth is concerned with moving from what is held in common to recognizing the contrasting forms and regional distributions of knowledge in South East Asia and Melanesia, this chapter shows how a similar model in Africa can be used to identify what is common in divergent cultural forms. The problem with such an approach is the inevitable tendency to reduce the past to the present, in particular when there is pressure to respond to the need to establish the bases for a sense of commonality on which future political growth may depend. My theme is Barthian, therefore, in the sense that my concern is also to see how a reservoir of potential images and ideas have been selected and used over several millennia leading to irreversible trends towards regional differentiation, variation, and hybridity of cultural forms. As Barth (1990: 650) says, "culture areas are then not only the product of past history; in a very real sense they are being made now, by the efforts of different intellectuals elaborating different kinds of knowledge".

If common elements can pass back and forth between culture areas and be transformed in the process, then their commonality remains, as the generative power of underlying structure would have it, in their co-presence even though different historical processes and dynamics will ensure a reproductive difference in specific social contexts. We need, therefore, to complement the notion of a common repertoire of cultural elements with a more dynamic approach that selects for different combinations (without it being a matter of logical necessity or the free will of transactional agents). Kopytoff's (1987) frontier thesis suggests that in Africa this process may be the expansion and splitting off of smaller polities from more complex societies as part of the historical expansion of African populations over the last two or so millennia. People moving into new areas either join an existing group or form a new society, not starting but bringing with them a "cultural inventory of symbols and practices that were brought from a metropolis and predated any particular society being observed" (Kopytoff 1987: 34). What might be designated therefore as a common repertoire of ideas, images and practices in the African setting were exposed to a historical process of rapid expansion and migration of population that would account for local divergence and difference. This could explain why so many political communities are socially heterogeneous and interdependent, with traditions of leaders coming from the outside and bringing with them new crops or new technologies as the basis for a culturally sanctioned hierarchical relationship.

Since Frobenius, there have been numerous attempts to describe a symbolic repertoire of common elements for Africa as 'ways of knowing' that can pass back and forth across different regional and cultural boundaries (e.g. Herskovits' (1926) East African 'cattle complex' or Murdock's (1959: 108) reconstruction of original Bantu social organization). Writing on ritual knowledge in Africa, de Heusch (1985) emphasized that African sacrificial rites as a whole could be distinguished from those of biblical, classical and Christian origin. African rituals, he claimed, were not concerned with keeping apart the sacred and the profane and mediating between them. Nor were they about overcoming tragic splits between gods and men (as in the separation of ritual priests and kings in Hindu cosmology or the tricks played between men and gods in ancient Greek mythology). Ancestors and spirits are managed in African social worlds precisely because they have access to powers that, although dangerous, are needed and must be controlled. What links the living and dead is the need to capture, cajole, attract or expel spiritual forces whose powers are deeply ambiguous and capable of both benevolent and evil acts. De Heusch and others have emphasized the pragmatic and grounded nature of African cosmologies. Misfortune is not the outcome of vengeful and distant deities manipulating human frailties but is the consequence of the actions of real others, possessed or otherwise, acting with evil intentions. Spirits of the dead, disease and impurities derived from antisocial acts are the 'things' that communities wish to be rid of. Failure to expel them from a community brings misfortune. The fact that this is quite material (i.e. it is children who die, women who cannot conceive, crops that fail) means that not only are the consequences real but also the cause can be detected through mediations such as divination and oracles and the causes neutralized through the use of appropriate medicines, purification ceremonies and cult practices that will detect and defeat the malefactors. Action on the agency of others addresses itself ultimately to conditions of life and death, that is, to conceptions of bodily substances, to praxaeology in forms of corporeal materialities and to the giving and receiving of life as constitutive of social relations.

If these general points are to be of comparative significance we need to explore their working out in a number of discrete settings that are sufficiently diverse to ignore mutual influence, and yet sufficiently related in terms of long-term historical processes of population movements to suggest common origins, without needing to specify what these might have been. The overall theme is the politics of inclusion and exclusion and the management of the practical conditions that cause and cure misfortune. However, each example presented below represents a distinct historical trajectory within the overall repertoire of the images and ideas available as 'ways of thought and practice'.

A politics of closure

In the Grassfields region of Cameroon, Warnier (1993) has described objects as containers to represent ideas concerning procreation and nurturing, misfortune, illness and death. Pots, stones, bowls and bags (woven from raffia or cord) are only part of a range of artefacts that, once treated with medicines, can become containers for spirits that can influence human affairs for good or ill. The spirits of the dead or of the wild have to be attracted to come and inhabit a locality and be satisfied sufficiently either not to cause harm or to be of benefit to the people living there. Objects must therefore be the subject of libations, of offerings, of food and drink or of sacrifice in order to attract spirits to come and reside in them. Moreover what is being sought by supplicants is evidence that a special relationship exists between such spirits and people living either in the same locality or belonging to the same kin group. Containers are therefore intricately bound up with the creation of social relations and the conditions in which they can be maintained or dissolved. The relationship between humans and spirits is quite pragmatic and in some senses utilitarian. At the heart of this arrangement are rituals of commensality in which a certain intimacy expressed in the sharing of food and drink is recognized between people who identify themselves as having a common relationship. In the most powerful cases these are members of the same kin group who, in light of where their ancestors are buried, recognize a particular locality as being of especial significance to them. Ritualized objects are therefore potentially transitory in the sense that it is the role which they play for a while in articulating a more complex set of metonymic relationships between the people, substances and things that make up a social group. The assumption is that these can be maintained for the benefit of the group, but whether this is really so is by no means certain. The linking of elders and chiefly powers with ensuring conditions of fertility is matched by the fact that they can also bring hurricanes and diseases into the community. Pots can contain spirits that bring diseases as well as those that embody good intentions.

It is not surprising, therefore, that Grassfields material culture (also its folklore, songs, jokes) is dominated by an iconography of containment (Warnier 1993). Food is always prepared and served in packages made from plantain leaves; raffia wine is mixed and served from special pots; and the sauces used as a condiment for yam or maize base staples are served from bowls made specially for that purpose. Food and raffia wine are ingested and there are complex words for describing the soft, ground foods and liquids that are eaten as part of taking into the body those substances that will promote well-being and protect against illness and disease. A specially carved wooden bowl is used to mix palm oil and camwood to make a red paste that is smeared on a person's body to protect against misfortune. The independence of a lineage is defined by the head being able to rub this ritual substance on the bodies of his people. An elder should also drink from a special cup and his dried saliva on its rim, mixed with that of his predecessors, is seen as a means of establishing continuity with ancestors and drawing upon their mystical powers. Bridewealth is comprised of 'bags' given to men and 'bundles' given to women. The most important bag is the 'bag under the bed' given to the bride's father, which amounts to half the expenditure. The body of a woman at marriage is treated as a container that promises to be fertile. Before leaving her father's house, he will rub her body with a mixture of camwood and palm oil and he will allow her to drink raffia wine from his ancestral cup before the women of the house escort her to her husband's house. Through these seemingly endless chains of signifiers we see how many gestures, images and words in the Grassfields ethnography are predicated on the assumption that bodies and objects are *continua* of each other when treated as containers for the substances for protection and ritual manipulation. The human body is itself a container of powerful substances and can be manipulated to attract external forces to come and inhabit it. The installation ceremony of a titled elder or chief literally involves the remodelling of his body into a container by his ingestion of substances and medicines during a period of seclusion.

Parallels with purification rites can be found widely in Central Africa involving the remoulding of a patient's body, or as Devisch (1993: 38) put it: in a Yaka healing ritual "the patient moves from a state of being tied, closed up, emptied out towards a remoulding of the body's shell and content, while simultaneously being gradually reinserted in the complex interweave of body, group and world".

Containers including pots, houses and bodies are intimately tied to conceptions of the person. In their study of Mandara pottery, David *et al.* (1988) describe how pots are assimilated to persons and may contain the spirits of the living and the dead. The argument is not therefore symbolic in the sense that a material object represents a more diffuse concept of the person, but metonymic in the sense that literally the pot/person distinction is dissolved and the container is a means to act directly on both the physical body for curing and other purposes and through this on the social body as a whole. In the Grassfields this association between material containers and the human body is associated with ideas of procreation, with the origins of the various substances that make up a human body and with what happens to them at death. What appears as a strong distinction in gender roles in conception is embedded in patrilineal and matrilineal kinship. Indigenous conceptions of procreation relate the sexual act to cooking and the application of heat to the contents of a pot. Whilst semen feeds the foetus in the womb it is breast milk alone that feeds the baby and the two should not be mixed. Hence the wife should avoid sexual intercourse with the husband until the child is weaned because this will affect its health. The fact that witchcraft substance is thought to be passed through the matriline also accounts for a particular anxiety over the relation with the mother's father, since his anger or a formal curse can activate the substance to cause illness and death of his children's offspring.

Chiefdom organization and hierarchy have a basis in the accumulation of ancestral and material substances that are held and transmitted in bodily containers – those of chiefs and notables – and from them dispersed to subjects for them to absorb. These substances may be bodily (such as semen, blood, saliva or breath) that may be dispersed among subjects or food to be ingested (such as raffia wine and palm-oil), or cosmetics such as the mixture of oil and red ochre to be rubbed on the skin. Kin groups can in this sense be seen as containers that hold vital life substances in common to be transmitted to future generations. In a cosmological sense it is possible to trace boundaries and containers from the notion of the person outwards to kin group, to communities of co-residential groups, and to the chiefdom. These form a schemata of envelopes that reach deep into the subjectivity of people through treatment of the body, use of material objects, emotions and movements, images and speech that combine to form a single act. This takes the form of rituals held either regularly, such as giving libations to ancestors, or less frequently but significantly at times of either installation of a successor to a title or at funerals. The installation of a chief involves his seclusion for a period when he literally ingests the medicines and foods that will transform his body from that of a person into a 'magical entity' that can protect and ensure the well-being of his subjects. The general notion of containment is therefore an effect of rituals of closure concerned with enclosing the means of transmitting life and defending these against loss or diminishment due to the hostility of others.

I argue that whilst there are significant differences in the way these principles are objectified, parallels exist in these basic ideas over a large part of western Central Africa. On this 'same but different' theme David *et al.* (1988) have described comparable ideas for the Mandara region of northern Cameroon and Pradelles de Latour (1991) for the Bamileke area extending to the south. Wider still would be the arguments of MacGaffey (1980) and Vansina (1990) for a certain commonality of cultural form from the Grassfields to northern Angola. Related to this is Vansina's wider linguistically based argument about Bantu migration (Vansina 1984). His argument is not based on a decontextualized diffusion of attribute traits but on the co-presence of syncretized complexes of material culture and language attributes that have been transformed by millennia of adaptation and interaction. Essentially I am arguing that a commonality can be recognized that can be detected through continuity of cultural form, to which local adaptations of meaning provide variation and difference. It is an observer perspective concerned with the recognition of pattern, despite the range of meanings and uses made of it by people in local circumstances. So what is the continuity of form in what has been detected so far?

Inclusion and exclusion

It is now widely recognized that we find a notion of heat mediated transformation of materials in much of Bantu speaking Africa (e.g. de Heusch 1980). The inspiration for this derives from Lévi-Strauss's association of cooking with physiological processes (Lévi-Strauss 1970: 336). De Heusch, applying this metaphor to Southern Bantu cosmology, argued that the biological development of the person was seen as following the path of ritual cooking. The sexual act as a feature of heat applied to substances to produce a foetus establishes a relationship with nature that, he argues, has to be cooled down during the successful development from childhood to adulthood. The cooling down process is therefore a metaphor for gestation and growth; cooling down is also a metaphor for healing and for being incorporated into the social world of adults. A cosmogonic code is elaborated by de Heusch (1980) that links procreation and growth with healing and social order.

Analogues with the Grassfields material suggest that de Heusch's argument based on Southern Bantu ethnography can be found widely in Africa. There are similarities in the use of the heat metaphor to describe processes of gestation and birth. This recalls Evans-Pritchard's (1937) argument that in Azande thought there was no concept of nature as separate and autonomous and dominated by human physical intervention. Instead, human and natural growth were part of the same process and depended on each other. Human practices such as hunting or agriculture were therefore means of facilitating a natural process of which they formed a part. An exterior world of threat or menace to human/natural order exists in acts of sorcery, in violence, illness and death. This dualism in the social order has, therefore, strong inclusionary/exclusionary metaphoric associations – a point made more frequently by de Heusch (1982) in his symbolic analysis of African kingship in which he distinguishes, on the basis of oral history, the emergence of a 'divine' (celestial) kingship in opposition to an indigenous, terrestrial authority.

Adopting a semiotic approach, Collett (1993) also argues for a conceptual linkage between smelting, cooking and procreation in precolonial eastern and southern Africa. The gestation of the foetus and of iron are linked together because they both involve the transformation of one substance into another, through the mediation of heat. He also includes pots in such mediations and, by extension, relates pots to furnaces, and both to women's bodies as containers within which a process of gestation and growth takes place through an irreversible change of substance. A similar argument has been adopted by others writing on Central African metallurgy. There has been a tendency to reinforce a domesticated/wild dichotomy and the apparent paradox that whilst the symbolism of iron-working draws analogues between women's bodies and smelting furnaces, the actual process is in the hands of men and demands the exclusion of women for it to be successful (Barndon 2001; Bekaert 1998; Childs and Dewey 1996). The association of iron smelting with human life cycles has also been recognized by Herbert (1993) and the centrality of notions of reproduction to both processes. The linking of iron smelting to procreation gives African smelting a cosmic power implying that the combination of the cultural categories 'male' and 'female' provides different views about the combinations of substances in the human body and, by extension, production in general. Rowlands and Warnier (1993: 55) also recognized that male and female substances were combined in the production of precolonial iron in the Grassfields, and a similar pattern has been recognized by Childs (1991: 344) and Barndon (1996) and others in Central Africa. Willis (1967) also accorded embodiment and gender a central structuring role in Fipa myth. He argues that in Fipa mythology the body parts of head and loins are separated to represent maleness and femaleness, in order to show that their combinations were important metaphors for understanding and transforming their social world.

These observations concerning precolonial iron-working are consistent with a more general pattern established in the case of Grassfields material culture. Ideas of gestation and growth, production and reproduction, pervade both natural and social worlds. Success and failure are related to the virtues of containment and locality, as a means of ensuring the conditions of growth; hence the strong focus on material metaphors that define a cosmology of space as metaphorical domains. So far what has been omitted is precisely the sources of evil that undermine a carefully ordered world. Whether the entrances of compounds or the protection and well-being of bodies in the Grassfields or ensuring the balance of hot and cold substances in Central African iron-working, ideas of fertility and reproduction are inseparable from magic. What is being called 'magic' refers to medicines and treatments that effectively protect containers against the influence of evil and malevolent forces. The essential idea is that disease in human bodies, failures of iron smelting furnaces, stillbirths, and 'natural disasters' in both ethnographic/historical cases share a similar motif analogous to the invasion of the physical/social body by an external hostile force. It is intrusive agencies rather than an internal malady that cause illness, or it is said to be the infidelity of smelters or the presence of a menstruating woman in the workshop that causes the failure of an iron smelt. The theme goes back to Evans-Pritchard's (1937) equally moralistic explanation of Azande witchcraft as caused by social conflict and the actions of witches. Violence, quarrels and the spilling of blood are therefore dangerous because they breach the social order and allow malevolent forces to gain entry. Magic stands at the intersection of two lines of thought: one associated with fertility and reproduction, the other with violence and killing. The substance they have in common is blood; as an ancestrally transmitted substance contained in the body and as a potentially polluting substance of wounds, warfare and death. Sacrifice is one mediator between these two trains of thought since it spills the victim's blood yet does so in order to regenerate and renew the mystical conditions of life and growth. As a mediator between these extremes, sacrifice is fundamental to the practice of sacred power since it resolves the contradiction between destruction and regeneration, or between life and death, by transforming impotence in the face of externalized evil into ritualized omnipotence and mastery. Therefore, themes of commensality and well-being are part of the essential process of maintaining the boundaries within which safety lies. But the basic contradiction lies in concepts of witchcraft which in both of the above cases are detected as substances passed through the matriline and found, through autopsy, in the bodies of witches. Such persons are already part of the social order and it is only through the ambivalence of their actions in their use of witchcraft powers for good or evil that they are betrayed as 'enemies within'.

It is this ambivalence that sets the practice of precolonial iron smelting apart from other experiences of production and reproduction. Iron is both a source of value and a means of violence. From it are produced hoes and tools for clearing vegetation for agriculture and the weapons for hunting and killing in warfare. The fact that the iron smelting workshop is associated with violence would seem to be consistent with its treatment as a place to be set apart and inimical to domestic order. In both the Grassfields and the Central African case, iron smelting is associated with the wild, and furnaces were built in the bush and away from settlement. Herbert (1993) argues that hunting is associated with iron smelting in the way that both practices are associated with dangerous forces and both forbid sexual relations. Whilst the furnace may have been decorated with female attributes among the Fipa/Pangwa, to assume that the furnace was literally treated like a woman's body is inconsistent with the rigorous exclusion of pregnant or menstruating women from the workshop (e.g. Barndon 2001: 205, 221). Ritual prohibitions would be consistent with the workshop being treated as dangerous, and it being inimical for smiths to have contact with the processes of fertility. Herbert also emphasizes the role of smelters in performing dangerous transformations, such as smelting, royal coronation and royal burial, which can all be seen in terms of containment as movement from one state to another across dangerous thresholds (Herbert 1993). It is also the association of iron with failed production, with witchcraft and the causes of violence which seem to necessitate this exclusionary state.

We are not concerned here with a simple binary form of social order, reproduction, disorder, sterility type of argument, or a cosmic drama that opposes fertility and sterility since it is the presence of both in the social order that can be recognized in the myth/material culture patterning. It is reminiscent of Bloch's (1992) argument that, almost universally, rituals turn human beings into prey as sacrificiands. His dialectical argument describes a process in which human vitality is first opposed to social order as wild; sacrifice brings that vitality under the sway of social order through an act of ritual killing. Vitality is then restored through the final stage of re-incorporation of humans into social order, now altered by this external force. A conspicuous feature of Bantu mythology is the depiction of the hunter as a stranger. He comes from the outside, challenges existing authority, sometimes by killing, and then takes indigenous women to have children. This 'stranger-king' theme is widely found (cf. Sahlins 1985) but in Bantu mythology it is not simply the opposition of external dynamism to interior passivity that is important, but rather the culmination of the act in reproduction so that civilization can begin to work.

Like all origin myths, the explanation is that of a social order which is able to contain the worst aspects of violence and turn it into a dynamic and vital force. Yet this is never certain, hence the need to have skilled persons able to mediate between the two. Chiefs, diviners, witches, smiths and earth priests in different settings are able to move across the boundaries between lived and spiritual worlds, to influence or attract the actions of spirits or occult forces for social ends. To do this is a source of power but it also implies knowledge of invisible worlds – to see into them, affect them, and use this to impose moral and aesthetic order upon experience in the visible world of daily life. Efficacy in mediation is judged by results: the ability to provide protection from death and disease, famine and sterility through a proven ability to transform the invisible into the visible world of real effects.

Sacrificial economies as embodied practice

Seligman (1934: 5–6), applying Frazer's *Golden Bough* to Africa, claimed to recognize a common theme of the sacred king who derives his power not from birth but by ousting his predecessor and who, in turn, will be killed by a successor. The role of sacred king as sacrifice who in turn becomes himself a sacrificiand fits the above argument. Whilst the Christian bias in this formulation and the ethnographic veracity of some of the ethnographic cases used by Frazer have been criticized, the significance of sacrifice as an offering involving the death and consumption of a victim remains the distinctive characteristic (cf. Valeri 1994). The key to understanding sacred power is sacrifice and its mediation through the body of a ritual leader. However, there are significant differences in the particular culture histories of sacred power. The arguments of the previous two cases recognizes that sacrifice of ritualized bodies has to take into account how the body as container forms a metonymic part of a larger whole, and how the body both encloses a notion of vital force and contains a capacity for violence on which social reproduction depends. It is the combination of these two features which in turn shapes the argument for a scheme that, we argue, can be of more widespread African relevance.

Chiefdoms of south-west Cameroon, now grouped under the title of Bamileke, are described in the literature as wielding deeply ambiguous and dangerous powers. One description recorded by Miaffo (1977) describes a Bamileke chief as "good, illustrious, powerful certainly but dangerous and arbitrary, capable of every kind of bad act". He is often discussed using a term such as "if you kill his mother he eats her, sell her and he will take the money" (Miaffo 1977: 99).

The foundation legends of several Bamileke chiefdoms share motifs we have already encountered in Central African myths of chiefly origin (e.g. Pradelles de Latour 1991). The founding ancestor is an immigrant who has left a mother chiefdom over a succession dispute. He arrives as a hunter, deposes an indigenous earth priest, marries and produces children. The immigrant hunter establishes himself through gifts of wild game and attracts people to him through generosity. Through a ruse, he deprives other chiefs of their independence and founds the chiefdom. Ambiguity lies therefore in the fact that what is unified in Bamileke chiefship are two contradictory principles that, in a just and moral order, ideally should be kept separate. They can be represented as follows:

Sorcery	Ancestors
Power	Legitimacy
Forest/Hunting	Earth/Fertility

And when combined with the means (technical/mystical) of exercising these functions:

Witchcraft	Divination/Oracles
Magic/Medicines	Libations/Sacrifice

we arrive at the following functions occupied by positions of varying degrees of ambiguity in legitimacy/power:

Witchfinders	Rain/Earth Priests/Prophets
Power/Witches/Sorcerers	Legitimacy/Healers/Witchcleansers
Regulatory Societies	Elders/Diviners/Herbalists

Chiefs

In this model, chiefs mediate between principles since they have both ambiguities of power (like witches, they have the power to kill), and legitimacy (based on their relation to ancestors which may be used, for example, to detect witches). Whilst elders should be excluded from the contamination of killing, the power of chiefs usually involves the killing of criminals as well as hunting and other potentially polluting acts. In this sense chiefs overlap with (and can become) witches in the power to kill. Conversely, earth priests and magicians are healers who exercise the power of life in the public interest. Not only do they manage rain, fertility and conditions for life but they also provide some of the means to protect these resources against powers of witches and the legitimacy of ancestors. Finally, there are witchcleansers/diviners/healers who detect the work of witches, and those such as chiefs with witch-like powers that have used them for personal ends. Given the ambiguity of chiefly powers to combine life giving forces with the power to kill, it is perhaps not surprising that they are treated as 'divine' in much the same way as the ambiguous powers of the iron-working furnace, i.e. that they are to be kept away from.

This scheme is a model for sacred power in precolonial Africa (with postcolonial continuities in mind) devised to help generate comparison of various local histories that represent different trajectories. Each trajectory would have its own peculiarities of transmission and agency but in this analysis I have been more concerned with tracing commonality of principles on which to base comparison in Africa. I would argue that some such scheme is applicable to both Bantu and non-Bantu speaking peoples more or less widely in sub-Saharan Africa (MacGaffey 1980). Combined with the principles of containment and body substances, it is possible to locate the sources of these means and functions within different modes of embodiment. The argument about containers, for example, could be reduced to the single statement that whatever form they take, they are in fact transforms of the human body (Warnier 1993). A useful if speculative contrast between 'house societies' and 'embodied societies' could be made if we wished to characterize the distinctive nature of this schemata (cf. Lévi-Strauss 1983: 163–170). Sacred power in ancient Mesopotamia and more widely in the ancient Near East seems broadly inseparable from the identification of the person with the 'house', whether temple, palace or residence. This is not to deny that the house and the body are intimately linked and in constant interaction as both physical structures, objects of thought and a way of imagining social relations. Symbolizing the house as a body has a widespread distribution including significant type cases from Africa (one of which is Bourdieu's 1977 classic paper on the Kabyle house). But Lévi-Strauss' (1987: 151, cf. Carsten and Hugh-Jones 1995: 10) original definition of 'house societies' related them to 'transitional societies' by which he meant, cast in a rather evolutionary language, a form transitional between kin-based and class-based social orders. In such systems the prescriptions of elementary kinship are undermined by economic and political interests that may subvert and use the latter and convert them into the bases for rank and hierarchical differentiation as in the formation of aristocratic houses or noble lineages. Carsten and Hugh-Jones (1995) also make a connection between Lévi-Strauss' characterization of 'house societies' as transitional between elementary and complex structures and his discussion of Crow/Omaha kinship systems where marriage alliances are constrained by rules prohibiting further marriages between clans that have intermarried within certain generations. The logic is expansionist and in fact some of the more complex explorations of these forms have been made in West and South Africa (e.g. Heritier 1981), so a simple Africa versus Eurasia contrast in the manner of Jack Goody will probably not do. But unlike proto Indo-European kinship that has been broadly categorized as Omaha in type (cf. Mallory and Adams 1997), no such generalization would characterize proto-Bantu or

non-Bantu Africa. On the contrary, the cases of transitional 'house societies' in Africa could be linked to more recent historical events such as the expansion of long distance trade and the impact of European settlement.

I would suggest, therefore, that embodied societies are linked to elementary systems where bodies as containers of substances – regenerative, reproductive and life sustaining – are more directly implicated both as the 'raw material' out of which the social order is wrought and potentially as a source of danger to it. In contrast to the simple/complex dichotomy used by Lévi-Strauss, principles of embodiment are quite compatible with forms of hierarchy that exemplify the 'chief' as literally the 'father' or 'progenitor' of his people. In this context, power and sexuality are strongly entwined both in the benign form of the dispersal of reproductive substances and in hostile, violent forms of sexual conquest and the sacrifice of enemies.

To make a link with Ancient Egypt, I may posit analogues between Egypt and sub-Saharan Africa as sharing a proto-cosmogony.

> One could argue that pharaoh is ritually treated as a uniquely shaped container, who attracts powers relevant to life, productivity and order from the divine world and transmits them to his subjects. In this he is analogous to the creator god, whose bodily emissions (tears, saliva, semen, blood, air and light) are involved in the cosmogony, and the subsequent process of maintaining cosmic order.

(O'Connor, pers. comm. 2002)

Pharaohs, O'Connor suggests, also apparently shared in the possession of negative and highly dangerous powers that could be put to 'good use' in maintaining order and protecting social order from intrusive chaotic forces which threaten that order and well-being at every level, from the individual through the state to the cosmos. It is pharaoh also that authorizes executions and, like a Bamileke chief, mediates between principles of violence and legitimacy and who therefore is a figure of avoidance as well as ambivalence. Such features may characterize sacred kingship more widely than Egypt, but the focus is very distinctively on the king's body as autochthonous container and a conduit for the dispersal of substances.

A very useful analogue is provided by O'Connor's (forthcoming) discussion of the representation of pharaoh on the eastern High Gate of the mortuary temple of Ramesses III at Medinet Habu. The internal programme has carvings of the king and groups of attractive women described as "beautiful ones" or "not yet stretched by childbirth". O'Connor suggests that the programme celebrates the king's potency, his capacity to experience sexual arousal and achieve intercourse in his symbolic role, for the Egyptians, as the exemplary representative of male potency and fertility. "Overall, the emphasis is upon the benevolent aspects of the king's sexuality, which manifest themselves in the Egyptian context, and actually or exemplarily in relationship to Egyptians" (O'Connor forthcoming). By contrast to the eroticization of the relationship of pharaoh to his subjects, relations to enemies and the outside generally depict the aggressive force through which he achieves complete domination over foreign males. The external programme provides diverse images of foreign enemies being rendered helpless by pharaoh, of great battle scenes which are visually structured as hunts in which large numbers of enemies are ridden down and slaughtered or are harvested by him as if they were vegetation. Contextually,

reference is made to the slaughter of the younger generation rendering the living older generation of foreign enemies impotent and without progeny. Foreign male enemies become the victims of the king's own virility, portrayed perhaps in the symbolic homosexual rape of the victims but also heterosexually, when describing overwhelmed enemies as "spread out" before the king, like women in childbirth (O'Connor forthcoming). The internal and external programmes form a conceptual unity by entwining themes of power and sexuality in both, and in the way that the body of the pharaoh mediates between, and unifies, the two principles.

Since the Ancient Egyptian case relates to a period before Bantu expansion in sub-Saharan Africa, it is clearly difficult to suggest any kind of synchronic comparison. But the elaboration of principles in the cases discussed in this chapter suggest certain basic commonalities. The focus on reproductive substances and the body is one aspect of more fundamental ideas within an ontology of growth and procreation specifying the conditions of decay and sterility. The body as container is *not* used metaphorically to grasp the meaning of other forms of containment but quite literally, through the ingestion of substances and ritual practices, shapes and forms them. The nature of malevolence is nurtured by the fear that 'life force', however configured, is a 'limited good'. The extraction and dispersal of such substances by malevolent 'others' can be used to explain conditions of famine, unnatural deaths, illness and loss. Reconciling the two principles seems to be at the basis of a notion of power that, before colonial interference, was simply one form of attachment. But if attachment (and dependency) is therefore a prerequisite for life, it is also true that the form it takes may sometimes imply the opposite.

Conclusion

The incentive to explore the possibilities of arriving at a schema that would be applicable comparatively to the whole of sub-Saharan Africa is unashamedly political. It is justified in so far as it responds to the call for a revitalization of a sense of African unity. The role of embodiment and containment of life giving/destructive forces that we gloss by Europeanized notions (such chiefs as witchdoctors, diviners and prophets) has, I argue, a certain relevance for understanding the distinctive features of the politics of contemporary Africa. If such a recognition of the fundamental questions being discussed recently constitutes an endorsement of an Afrocentrist position which seeks an African renaissance to construct a new African history, identity and culture and to reassert the notion of Africanness, then so be it.

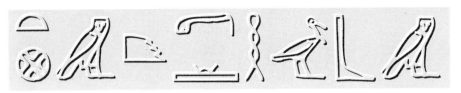

CHAPTER 5

ANCIENT EGYPT AND THE SOURCE OF THE NILE

Andrew Reid

This chapter explores speculation about relations between Ancient Egypt and the Great Lakes region of eastern Africa and how, over time, external factors, rather than conclusions derived from established evidence, have shaped discourse. Understanding of both Ancient Egypt and Great Lakes Africa was firmly entrenched in how Europe saw itself in relation to the wider world. This chapter illustrates an element of the process of locating Ancient Egypt in the broader European worldview, specifically examining Ancient Egypt's relationship with distant parts of the African continent. This location of Ancient Egypt can be contrasted with the treatment of sub-Saharan Africa and how Africa was considered to relate to the European world. Ancient Egypt and Great Lakes Africa make for particularly intriguing comparison because now they are both considered to be examples of indigenous state formation on the African continent. Their very different treatment in the past reveals much about the manner in which Europeans order(ed) the past and present worlds around them. In the absence of any real evidence for contacts between Egypt and the Great Lakes, the links that were drawn between the two demonstrate European unease in categorizing Ancient Egypt and sub-Saharan Africa. As will become clear, the quandary was essentially whether Ancient Egypt was African and not so sophisticated, or non-African and highly civilized. It would seem that a third possible option, that it was African and highly civilized, was unthinkable.

The absence of evidence for direct links between the two regions did not stop writers from drawing on a wide body of evidence to support their ideas. In what follows, extensive use is made of quotations in order to critically examine the psyche of 19th and 20th century pioneers in a range of fields. Detailed examination of the claims made of archaeology, history and ethnography makes it possible to explore why writers came to regard evidence to be so convincing that they could state that "an Egyptian influence has been at work in Uganda is I think certain" (Tucker 1908: 85). Most worryingly, ideas generated by explorers, missionaries and administrators in the late 19th century can be seen to be behind many of the academic interpretations of African history in the 20th century.

A question of geography

It is difficult to imagine two more disparate areas than Egypt and the Great Lakes region of eastern Africa, although environmental differences would not by themselves rule out meaningful human contact between the two. Egypt's harsh, arid, flat desert contrasts the extravagant verdance of the Great Lakes' swamps, rainforests and occasional snow-capped peaks. The Great Lakes' most arid locations receive considerably more rainfall than Egypt's wettest. The northern shores of Lake Victoria, the wettest part of the Great Lakes region, currently experience over 250 thunderstorm days a year, accumulating rainfall of more than 2,000 mm annually. Yet such disparate locations, separated by a distance of over 4,000 km, are connected to one another by a unique geographical feature – the Nile. This geography encouraged some commentators to draw links between the two regions. In the rapidly expanding European worldview of the 19th century, writers attempting to explain new discoveries needed to rely on existing knowledge to order the world around them.

The major polities of the Great Lakes were first encountered as an accidental consequence of the 19th century European quest for the source of the Nile. With hindsight, the efforts of European geographers and explorers investigating and debating the source of the Nile were an archetypal Victorian folly. European explorers were aware of centuries and even millennia of debate regarding the origins of the Nile and on their travels encountered people with local knowledge. Their expeditions were intended to test hypotheses. However, the briefest glance at exploration journals indicates that these geographical goals were secondary to actively constructing a sense of adventure and exploration of the unknown and, most importantly, establishing a sense of the 'other' in their encounters with African populations, thus placing Europe and Europeans in a privileged position in relation to these communities. "Discovery" of the source of the Nile was a necessarily eurocentric perspective, ignoring indigenous knowledge systems, which had understood some of this geography for some time, best indicated by Stanley's ironic account of his encounter with the 'Geographical Society of Karagwe' (Stanley 1899: 368). In addition, something approaching the correct origins of the furthest extension of the Nile, or at least the snow-capped Ruwenzori Mountains, were mentioned as one of three possibilities by Herodotus, writing in the fifth century BC (see Stanley 1878 for a summary of early exploration of the Nile). However, Herodotus reasoned that snow could not form in the heat of the Sahara, and therefore discounted this hypothesis. Subsequently, interest was expressed over the centuries by Greek, Roman, Arabic and northern European scholars as to the river's origins, with several early expeditions reaching as far south as the vast inland Delta of the Nile, the Sudd (Figure 5:1). Ironically, the focus of their attention, the White Nile, which originates from the Lake Chad and Lake Victoria basins of Equatorial Africa, does not in fact provide the greatest volume of water flowing in the river, although it does form the longest extension of the Nile. Despite its high rainfall, outflow from the Great Lakes is constrained by the trapping of water in Lake Victoria, the world's second largest freshwater lake. Instead, rainfall between April and June in the Ethiopian highlands swells the Atbara and the Blue Nile and causes the floods in Egypt between June and September, which were the cornerstone of ancient Egyptian agriculture prior to the construction of the Aswan Dam. During these floods, the Ethiopian tributaries may

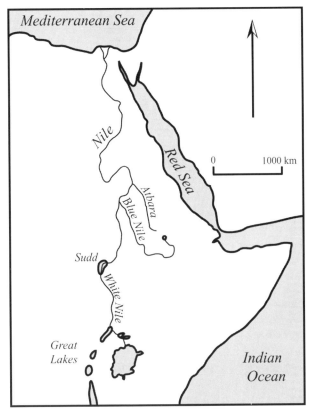

Figure 5:1   The Nile.

supply up to 100 per cent of the water reaching Egypt. By contrast, the White Nile supplies the bulk of water in the river throughout the remainder of the year, when levels are at their lowest. Therefore, lower annual minima in the Egyptian Nile reflect declining rainfall in the Great Lakes.

Obviously, water levels in the Nile are the result of the complex interplay between the climatic regimes in Equatorial Africa and in Ethiopia. Fluctuation in the actual timing of the rains can have considerable consequences, and it is therefore difficult to isolate a single subsidiary source as the sole factor controlling one aspect of river flow. Although its contribution to river levels in Egypt is considerably less than the Blue Nile, the White Nile is none the less significant for sustaining water levels. Rains in June and September in the Great Lakes generally determine the rate of decline of the main flood levels in Egypt. Good rains result in a gradual decline; poor rains cause a rapid drop. This uncertainty has important, if secondary, consequences for the agricultural cycle in Egypt in helping to determine the agricultural potential of different parts of the floodplain, the levels in the backwaters on the margins of the floodplain, and the need to lift water to agricultural land. Between November and April in Egypt, low rainfall supplying the White Nile leads to low river levels downstream, which affects river transport by reducing current and creating treacherous shallows. It is unclear, however, to what extent major river transport was attempted outside the season of the floods.

Logically, the Great Lakes environment had significant bearing on the course of life in Ancient Egypt. However, European observers were divided as to whether, culturally, the current ran in reverse. Whilst those most concerned with exploration and the creation of new colonies in the Great Lakes often perceived Ancient Egypt as a likely source for Great Lakes civilization, some early 20th century scholars saw Great Lakes societies as an inspiration for Ancient Egypt.

European contact with Great Lakes Africa

European exploration of the Great Lakes took place as part of increasing domination of the world in the 19th century. Dominance of the world economy was supported by ideological rationalization of this apparent superiority. The late 19th century witnessed European expansion into the last of the major continents, in what is now known as the 'Scramble for Africa'. By the 19th century, Europeans had constructed elaborate evolutionary frameworks representing Africans as the lowest form of human development. Europeans entering Africa believed they were confronting the base character of human nature, the antithesis of European civilization, and that they had a moral obligation to effect change, regardless of the reluctance of the continent's inhabitants. A casual perusal of titles of explorers' journals, published at the time, indicates the emotive appeal of travelling through the 'Dark Continent'.

There were stark differences in the preconceptions of Ancient Egypt and of African societies, which explorers, missionaries and administrators took with them to the African continent. Ancient Egypt had long been known to Europeans, principally because of its appearances in the Bible and its perceived peripheral location in the classical and medieval worlds (Ucko and Champion 2003). Its incorporation into Greek, then Roman and latterly into Arab worlds had served to continually mark its presence. In the late 18th century, Ancient Egypt was readily perceived as African and as a minor polity of little significance. The discoveries arising from Napoleon's expedition to Egypt (Jeffreys 2003b) demonstrated that Ancient Egypt went beyond this peripheral status, and served to keep Ancient Egypt in the public consciousness throughout the 19th century. This implied, under prevailing perceptions, that Ancient Egypt was highly sophisticated and African. Not surprisingly, thought changed rapidly to describe Ancient Egypt as a 'white' civilization (Bernal Chapter 2, this volume). The contrast between the theoretical treatment of Ancient Egypt and that of the African interior was immense. During three centuries of slaving by Europeans, principally in western parts of Africa, there was no perceived need to investigate the African interior. Slavery was no doubt easier on the conscience if the enslaved were dehumanized and the continent demonized. Indeed, perceptions of Africans changed from seeing them as the lowest form of human, inspired by Christian thinking, to the Enlightenment view of regarding Africans as being sub-human or non-human in nature (Sanders 1969). In the mid-19th century, early Victorian society's perception of Africa began to change, at least in some sections of society, informed by the writings of a few missionaries, most notably David Livingstone. Livingstone articulated a desire to counter the activities of Arab slave-traders along the East African coast and to alleviate the suffering he perceived amongst the populations of southern and eastern Africa. More important, he communicated with a large and receptive British audience. Not surprisingly, he considered the root-cause of eastern and southern African peoples' problems to be their ignorance of the Bible, which he and other missionaries saw as a prehistoric falling away from Christianity (see Bennett Chapter 8, this volume). His recommendation was that these impoverished people could only be properly assisted to re-establish themselves by wholesale European colonialism. European society was therefore encouraged to think of Africans as simple human beings, practising primitive and base lifestyles and living in small, non-hierarchical societies, who needed the help of European civilization. Not surprisingly, there was no appreciation of the contribution of European mercantile capital in destabilizing African communities in eastern and southern Africa in the 19th century (e.g. Koponen 1988: 361).

In 1861, Europeans (Speke and Grant) first encountered the kingdoms of the Great Lakes region (Figure 5:2). No matter how observers wrote about these states, they clearly did not conform to the stereotypes of impoverished African society. In the Great Lakes region kings sat within highly organized courts, with hierarchical lines of communication stretching across the state (Connah 1987; Reid 1997). In states such as Nkore, Rwanda, Karagwe and to a certain extent Bunyoro and the Buhaya kingdoms, economic power was exerted through the control of cattle. In Buganda, by contrast, extensive banana plantations developed, leading to conflict over the control of land.

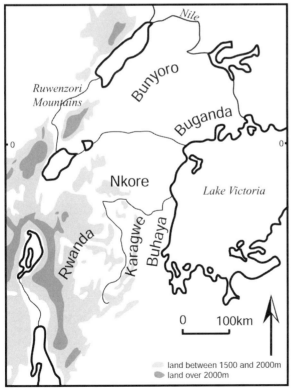

Figure 5:2   The Great Lakes region of Africa.

Kings were responsible for ensuring the fertility and fecundity of the state, which they did in regular elaborate rituals, such as the New Moon celebrations. Governance was extended through chiefs, delegating power over successively smaller units of people. The centres of government were large capitals (Figure 5:3), including highly impressive architecture. These capitals were regularly rebuilt, and their careful symbolic layout served to confirm the authority of the king (Ray 1991: 133–138). Kings had at their disposal large armies and, in the case of Buganda, navies. The diverse products of the region were efficiently circulated through regional markets, routinely moving products several hundred kilometres over land or across the lake. Movement in places like Buganda was further facilitated by the building of roads, which included the construction of causeways across its wide swamps.

Ancient Egypt in Great Lakes Africa

The earliest encounters Europeans had with Great Lakes Africa were largely recorded in the accounts of explorers, missionaries and subsequently administrators. Explorers had to appeal to readers of newspapers and books in order to get funding for further expeditions. Missionaries had to demonstrate the need for their presence in spreading Christianity and in improving the lives of fellow human beings. Administrators had to satisfy taxpayers that establishing yet another colony was an important issue worthy of public expenditure.

For most of these Europeans, writing for these various purposes, it was unthinkable that these states of the Great Lakes could have arisen without some external stimulus. Many writers, it has to be admitted, chose not to discuss the origins of the kingdoms, often ignoring the kingdoms entirely, but those who did were

Figure 5:3   A capital of the Buganda kingdom (Stanley 1878: facing page 308).

unanimous in looking for what they considered to be non-African elements, reflecting the disregard for African capabilities inherent in 19th century European society. The scope of these purported external stimuli was by no means restricted to Ancient Egypt but also included variously 'Abyssinia', 'Rome' and 'Arabia'. Reference to these civilizations was made in a manner which would now be described as both casual and interchangeable.

European opinion was guided by preconception and the impressive Great Lakes states themselves. As Tucker (1908: 86) put it somewhat paradoxically, the most "striking testimony to the influence of some ancient [i.e. non-African] civilization is the complex system of unwritten law, and of national government, which from time immemorial has prevailed in Uganda". Diffusion was of course a well-regarded explanation of cultural change in the late 19th century. Thus, Stanley (1890, 2: 359), in providing his account of his third major expedition, talks about the development in Great Lakes Africa that "has been effected during fifty centuries by long successive waves of migration from Asia into Africa". All had a stake in establishing that the states were a non-African phenomenon. Explorers, particularly in the case of Stanley, were obliged to fuel preconceptions regarding the African continent in order to satisfy their readership and to continue to be funded by publishers. The political significance of this writing was clearly increasing in the late 19th century.

It is intriguing that in the account of his second major expedition, between 1874 and 1878, Stanley (1878) failed to make any mention of the external origins of the kingdoms or their inhabitants, despite travelling extensively in the region. In between expeditions, of course, Stanley had enjoyed a period of employment in the service of King Leopold in the Congo. Leopold's devastation of this territory, prosecuted in part under the direction of Stanley and leading to the death of at least five million people, was considered excessive even in the late 19th century (Hochschild 1998). Additionally, in 1885 the Treaty of Berlin was signed which created the effective division of Africa between European countries and the creation of commercial territories. Stanley's newly developed colonial zeal is most aptly demonstrated in his preface to the second edition of his account of his 1874–1878 expedition, in which he berates British colonial inactivity by comparison with German and Belgian commercial success (Stanley 1899). By the end of the 19th century, exploration, colonialism and commercialization were obviously closely linked. Missionaries also advocated European expansion. Although missionaries presented a picture of poor, helpless, uneducated folk in need of salvation, they thought salvation would come as readily from capitalism as from Christianity. Investment and development, they believed, would help nurture Christian values. Mackay, writing in the context of Great Lakes Africa in 1878, revealed his hopes for development, alongside his lack of understanding of the workings of the Nile watershed:

> The wheat and rice and cotton fields of Egypt are of no small importance in the world's supplies; and considering the amount of English money invested in the country, capitalists would do well to turn their attention to Lake Victoria, for the rise and fall of the waters in that tank determine the amount of produce in Egypt.

> (Mackay 1890: 93)

Subsequently for administrators of the new Uganda Protectorate, it was important to present their role in promoting effective government throughout the entire territory. As in other parts of the British Empire (e.g. Leach 1990), extant, indigenous myths regarding outside civilizing peoples and their political innovations were greatly encouraged. Tales of Cwezi, previous ghostly, pale/white innovators, created an important precedent for European imperialism in the Great Lakes. Now, Cwezi are regarded as key elements in defining the indigenous development of ritual and political power in the Great Lakes kingdoms (Robertshaw 1999; Tantala 1989). At the end of the 19th century, the origin of these political innovators was, for some, apparently self-evident: "the Negro, in short, owes what little culture he possessed, before the advent of the Muslim Arab and the Christian white man, to the civilizing influence of ancient Egypt" (Johnston 1902: 487). Within this context of external origins, the kingdoms were then promoted and became the cornerstone of indirect rule. Buganda, "perhaps one of the best organized and most civilized of African kingdoms" (Johnston 1902: 636), was central to this enterprise, and Buganda administrators and missionaries were sent throughout the Uganda Protectorate.

Various items of material culture and elements of cultural practice were drawn upon to demonstrate the connection between Ancient Egypt and the Great Lakes. These links were made on an extremely casual and often contradictory basis. Stanley (1890, 2: 366), in the account of his last major expedition, drew explicit comparison with illustrations of Ancient Egyptian material culture published in popular form by Wilkinson (1854). Attention was drawn to the cloth wrappers worn around the waist by some individuals in Ancient Egypt and common amongst pastoralist societies in the Great Lakes (Figure 5:4). Bow-harps were also noted from both ancient Egyptian tombs and ethnographic encounters (Figure 5:5). Besides these explicit comparisons,

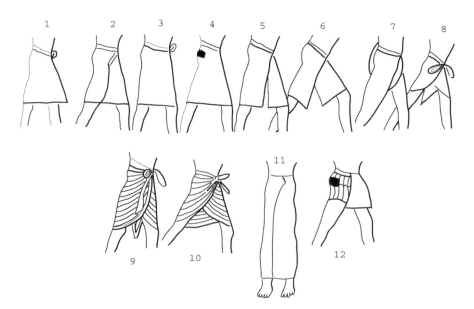

Figure 5:4   Styles of clothing in Egyptian art (after Wilkinson 1854: fig. 459).

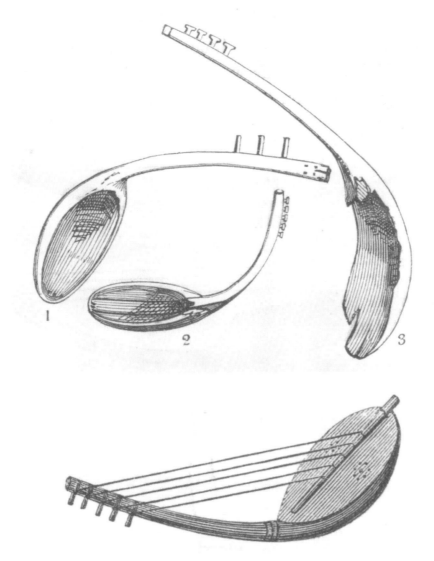

Figure 5:5   Bow-harps recovered from Egyptian tombs (Wilkinson 1854: figs. 135, 136).

Stanley (1890, 2: 366–368) also suggested a plethora of other items linking the two regions:

> The hafts of knives, the grooves in the blades and their form, the triangular decorations in plaster in their houses, or on their shields, bark clothes, cooking utensils, and in their weapons, spears, bows and clubs; in their *mundus*, which are similar in form to the old pole-axe of the Egyptians, in the carved head-rests, their ivory and wooden spoons; in their eared sandals, which no Mhuma would travel without; in their partiality to certain colours, such as red, black and yellow; in their baskets for carrying their infants; in their

reed flutes; in the long walking staffs; in the mode of expressing their grief by wailing, beating their breasts, and their gestures expressive of being inconsolable; in their sad, melancholy songs; and in a hundred other customs and habits, I see that old Egyptian and Ethiopian characteristics are faithfully preserved among the tribes of the grass-land.

Another item "which in their beauty, speed and strength speak, to my mind, so eloquently of that ancient Egyptian influence" (Tucker 1908: 86) was the plank-sewn canoe of the Buganda (Figure 5:6). Their form, in particular their prow, "seems to be very clearly of Egyptian origin" (Tucker 1908: 85). Not renowned for his sympathy towards his Buganda hosts, Tucker (1908: 85) offered faint praise: "The Uganda canoe is very impressive in the silent testimony which it bears to the comparatively civilized condition of the people. It is a wonderful contrast to the shapeless dugout which creeps along the shores of Usukuma in the south."

Johnston was also keen to point to items which proved external origins. "The Kavirondo cultivate the sesamum and make oil from its seeds, which they burn in *little clay lamps* strongly resembling in form those of Egypt and Rome" (Johnston 1902: 741). A curious artefact category, which Johnston discusses on several occasions, was "blue beads of a large size and dull appearance" (Johnston 1902: 36), worn as earrings by Luo in the north-eastern corner of Lake Victoria. These beads were claimed, by those they adorned, not to be trade beads, but were said to have been collected from fields near the 'Maragolia Hills'. Johnston (1902: 784–785) imagined that "the original possessors of these beads made considerable settlements in the neighbourhood of the Maragolia Hills and that the beads were constantly being dropped and lost in the fields", and hence concludes that "ancient village sites" (Johnston 1902: 209) must be present. The significance for Johnston (1902: 783) is clear:

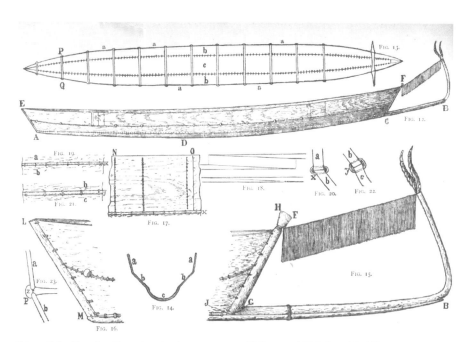

Figure 5:6   Construction of a plank-sewn canoe (Kollmann 1899: figs. 12–23).

These beads, and the custom of building clay walls with arched doorways round the villages, may possibly indicate that in ancient times representatives of a superior, not wholly negro, race may have come down from the north, and have dwelt as traders, miners, or settlers in these countries to the south of Mount Elgon.

Besides being an illuminating example of the manner in which archaeology was constructed in the colonial past, if the source of these beads were to have been accurate, that is from archaeological sites of whatever antiquity, these stories would also have been an intriguing example of indigenous African archaeology practised prior to the arrival of Europeans. Needless to say, evidence for these beads does not now exist and there is nothing to indicate that they were anything other than trade beads regularly available in the 19th century. Also, the location of the 'Maragolia Hills' is unknown and no such sites have been found by any of the archaeologists who have worked on the later archaeology of the area.

A further element receiving regular attention was religion. Casual references suggest religious connotations. For instance, Buganda oral traditions recognize the founder of the kingdom as a mystical character by the name of Kintu whom Stanley (1890, 1: 345), "from his character", describes as "probably a priest of some old and long forgotten [non-African] order". Naturally, missionaries took a special interest in indigenous religious practice, if only to assess the nature of the opposition. Buganda was the main focus of missionary activities. In Buganda, the Lubaale cults recognized a pantheon of deities, which missionaries considered to be more sophisticated than regular African religious practice. Writing in 1885, a Mr O'Flaherty suggested that "Lubare [sic] is not a cold, bare unmeaning system of devil worship, as some have reported it to be, but rather an attractive service calculated to fill the heart of the simple-minded native with awe and wonder and to captivate him with its charms" (in Tucker 1908: 85). This degree of sophistication in Africa could mean only one thing: "it is a mixture of Alexandrian Gnosticism and ancient Egyptianism in which Lubare incarnate takes the place of Christ and the whole system the place of a corrupted Christianity" (in Tucker 1908: 85). This may suggest that O'Flaherty agreed with religious commentators in southern Africa at around the same time who saw African societies as fallen from Christianity (see Bennett Chapter 8, this volume).

Hamites

An important strand in these arguments was that there was a major influx of a more sophisticated people in the distant past. These ideas were encouraged by the popularity of Hamitic explanations for the origins of ancient Egyptian civilization (Folorunso Chapter 6, O'Connor and Reid Chapter 1, Wengrow Chapter 9, all this volume). The notion of Hamites has a long and curious history. It had been adopted into Christian Europe from Jewish sources by the 16th century. These representations derived from Ham, the cursed son of Noah, whose offspring, as well as being sinful and degenerate, were originally represented as being dark, but in later texts were said to have been black (Sanders 1969). These perceptions helped to provide moral justification for the development of the slave trade, exploiting what became known as the Negro-Hamite. During the 18th century Enlightenment, the popularity of this Hamitic concept waned as ideas of a separate creation gained. The latter idea relegated Africans to non-human status. Towards the end of the 18th century, some writers began to see Egypt as an African creation (Bernal Chapter 2, this volume). The Napoleonic encounter with Ancient Egypt revealed the extent of Egyptian civilization, and throughout the 19th century this civilization was increasingly perceived to be incompatible with an African origin. During the 19th century the notion of Hamites was resurrected by a subtle shift in biblical interpretation, which allowed Hamites to be reconstituted as Caucasoid; as such they could then be considered capable of civilization. Towards the end of the 19th century, the emerging ideologies of colonialism and racism promoted the concept of the Caucasoid Hamite to such an extent that writers from 1890 onwards demonstrate a remarkable uniformity in their application of the idea. This contrasts with the ambiguities inherent in the earliest use of the term in relation to the Great Lakes. Speke (1863: 246), encountering the pastoralist populations of the Great Lakes, remarked that it was "impossible to believe, judging from the physical appearance of the Wahuma, that they can be of any other race than the semi-Shem-Hamitic of Ethiopia".

Subsequently, it became readily accepted that a migration of Hamites was responsible for all political development on the African continent.

> In this way, and through Uganda as a half-way house, the totally savage Negro received his knowledge of smelting and working iron, all his domestic animals and cultivated plants (except those, of course, subsequently introduced by Arabs from Asia and Portuguese from America), all his musical instruments higher in development than the single bowstring and the resonant hollowed log, and, in short, all the civilization he possessed before the coming of the white man – Moslem or Christian – 1,000 years ago.
>
> (Johnston 1902: 486)

This influx was considered to have had a major impact on the human populations they encountered. From Hamites "more than a third of the inhabitants of Inner Africa had their origin" (Stanley 1890, 2: 355). Through miscegenation "the Semitic became tainted with Negro blood, the half-cast tribes intermarried again with the primitive race, and became still more degraded in feature and form" (Stanley 1890, 2: 355). Evidence for Hamites was readily found in the very different countenance of pastoralist groups, such as the Tusi and Hima, who were associated with the more westerly cattle-based Great Lakes states. These states were characterized by cattle-keeping and agricultural classes who were regarded as culturally and socially (and therefore ethnically) distinct. Thus, the cattle-keeping Hima were "tall, light-colored, with comparatively intellectual features, they remind one in their cast of countenance of the ancient Egyptians. Here is a man the very image you would say, of a Ramses II" (Tucker 1908: 233). By contrast the agricultural Iru were seen to "have the usual Negroid cast of countenance, and neither their physical nor intellectual capacity is of a high type" (Tucker 1908: 233).

There was, however, a problem with this overview, because the Buganda kingdom, generally recognized as the most significant of the Great Lakes states, did not have a resident pastoralist population. Kollmann (1899: 9) articulates the problem:

> the high culture of the Waganda, their furniture – often of artistic make – and all the other articles in ordinary use, are incomparably better than those in the neighboring countries and the other countries occupied by Wahuma. In spite of this indisputable

Hamitic influence, the genuine Mganda belongs to the Bantu race as to his exterior, and his bodily type often exhibits the true Negro type. On the other hand, these countries in which the Wahuma blood has maintained itself more from admixture, as Nkole, Karagwe, etc., present forms of noble, elegant, and graceful bearing; but here again civilization stands at a markedly lower level than in Uganda. Why and wherefore is a difficult problem to solve.

Kollmann's solution was to suggest that two migrations of distinct Hamitic peoples had occurred, with all traces of one group having disappeared. Johnston (1902: 214) suggests an alternative hypothesis reliant on Victorian notions of civility, virtue and sexuality.

Though the [B]Uganda dynasty, no doubt, belongs in its origin to this Hima stock, which is Hamitic and of the same race from which most of the earlier inhabitants of Egypt proceeded, nevertheless, as for several hundred years it has married Negro women of the indigenous race, its modern representatives are merely negroes, with larger, clearer eyes, and slightly paler skins.

Johnston seems to have believed that racial difference, and degree of social evolution, led to a difference in sexual appetite and fertility, acting against the more refined. "The women of pure Hima blood are not very fertile, and the men augment their households with wives or concubines from the Negro tribes around them" (Johnston 1902: 630–631). By contrast, what he considered to be the indigenous peoples of the Great Lakes had an unfettered desire for sexual activity, which had led to unfortunate consequences. "It would almost seem as though the Baganda had lost much of their original vigour as a race through the effects of former debauchery and the appalling ravages caused among them by syphilis" (Johnston 1902: 640).

Roscoe (1923: 7), in an uncharacteristic digression from his extensive and highly focused ethnography, describes the process in Bunyoro:

The pastoral people at first forbade intermarriage with the agricultural tribes on the land. The custom of allowing favoured peasants to marry into the ranks of the pastoral people arose after a certain amount of laxity had already crept into the observance of milk-customs, and when intermarriage had become more common the old strict laws and taboos were rapidly forgotten. The effect of these mixed marriages was also apparent in the physical appearance of the race, though, owing to the fact that some pastoral clans have kept themselves apart, there are still to be found people who show little trace of negro blood, and whose purity of descent is traceable in the early Egyptian or Roman type of their features.

Ultimately, most authors seem to have recognized that there was no clear evidence for these Egyptian or other external origins. This is reflected in the contradictions within many of the writings. They were evidently unsure whether this evidence represented a result of contact during the height of Egypt, a pre-existing state or subsequent movement of peoples up the Nile. A pre-existing state is suggested by Stanley's opinion that "thus, the unlettered tribes of these long unknown regions are discovered to be practicing such customs, habits and precepts, as must have distinguished the ancestors of the founders of the Pyramids in the dark prehistoric ages of Egypt" (Stanley 1890, 2: 368). Writers were, however, equally unsure that Ancient Egypt was directly responsible. Johnston (1902: 486), in a statement directly contradicting other comments of his own in the same publication, admits, "Rather it would seem as though Ancient Egypt traded and communicated directly with what is now Abyssinia and the Land of Punt (Somaliland), and that the Hamitic peoples of these countries facing the Red Sea and Indian Ocean carried a small measure of Egyptian culture into the lands about the Nile lakes".

Great Lakes Africa in Egypt

Bernal (Chapter 2, this volume) has examined how 19th century thinking on the origins of Ancient Egypt, faced by the civilized/African paradox, changed from considering Ancient Egypt as having an African origin to seeing its roots in western Asia. By the early 20th century ideas promoting the latter origin were predominant, fuelled concomitantly by increasing recognition of the significance of ancient Egyptian civilization and by mounting interest in rationalizing territorial acquisitions on the African continent, which were perceived to be incompatible with examples of African self-government. Encounters with major political forms in the Great Lakes and in other parts of the African continent began to make available new sources of information for anthropologists. This increased awareness of ethnography then offered a new source of some potential with which to reconsider ancient Egyptian evidence. Foremost in this endeavour was the Egyptologist E. A. W. Budge, who drew on elements of the ethnography of many African societies, demonstrating similarities between them and the myths and rites of Ancient Egypt. The work was stimulated by Budge's own sojourn as a government official in the Sudan, commenced in 1897. As a result of successive visits to the Sudan, he

> became convinced that a satisfactory explanation of the Ancient Egyptian religion could only be obtained from the Religions of the Sudan, more especially those of the peoples who lived in the isolated districts in the south and west of the region, where European influence was limited, and where native beliefs and religious ceremonies still possessed life and meaning.
>
> (Budge 1911: xvii)

Budge recognized that some might consider these contemporary African societies to be "survivals of ancient Egyptian religious views and opinions". However, against this he cited the great time depth and "that many of the most illuminating facts for comparative and illustrative purposes are derived from the Religions of peoples who live in parts of Africa into which Egyptian influence never penetrated" (Budge 1911: xvii). Budge concluded that since the beliefs underlying "modern" African religions were "almost identical" to those of Ancient Egypt and "they are not derived from the Egyptians, it follows that they are the natural product of the religious mind of the natives of certain parts of Africa, which is the same in all periods" (Budge 1911: xxv). His conclusion on Egyptian religion was that "the beliefs examined herein are of indigenous origin, Nilotic or Sudani in the broadest sense of the word" (Budge 1911: vii). Unfortunately, such engaging and seemingly progressive scholarly enterprise is then put firmly within its historical and social context. For Budge, evidently, Egypt was not one of the great civilizations and therefore could safely be considered to be African:

> it is wrong to class the Religion of Ancient Egypt with the elaborate theological systems of peoples of Asiatic or European origin, and worse than useless to attempt to find in it systems of theological thought which resemble the Religions of peoples who live on a

higher level of civilization than the primitive Egyptians. The fundamental beliefs of the ancient Egyptian belong to a time when he was near to Nature.

(Budge 1911: xxvi–xxvii)

Where immediate correlations could not be found in evidence from the Sudan, Budge searched societies further afield for what he considered relevant parallels. Thus, he drew on a number of Great Lakes societies for evidence of kingship, including Buganda, Bunyoro, Karagwe, Nkore and Rwanda. This evidence largely consists of simple reference, rather than detailed consideration. Ray (1991: 185) summarized five similarities which Budge drew between Buganda and Ancient Egypt: the royal jawbone, the royal umbilical cord, observation of lunar ceremonies, the association of the king with a bull, and the king as the embodiment of the nation. Evidence from other Great Lakes kingdoms was used to corroborate these similarities and also served to enable discussion of royal burials, spirit possession and illness and the significance of the throne. Of the similarities with Buganda, according to Ray, the emphasis placed on the royal jawbone and umbilical cord are key features of Buganda royal ritual, not present in Egypt. Conversely, the association of the king with a bull and the king as the embodiment of the nation are characteristics key to Ancient Egypt but not Buganda. The other element, the observation of lunar ceremonies, was practised in both locations, but in very different ways; in Egypt the moon was associated with the deity, Osiris, but in Buganda the rising of the moon, and the securing of fertility, was reason to give thanks to all deities and spirits.

Budge's ideas were novel for the day and do not appear to have found much favour. One of the major impediments was that of race. Even if there were cultural grounds for drawing similarities between Ancient Egypt and sub-Saharan Africa "it would not justify us in inferring an ethnical affinity between the fair or ruddy Egyptians and the black aboriginal races" (Frazer 1914: 161). Seligman's notion of the Hamitic migrations, and his collation of anthropological evidence with which to prove it, incorporated this racial perspective. Intriguingly, Budge does not mention Hamites in his entire two-volume work, either to support or refute the idea, despite readily acknowledging the contribution of the work of Stanley and Johnston, amongst others, to his data. Seligman's view was that the Ancient Egyptians were a significant offshoot of the Hamitic race, a culturally superior immigrant Caucasian population who intermixed with the indigenous population and became the source of civilization in Africa. For Seligman (1930: 96) "the civilizations of Africa are the civilizations of the Hamites" and this was a consequence of their being "better armed as well as quicker witted than the dark agricultural Negroes". Thus, all African civilizations, Ancient Egypt included, arose as a result of this Hamitic incursion and therefore shared Hamitic traces (a point which Rowlands Chapter 4, this volume, uses to constructive ends). By comparing ancient Egyptian society with modern 'Hamitic' societies in eastern Africa, Seligman considered it possible to define the major elements of early Hamitic culture. Since Seligman believed the Ancient Egyptians to be the most pure of Hamitic societies available for him to consider, he then looked for ancient Egyptian traits in East African societies to confirm his hypothesis. Subsequent writers, such as Frankfort (1948), maintained that Seligman's ideas could work with regard to cultural continuity and could demonstrate that Egyptian culture arose out of a preceding East African culture.

Seligman's evidence was heavily based on ethnography from the Sudan, particularly concerning the Shilluk, but he also drew on the ethnography of the Great Lakes kingdoms. Whereas Budge saw links with many African societies, including those of West Africa, Seligman was much more selective in distinguishing what he termed Nilotes, half-Hamites and the Southern Bantu from West African Negroes. According to him (Seligman 1913: 636 n. 2), Budge's "explanation implies that the 'African' religion of which he writes as forming the basis of Egyptian belief in predynastic times is essentially Negro in origin". Seligman regarded this view as "inherently improbable" and "even more difficult to accept since Elliot Smith [Champion 2003a] has shown that the predynastic Egyptians and earliest Nubians were not even Negroid. It seems scarcely credible that the White Race borrowed its beliefs from Negroes, with whom it had so little contact that miscegenation seldom or never occurred" (Seligman 1913: 636 n. 2).

Ray (1991: 191) discusses five features of Egyptian kingship that Seligman believed could be linked with Buganda: the treatment of the royal placenta, the royal brother–sister marriage, royal renewal rituals, the treatment of the royal corpse, and the royal falcon symbol. The first two of these Seligman attributed to Hamitic heritage and the remainder he believed were the result of the later spread of Egyptian ideas during the New Kingdom. Other elements from the Great Lakes, which Seligman highlighted, were the exclusive consumption of milk by Bahima pastoralists and the apparent evidence for regicide in Bunyoro. For Seligman, clearly, contemporary African societies had been moulded through their contact with a superior society, and had preserved this evidence of contact for 5,000 years. This view was articulated by Frankfort, who, in discussing Maasai ethnography, claimed that he had obtained "proof positive that certain objects, and a very high degree of probability that certain customs, have survived in Africa without change these five thousand years" (Frankfort 1932: 451).

Frankfort's ultimate goal was the explanation of Egyptian kingship. One of the sources he employed was ethnography: "there are alive today in Africa groups of people who are the survivors of that great East African substratum out of which Egyptian culture arose" (Frankfort 1948: 6). He believed that cultural ties could be shown to link Egypt with people such as the Buganda; "people who at least in their Hamitic traits, are related to the ancient Egyptians. We seem here, again, to touch upon that North and East African substratum from which Egyptian culture arose and which still survives among Hamitic and half-Hamitic people today" (Frankfort 1948: 70).

The theoretical premise under which Frankfort operated was carefully stated. Thus, in comparing the royal twin symbols of Buganda with an object from an Egyptian depiction, Frankfort (1948: 70–71) rationalizes: "Since we know absolutely nothing about this object from Egyptian sources, one is inclined to explain it tentatively by reference to modern usages belonging to a group of people demonstrably related by some of their cultural, as well as by linguistic and physical traits, to the ancient Egyptians." Yet, such seemingly reasonable academic endeavour, concerning material culture, is yet again founded on a racial premise. When using ethnography, "this evidence requires correction, for we are dealing here with savages who, either by tenacity or by inertia, have preserved through several thousand years the remnants of a primeval world of thought, while Pharaonic culture was the most highly developed and most progressive of its age" (Frankfort 1948: 6).

These notions of the broad cultural influence of Ancient Egypt on the African continent have persisted into more recent times (e.g. Meyerowitz 1960). In discussing the significance of Ancient Egypt, a standard African history textbook, used widely in university education across the continent, opines:

> It is surely *only reasonable* to infer that politico-religious ideas and practices, which later became very widely distributed, had their origin and growth in this uniquely fertile soil. Later, much later, they would be exported, directly to Nubia, and, at tens and hundreds of removes, to more distant parts of Africa, where migrants establishing 'conquest states' would try in absurdly different circumstances to apply some already greatly modified form of the Egyptian idea of the state. So it would come about that four thousand years and more after the Old Kingdom had reached its peak, a Monomatapa ruling to the south of Zambezi would marry his 'Queen Sister', or that on his accession an Omukama of Bunyoro in western Uganda would ceremonially 'shoot the nations' by firing arrows to the four points of the compass.
>
> (Oliver and Fage 1962: 37; emphasis added)

It is only with this volume's sixth edition in 1988 that this paragraph was slightly modified – and then only by altering the opening statement to "It is surely *at least possible* to infer that ..." (Oliver and Fage 1988: 24; emphasis added).

Thus, views developed on the infirm foundations of racism and imperial conquest are found to still have currency almost 100 years later. Indeed, discussing the historical evidence, whilst Ray (1991) is clearly unimpressed by any such suggestions, Wrigley (1996) is more circumspect in his discussion of the possibilities of African contacts with Ancient Egypt. Viewed from a historiographical perspective, it is possible to understand how these essentially unsubstantiated conclusions were readily accepted in the past. Using this same historiographical perspective to demonstrate how such ideas were rooted in 19th century racism and colonialism, it is difficult to see how these ideas could still be considered to have some merit. It is particularly curious that historians appear to have encouraged the view of Africa as timeless, a continent without history, implying that African societies 5,000 years on were incapable of effecting historical change.

Archaeological perspectives on diffusion and contact

There is no single piece of archaeological evidence to indicate direct contact between the Great Lakes and Egypt, or any other centre of civilization within or outside Africa. As Wayland, when discussing putative Roman connections with Uganda, was able to state so succinctly in the 1930s: "reconstruction of some broken pots found at Ntusi calls to mind an *ampulla* – much as a queen termite calls to mind a sausage" (Wayland 1934: 30). Despite this it is only in recent decades that archaeologists have coherently and irrevocably established the independent nature of archaeology in eastern Africa. This is partly because it was only in the 1960s that archaeologists began to focus on the 'Iron Age' as a period worthy of study, rather than a recent short-lived epoch of tribal infighting and degradation (Robertshaw 1990). Earlier viewpoints were typified by

Cole (1964: 316), who described the Hamites on archaeological grounds as being "skilled builders in stone, road makers and irrigators", and stated, "In Uganda, there is little doubt about the presence of Hamitic peoples during the early part of the second millennium AD who left substantial relics of their occupation in Bunyoro, Buganda and parts of Ankole" (Cole 1964: 319). Some studies in archaeology and related disciplines continue to employ ideas rooted in the Hamitic premise (e.g. Desmedt 1991; Exchoffier *et al.* 1987). Since the 1960s, recognizing the essential independence of the East African record, archaeologists have had to find new explanations for the presence not only of sophisticated polities, but also towns, plant and animal domesticates, metallurgy, and ceramics. Many of these items had previously been assumed to have been introduced from further north, but now the burden is on proving these contentions. Plant and animal origins are generally easier to define because of their limited wild distribution. Sorghum and finger millet are now thought to have been developed as cultivated plants in north-eastern Africa (Rowley-Conwy *et al.* 1999). Cattle, long thought of as being a Near Eastern domesticate, were probably domesticated in the Sahara (Bradley and Loftus 2000). Importantly, explanations of the arrival of these domesticates now revolve around more local innovation and their exchange from society to society rather than their arrival as part of the baggage of a migratory population. In the case of metallurgy, Meroitic furnaces were thought to provide proof for the diffusion of iron smelting technology into Africa, but were subsequently discovered to be later, relating to the Roman occupation of Egypt. Schmidt's extensive investigation of iron smelting in Buhaya, on the western shores of Lake Victoria, suggested early dates and a distinct technology, possibly indicating an independent innovation of iron smelting (Schmidt 1981).

There appear to be good grounds for diffusion of new developments southwards, but there are obvious dangers in becoming too reliant on such ideas and in failing to see other patterns in the archaeological record. The persistence of north–south models of cultural diffusion in eastern African archaeology is a theme that has been highlighted, in particular, by scholars from the region (e.g. Abungu 1998; Chami 1994; Kusimba 1999). Indeed, Chami (1994: 32) suggests that the continued use of such models is a direct result of "how difficult it is to disentangle the mind from the diffusionistic/migrationistic and Hamitic paradigms". Instead, archaeologists have been urged to consider much more carefully the abilities of East African populations to produce innovations independent of other regions of the world, with the burden of proof being shifted to proving external origin, rather than internal innovation (Sinclair *et al.* 1993). It is also important to recognize that many conclusions have been based on the absence of data, always a difficult element to rely upon. This absence is matched by a general absence in appropriate research which would identify such features.

Egypt and Great Lakes Africa: substance or nonsense?

It is no surprise to learn that attitudes towards connections between Ancient Egypt and the Great Lakes have varied according to the cultural and historical context of the individuals concerned. Thus, the likes of Stanley and Johnston saw in Ancient Egypt a powerful tool for justifying colonialism in the Great Lakes region. Budge, Seligman and Frankfort each in their own way regarded the polities of the Great Lakes as relics of a society ancestral to both Ancient Egypt and the Great Lakes. And indeed, Chami and others, developing archaeology as a new discipline for Africans, would regard the suggestion of Egyptian contacts as another means of disassociating East African communities from their rightful heritage.

With such a diversity of conclusions it is not surprising to find that a range of different attitudes is evident in the present day, and that each can produce evidence to support their position. Consequently, despite the total lack of evidence, popular writers can still produce texts arguing for direct human contacts. Wicker (1990) surmizes that Egyptian civilization would have originated from people who moved away from the base of the Ruwenzori Mountains. Archaeological evidence is drawn from undated Late Stone Age sites in the vicinity of Ishango, on the Semliki flats in eastern Democratic Republic of Congo, where bone harpoons have been noted. Further evidence for contact is suggested on account of the modern existence of long-horned cattle and plank-sewn boats, similar to those depicted in Egyptian art, as well as various vague geographical descriptions in ancient texts.

It is hardly surprising that there is no good evidence for direct human contact between Ancient Egypt and the Great Lakes, given their great geographical separation and also because of the great disjuncture in time. Any suggestion that there are political connections between predynastic (or later) Egypt and the polities of the Great Lakes makes the untenable assumption that African societies were incapable of producing their own forms of political organization. Indeed of all the locations where African states emerged, the Great Lakes is the only one where there was simply no contact (of whatever kind) with non-African societies (Connah 1987). It is therefore possible to conclude, as a result of this Great Lakes evidence, that developments elsewhere on the continent were also the result of indigenous processes. Archaeological research in the Great Lakes demonstrates that there was no arrival of a foreign, highly civilized polity, but rather that from around 1000 AD there were successive developments in economy, class and settlement form, which gradually led to the formation of the later kingdoms. There is no evidence for Hamites, but there is good evidence to suggest that the Great Lakes pastoralists developed their pastoralist world, including improving their cattle, over the second millennium AD (Reid 2001), indicating that their pastoralism was honed in the Great Lakes and not imported from elsewhere. Sadly, the notion of Hamites is still the central ideology in fuelling continuing conflict in Rwanda and Burundi. In seeing connections between Egypt and the Great Lakes, there is also an assumption, made explicit in some of the quotations above, that Africans were incapable of generating their own history, either by way of initial innovation or subsequently in modifying purportedly inherited cultural systems over a 5,000 year period. This assertion was most notoriously made public as late as 1963, although it subsequently inspired African history across the entire continent. "Perhaps in the future, there will be some African history to teach. But at present there is none: there is only the history of Europeans in Africa. The rest is darkness, like the history of pre-European, pre-Columbian America. And darkness is not a subject for history" (Trevor-Roper 1963: 871).

Many elements of material culture were cited as evidence for contact between Egypt and Great Lakes Africa by early writers. Of these, many can be dismissed as superficial similarities, based on casual, uncritical comparisons. Where more detailed investigations of these similarities have subsequently been made, these have demonstrated significant differences. For instance, at face value the bow-harps may indicate a more direct form of connection. However, Egyptian bow-harps were played with the bow to the body, whilst Great Lakes bow-harps are played the other way round, with the bow pointing away (Figures 5:7 and 5:8). In some cases at least, the pegs on Egyptian bow-harps were fixed anchors, whereas in the Great Lakes pegs are loose to enable tuning (Trowell and Wachsmann 1953: 393–394).

Having made such a strong case to disconnect Egypt and Great Lakes Africa, there are, however, two elements which appear to indicate some form of connection. The first is the domesticated cat, almost certainly a domestication which took place in Egypt (Blench 2000: 320–321). One cat bone was recovered from the small 14th century

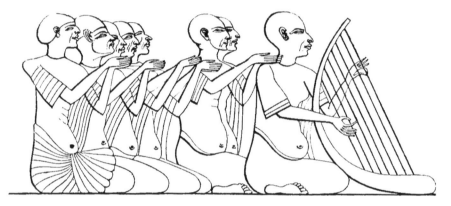

Figure 5:7   Relief image of singers and a courtier playing a bow-harp, Tell el-Amarna (Wilkinson 1854: fig. 106).

Figure 5:8   Bow-harp being played (far right) at the court of the king of Buganda (Speke 1863: 212).

site of Kasebwongera, in Mawogola, southern Uganda (Sutton and Reid forthcoming). A further cat bone has been retrieved from Mubende. Yet, it is not really surprising that cats should be present. These animals were probably kept around homesteads, as they are today, to curtail rodent populations. Almost certainly their presence in Uganda would have been the result of gradual diffusion further south from community to community and need not have been the consequence of population movement. The second element is the Nile itself, which of course represents a physical rather than a cultural connection. Since Nile minima reflect water almost exclusively sourced from Equatorial Africa, fluctuations in the minima in Egypt represent changes in rainfall in the Great Lakes. Therefore, records taken of Nile levels at the Rodah Nilometer from the seventh century AD can be used to infer climatic conditions in the Great Lakes (Hassan 1981). There are problems with these records caused by missing information, siltation and the tendency to misrecord levels in order to alter tax projections, but by grouping records into decadal results and allowing for siltation it is possible to generate time-sensitive climatic data (Figure 5:9), which is otherwise absent for the Great Lakes (Nicholson 1998). The significance of such results for interpretation of developments in the Great Lakes has already been demonstrated (Robertshaw and Taylor 2000; Schoenbrun 1998). Hence, records from Egypt, albeit made in medieval times, by reflecting Equatorial rainfall, rather ironically (given the absence of cultural contacts) do provide a means for understanding the archaeology of Great Lakes Africa.

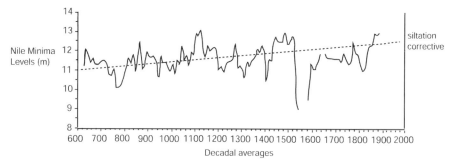

Figure 5:9   A sequence of Nile minima levels derived from the Rodah Nilometer (after Nicholson 1998: fig. 6).

Conclusion

Assessments of Ancient Egypt and the kingdoms of the Great Lakes were clearly mediated by the historical circumstances of their discovery, or more appropriately, their initial encounter with the European world. Europeans ordered this new information within their own culturally defined knowledge systems. These broader knowledge systems were linked to the relative position of Europeans and Africans in eurocentric constructs and were clearly founded on a racial base. They were also guided by the historical circumstance of European expansion into Africa. In the context of the expansion of European mercantile capital and imperialism, Egypt could not be understood as a sophisticated African political form. Concepts of race meant that Egyptian civilization was either highly sophisticated and therefore white, or not nearly as complex as western Asian societies, which would therefore enable it to be black. This was consistent with the ideologies of the late 19th century which provided moral justification for territorial acquisition, conquest and subjugation. These ideologies similarly served to deny Africans access to their past and indeed, as evidenced by a number of the quotations in this chapter, believed that Africans were incapable of producing history. Thus, interpretations of African history located Egypt and Great Lakes Africa in very different ways. Hence, this chapter has discovered little about the history of Africa (Egypt included) but much about the concepts of Africa and of Egypt, as they were constructed by Europeans. Of perhaps greater concern is the continued and largely unquestioned use of such models in recent times. This underlines the importance of all research employing a critically aware historiographical approach.

Such a critically aware approach must inform research on African history today. Whilst it is easy to understand why archaeologists and historians would now want to avoid north–south models of development, there are some unintended consequences of such a position. In rejecting Egyptian and general northern influences on sub-Saharan Africa, Africanists would appear to be confirming that Ancient Egypt was *in* Africa, but not *of* Africa. Conversely, those who propose African connections for Ancient Egypt would appear to side with the view that sub-Saharan Africa was incapable of its own development and sat inert over 5,000 years without being able to create political change. There are some items, such as domesticated plants and animals, which, on present evidence, are understood to have diffused southwards. There is therefore a historical process of diffusion which does require investigation. Care must be taken, however, not to assume that amongst these were socio-political elements such as kingship. Equally, there are valid historical questions to be asked regarding why Ancient Egypt had such apparently minimal impact on the rest of the continent. By framing questions in these ways, it should be possible to generate a positive image of the Egyptian achievement, the developments in sub-Saharan Africa, their differences *and* their possible connections.

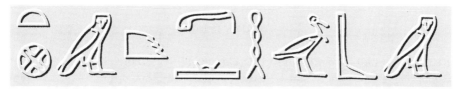

CHAPTER 6

VIEWS OF ANCIENT EGYPT FROM A WEST AFRICAN PERSPECTIVE

Caleb A. Folorunso

There are several different scenarios in which relationships between West Africa and Ancient Egypt have been claimed. The first three themes are broadly interrelated. One view is that Ancient Egypt was the source of civilization in the West African region, a view expressed by European diffusionist scholars. A second idea is that Ancient Egypt was the original home of some West African peoples before they migrated southwards. This latter view has been incorporated into oral traditions, for example from the Yoruba of Nigeria, concerning migrations of people from the 'East'. Evidence for this theory was also discovered in ethnographies. A third view is that of some African or 'Afrocentrist' scholars who take the authors of ancient Egyptian civilization to be black Africans and claim that evidence abounds to establish a link between the Ancient Egyptians and some present West African peoples. This 'Afrocentric' view claims that the assertion that the Ancient Egyptians were light-skinned has no proof, scientific or otherwise. A final and unrelated viewpoint, which has emerged for example in Nigeria, focuses on Egypt as expressed in recent Christian teaching and concerns the perceived role of Ancient Egypt in the Bible.

To most West Africans today, Egypt is a country in North Africa inhabited by Arabs. Many educated individuals know also that Egypt has a long history, part of which is recounted in the Bible, particularly in the story of the Israelite sojourn in pharaonic Egypt. Many are also aware of the pyramids of Egypt, but hardly bother to consider the builders of those pyramids, probably assuming that the present day Egyptians have always been in Egypt and were responsible for the ancient Egyptian civilization. Thus, if the study of Ancient Egypt is to be objective and scientific, the ideological presumptions that have tended to excise Ancient Egypt from the rest of Africa, emanating from both European and West African sources, must be reconsidered.

Egypt as the source of civilization in West Africa

Since at least the 1820s (Bernal Chapter 2, this volume) European scholars could not see Africans as having been capable of meaningful cultural development. Cultural manifestations considered to reflect human advancement on the African continent, particularly among black Africans, were explained as the result of influence from

Ancient Egypt and other ancient "non-African" civilizations. In the 19th and 20th centuries, the dominant explanatory model for cultural development on the continent of Africa was the so-called 'Hamitic Hypothesis' (Reid Chapter 5 and Wengrow Chapter 9, this volume). This theory focused on light-skinned peoples, of ancient Egyptian or Indo-European origin, who spread across Africa in a mission to civilize subject races who were mentally and physically inferior. According to theories which centred on Hamitic incursions, the highly developed state systems of West Africa, together with their renowned art, were inspired from outside (Howe 1998: 115–116). Delafosse (1900) was not unique in searching for evidence of "white" antecedents for West African states, which he duly claimed to have found in abundance in the Ivory Coast. The German anthropologist Frobenius (1913) proposed that the Yoruba art of Ife (see cover illustration, this volume), one of West Africa's most original artistic traditions, originated from Plato's 'Atlantis' and was therefore essentially Greek in origin, while the Hamites had been responsible for other characteristic West African artistic manifestations. Strangely, Frobenius, whose collection methods included outright theft from Ife, proved a major influence on Diop's work (Howe 1998: 116; MacDonald Chapter 7, this volume; and see below).

F. L. S. Shaw – better known as Lady Lugard, wife of the renowned British colonial enforcer – provides an extensive account of purported ancient contacts, derived "in part from original manuscripts, but chiefly from translations of Arab historians" (Shaw 1905: 6). This account is predictably problematic given the context of its production, but it is an illuminating and, it has to be said, vast compilation of 'historical' data which provides intriguing insights into the early colonial generation of history. A number of curious stories may be mentioned here. First is the story of "a Pharaoh of the name of Barkhou, of whom it is said that he left a trace of himself in every country through which he passed" (Shaw 1905: 231–232). Borgu in northern Nigeria, which "was often called by early Arab writers, Barkou" (Shaw 1905: 231) is suggested as evidence that this pharaoh marched through parts of West Africa. An idea of the confused state of Shaw's history is provided by the logic which she used to come to this conclusion:

> I abridge from Macrizi an account of an eleven years' expedition of one of the Pharaohs into the west and south, which seems definitely to confer upon Borgu the honour of connecting the existing territory of British Northern Nigeria with the Egypt known to us in the Old Testament. The expedition took place some 1700 years before Christ. The Pharaoh was king of Egypt when 'a young Syrian, of the name of "Joseph the Truthful", was sold by his brothers into Egypt'. The Pharaoh of Joseph was known by many names. Amongst them the Copts gave him the name of 'Barkhou'.

> (Shaw 1905: 229–230)

In similar vein, Shaw claims that Gao, the ancient capital of Songhay, was known "as a town of magicians, whence the Pharaohs on occasions summoned help" (Shaw 1905: 229).

A clear picture of how European thought was constructed is provided by Dubois (1897). In describing Jenné-jeno and the Songhai, he claims to

> show how the beneficent influence of Egypt, mother of all our western civilisation, penetrated the heart of the negro country; and by what means a reflection of its culture

spread and survived unto our day, containing in its afterglow all the glory and vivid charm of the tropical twilight.

(Dubois 1897: 87–88)

On the basis of Arabic texts, Dubois (1897: 90–95) developed an account whereby Dialliaman, ancestor of the Songhai, had moved from the Yemen to the Nile. Subsequently the Songhai had fled the Nile under Arabic attack and eventually had come to the Niger (Figure 6:1). Consequently, Jenné displayed many ancient Egyptian features. "Above all, the houses of Jenné-jeno display that essential characteristic of Egyptian art – the pyramidal form, which represented solidity to those ancient ancestors" (Dubois 1897: 150).

The decline of the civilization established by the purported white-skinned immigrants was said to have occurred because they interbred with their subjects. The result was a deteriorated racial type. Explanations provided for the decline in the civilization founded by the light-skinned Hamites in Nubia considered that the "smallest infusion of Negro blood immediately manifests itself in a dulling of initiative and 'drag' on the further development of the arts of civilization" (Smith and Jones 1910: 25). These racial theories were equally applied to West Africa. Ancient Egypt itself was seen to have at certain times succumbed to this process of degeneration through the infiltration of the Negro population (Howe 1998; Morkot Chapter 11, this volume).

Versions of this 'Hamitic Hypothesis' were still being taught to West African archaeology undergraduates in the 1970s to explain how every cultural development, commencing with the beginning of agriculture, had been introduced into West Africa, mainly through Egypt and the Nile Valley. The map of Africa became littered with arrows showing the supposed routes of such introductions. These theories failed to provide any explanation of how these alien elements could have been imposed on the West African region with its very different characteristics from those of the Nile Valley, including ecology, geology and social organization. There was no thought of

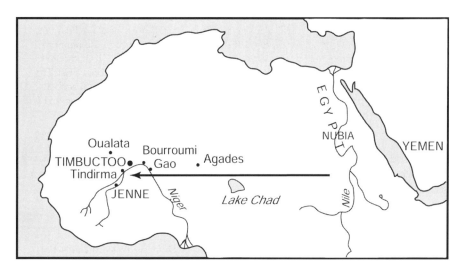

Figure 6:1   Dubois' (1897: 94) proposed Songhai migration.

any possible influence from the south northwards, nor of the more simple exchange of cultural elements between the north and the south.

Hatch (1970) presented a novel view, namely that the growth of the Sahara had had profound effects on the development of African society as most African peoples were severed from the Mediterranean, the Middle East, and Europe – supposedly the source of new ideas. Accordingly, much of Africa was effectively culturally starved and did not share in the urban revolution that developed in Asia, Europe and North Africa. On another tack, seemingly demonstrating that West Africa was a cultural and socio-evolutionary backwater, Oliver and Fagan (1975) noted that the last and, therefore by implication, most advanced phase of stone tools, prior to the adoption of iron, "were not even those of the more advanced, ground and polished kind made by Stone Age farmers" (Oliver and Fagan 1975: 1). According to them, the stone tools were more of the kind used by people "who were *still* hunters, gatherers and fishermen rather than farmers and stock-breeders" (Oliver and Fagan 1975: 1; emphasis added). The continent of Africa, it was maintained, went to sleep in the period beginning 10000 BC, and began to re-awaken only in the Iron Age. Nowadays some scholars still essentially follow this version of events, although most would disagree.

The Unesco *General History of Africa I*, published in 1981, is a good example of how attitudes were gradually changing and how Ancient Egypt was treated in relation to West Africa.

> By the fifth millennium before our era there were domesticated sheep and cattle in Egypt and cereals were being grown. At present we have evidence for domesticated cattle earlier than this in the Central Saharan highlands, and some evidence, though slender, for cereal-growing. The difficulty of starting up cereal agriculture in sub-Saharan Africa as a result of example from the Nile valley is that the crops anciently grown there, wheat and barley, are winter rainfall crops, which can only be grown with difficulty south of the inter-tropical front in the summer rainfall area. What was necessary here was the domestication of suitable indigenous wild grasses, which gave rise to the African cultivated millets; the most important of these was *Sorghum bicolor* or Guinea corn, which was domesticated by the first half of the second millennium before our era in the area between the Sahara and the savannah, from the Nile to Lake Chad.

(Shaw 1981: 626–627)

Although not explicitly stated, one can suggest the implication that West Africa's development is no longer incontrovertibly tied to the proposed beginning of agriculture in Egypt. Thus, it is stressed that wheat and barley would not do well in West Africa and therefore indigenous grasses had to be domesticated. By implication, this could either be read to indicate that the whole idea of domesticating indigenous grasses derived from Egypt or it could be taken to indicate that a distinct course of action was taken by West Africa.

Shaw further considered the use of metal. The application of the European Three-Age System of Stone Age, Bronze Age and Early Iron Age to Africa had revealed that the Bronze Age was absent in West Africa. Shaw (1981: 628–629) posed some questions and provided some answers for this distinct cultural development:

Why was there no bronze age in sub-Saharan Africa and why did Ancient Egyptian civilization not use it more? The reasons are partly to do with the fact that the third millennium before our era, which was the time when metallurgy, writing, monumental building in stone, the use of the wheel and centralized government became firmly established in Egypt, was also the millennium of the final desiccation of the Sahara when people were moving out of it and when it could no longer serve as an indirect link between Egypt and West Africa. The link was not re-established until it was achieved with the help of the camel, some 3,000 years later. Other reasons are connected with the later and slower build-up of an agricultural economy in West Africa, as described above. Some writers have sought to give dignity and luster to West African history by trying to show connections with Ancient Egypt, to enable West Africa to bask in its reflected glory. This does not seem necessary. Throughout the early part of the Iron Age there must have been many parts of West Africa which had no contacts with the outside, and in most cases such contacts as there were with the classical world were slender, sporadic and indirect. Much has been made of Hanno's supposed voyage, but the account is probably a forgery. Herodotus' account of the Carthaginians' silent trade for West African gold is almost certainly based on fact. Indeed, there must have been some reason for contact with the outside world, since it was at the beginning of this period that a knowledge of iron reached West Africa. This was not just an importation of iron objects, but also of the knowledge of iron manufacture, which, since there was no previous knowledge of metallurgy at all, is most unlikely to have been an independent invention.

From the foregoing passages it would appear that it was believed that the fortunes of West Africa were still, albeit ambiguously, tied to development in Egypt. The West African region was still at this time thought to have been essentially cast adrift for 3,000 years as a result of a break in communications with Ancient Egypt. Of course, at the time of writing – which was some years before eventual publication in 1981 – the innovative work of the McIntoshs on inland Niger Delta urbanism had not come to the fore (McIntosh and McIntosh 1980) and therefore trading and the development of towns in West Africa was also attributed to the same Trans-Saharan contact. In this sense, the criteria for urbanism such as the existence of classes of professionals, a religious hierarchy, a centralized authority and public building programmes, were said to be absent in sub-Saharan Africa (McIntosh and McIntosh 1993). Urban centres were said to have been the result of trade propelled by Berbers, Moors, Persians and south Arabians (Clark 1962: 26, 29).

Potential alternative hypotheses to those of Clark and Shaw proposing a food production revolution in West Africa as being separate from, and contemporary with, that of the Near East, were not considered. Shaw (1971) did not explicitly state the processes by which innovations were supposed to have reached West Africa from North Africa, whereas Clark (1976) postulated an influx of human and animal populations from the north into the Sahel and Sudan zones during the last two and a half millennia BC. Later, as has been seen above, Shaw (1981) became more cautious about the beginning of agriculture in sub-Saharan Africa. He stated that there was evidence for domesticated cattle in the central Saharan highlands earlier than in Egypt and some evidence, though slender, for cereal growing. He concluded (Shaw 1985: 73) that it was difficult to know whether there were independent developments in the Sahara or whether early food production was entirely due to influence and stimulus from outside.

The application of diffusionist and migrationist theories to explanations of cultural change in West Africa has been strongly questioned and thus by implication the exact nature of the role of Ancient Egypt in cultural development in the region can be questioned. Andah (1987) argued that the agricultural requirements for cereals differ from other forms of domesticated plant and therefore that different kinds of agricultural economies in West Africa had been erroneously grouped together in the literature, thereby minimizing the significant local differences that occur between the major ecological zones of West Africa and the Sahara. Although direct archaeological evidence is currently unavailable and indeed may not survive on archaeological sites, ecological and ethnoarchaeological studies suggest a local development of agriculture in West Africa. In particular, the ethnobotanical research of Harlan (e.g. 1989, 1993) served to emphasize the interplay between wild and domesticated African cereals in the Sahelo-Sudanic belt of the southern margins of the Sahara.

With regard to iron production in West Africa, Andah (1979) noted the complexity of the available evidence, and concluded that it was not currently possible to know when and how Iron Age complexes were established in each African area. Available dates for the 'earliest' iron working industries in sub-Saharan Africa, and evidence of the technical aspects of these industries, could well suggest independent development at one or more points south of the Sahara.

> If the knowledge of the processes involved in working iron did diffuse from either Carthage or Meroe or both places to different parts of Africa, one might expect that the techniques used in the donor areas were transferred to recipient areas at times that were appreciably later. But dates cannot by themselves constitute evidence of spread, so we would expect that the use of similar methods (processes and artefacts) in working iron would also be reflected by substantial similarity in other socio-cultural features.

(Andah 1979: 136–137)

Andah also noted that early dates for iron working in West Africa had been dismissed in the literature, and important differences between techniques of iron working in parts of West Africa ignored. According to Andah, a diffusionist thesis depended on a fragile framework of dates, and the available evidence could perhaps support the idea that iron working in the Sudan (and specifically Meroe) might have resulted from the transmission of ideas from Egypt, but it could not support the view that these same ideas spread from Meroe to the earliest known centres of iron working along the western Sudan belt. The earliest known instances of iron working in West Africa could have preceded those of North Africa (Andah 1979: 140; Woodhouse 1998), although the absence of preceding intermediate pyrotechnologies, which could have given rise to the independent development of iron smelting, is still problematic.

Recent archaeological findings have raised serious doubts about the influence of North Africa or Egypt on the beginning of urbanization in West Africa. As McIntosh and McIntosh (1993) observe, past characterizations of urbanism assumed that towns were the result of Arab traders and that truly indigenous African urbanism never existed. However, recent research has shown that distinctively African phases of urbanism existed long before the presence of Arab traders in West Africa (MacDonald 1998b; McIntosh and McIntosh 1988, 1993).

If diffusionist theories fail in the light of recent studies, so the proposed role of Ancient Egypt in cultural developments in the region needs critical re-examination. The nature of the link between Ancient Egypt and West Africa, as postulated earlier by diffusionist theories, is yet to be demonstrated in the archaeological record of the region. To reach this conclusion is not to reject outright any connections between Ancient Egypt and West Africa. However, the extent of influence on West Africa, which diffusionist theories attributed to Egypt, has yet to be demonstrated.

Claims of West African origin in Egypt or the Middle East

Smith (1976) observed that the Yoruba of western Nigeria and other West African peoples claimed to have originated from the east. Perhaps not surprisingly there are references to descent from a king in Mecca in the legends, but such legends are also often interpreted to imply an Egyptian origin. He argued that an eastern origin could to some extent be supported by the possibility that certain West African techniques of iron working and the *cire-perdue* (lost wax) process of casting metal objects, as well as forms of government and divine kingship, could have diffused from the Nile Valley (Smith 1976: 13).

Legends of migrations seem only to relate to the ruling classes, and may therefore represent narratives legitimizing the status of elites in different societies. Such is the story of the legendary Kisra, a prince from the 'East', claimed to be the founder of several chiefdoms established in precolonial Borgu. According to Borgu traditions, Kisra migrated westwards from Arabia after refusing to accept the reforms of the Prophet Mohammed. After a brief stay in Bornu, he and his followers moved westward to the Niger. After the death of Kisra, his three sons started the chiefdoms in the Borgu area (Crowder 1973). Descendants of the Kisra migration formed the ruling class, the 'Wassangari', and intermarried with indigenous Boko/Busa inhabitants (Jones 1998). Acceptance of the Wassangari as the political hub of the 'nation' is rooted in the fact that they represent a precolonial power with a warlike reputation. However, other oral traditions recount that the ancestral Wassangari were originally hunters who arrived in the area and gained influence through the distribution of the salted-down meat of the game they killed. Later they were able to acquire horses from traders and subsequently developed the ethos of mounted warriors, which led to their domination of political power. It could therefore be claimed that the traders of horses, who happened to be Muslim, were instrumental in the creation of the Wassangari-headed polities rather than that the Wassangari resulted from a migration out of Arabia (Moraes Farias 1998).

Zachernuk (1994) has provided a synthesis of the generation of historical models regarding West African history by Europeans, African Americans and West Africans. All three incorporated elements of the 'Hamitic Hypothesis' into their histories, a factor which Zachernuk suggests is a reaction to broader changes in western thought in the 19th century. In the early 19th century what Zachernuk describes as a Christian historical model developed. This, to some extent, was an offshoot of Bernal's 'Ancient Model' (Bernal Chapter 2, this volume). In these early 19th century accounts, Christian writers – reliant on biblical chronologies, which saw the entire history of humankind as having taken 6,000 years, through literal interpretations of biblical chronology

(Champion and Ucko 2003) – saw West Africans and black populations in general as having been fully integrated within the classical world. From Egypt, descendants of Ham had dispersed south and west, settling in West Africa and elsewhere. There was no doubt in these writings that Africans were just as capable of civilization as any other humans. Some writers suggested that these populations became black in West Africa through over-exposure to the sun.

As European thought drifted away from biblical interpretations, Victorian science saw humans in terms of polygenesis or multiple origins. These ideas helped to provide evidence for the moral justification of slavery and encouraged the demeaning of Africans and their disassociation with civilization. African American writers in the mid 19th century, who were mostly missionaries in West Africa, resisted these European trends which seemed "determined to pilfer Africa of her glory" in particular by denying that Egypt was "Africa's dark browed queen" (Garnet, quoted in Zachernuk 1994: 433). The main concern for these African American writers was to protect the association of Africans with classical civilization. Strangely, they held that after its Egyptian florescence African societies achieved very little. Many accepted "the sad and startling fact, that mental and moral benightedness has enshrouded the whole of the vast continent of Africa, through all the records of time, far back, to the earliest records of history … So far as *Western* Africa is concerned, there is no history" (Crummell, quoted in Zachernuk 1994: 434). This position was partly related to missionary needs, since this apparent absence of history helped to augment their claim that Africa needed external help. It is from these traditions of writing that the 'Hamitic Hypothesis' becomes incorporated into West African intellectual traditions. It may also be possible to see in these African American writings the forerunners of an Afrocentric approach.

There was a second source by which elements of the 'Hamitic Hypothesis' became incorporated into West African historical traditions: West African Islamic sources. For instance, Mohammed Bello, Sultan of Sokoto, attempted to justify his attempts to force Yoruba to accept Islam, by claiming that the Yoruba were descended from a character, or group of people, called 'Nimrod'. Nimrod in turn was a distant descendant of the cursed Ham. Denham and Clapperton (1826, Appendix XII: 165) published a historical account by Bello in which he claimed that:

> The inhabitants of this province (Yarba), it is supposed, originated from the remnant of the children of Canaan, who were of the tribe of Nimrod. The cause of their establishment in the west of Africa was, as it is stated, in consequence of their being driven by Yaa-rooba, son of Kahtan, out of Arabia, to the western Coast between Egypt and Abyssinia. From that spot they advanced into the interior of Africa, till they reached Yarba, where they fixed their residence. On their way they left, in every place they stopped at, a tribe of their own people. Thus it is supposed that all the tribes of Soodan, who inhabit the mountains, are originated from them . . .

Bello's claims may have helped him justify his attacks on the Yoruba. However, by the mid-19th century Yoruba traditions began to incorporate these elements of the 'Hamitic Hypothesis' in order to justify their resistance to Islam and to Bello (Zachernuk 1994).

Johnson's *The History of the Yorubas* (1921) was published posthumously, having been completed in 1899. He was one of the first Yoruba historians and an early and passionate Christian convert. Johnson noted that "the origin of the Yoruba nation is involved in obscurity" and in seeking to use oral histories he stated that "we can do no more than relate the traditions which have been universally accepted" (Johnson 1921: 3). According to Johnson, such traditions asserted that the Yoruba had "sprung from Lamurudu, one of the kings of Mecca, whose offspring were: Oduduwa the ancestor of the Yorubas, the Kings of Gogobiri and of the Kukawa two tribes in Hausa country" (Johnson 1921: 3). Johnson observed that these different groups "still have the same distinctive tribal marks on their faces, and Yoruba travellers are each recognizing each other as of one blood" (Johnson 1921: 3). He suggested that the name Lamurudu (or Namurudu) was "a dialectical modification of the name Nimrod" (Johnson 1921: 6). "It is known that the descendants of Nimrod (Phoenicians) were led in war to Arabia, that they settled there, and from thence they were driven by a religious persecution to Africa. We have here also the origins of the term Yoruba, from Yarba, their first permanent settlement in Africa" (Johnson 1921: 6).

Johnson accepted the fact that the Yoruba "could not have come from Mecca" (Johnson 1921: 5), explaining that reference to Mecca was necessarily inexact, because to the Yoruba "the East is Mecca, and Mecca is the East" (Johnson 1921: 5). He alleged that evidence for the Yoruba deriving from the East is reflected in "their habits, manners and customs" (Johnson 1921: 5), but he gave no details. He also saw the 'Ife marbles', which he claimed were "altogether Egyptian in form" (Johnson 1921: 6), as evidence of the Yoruba migrating from Upper Egypt. On Yoruba origins he (Johnson 1921: 6–7) concluded

- that they sprang from Upper Egypt, or Nubia;

- that they were subjects of the Egyptian conqueror Nimrod, who was of Phoenician origin, and that they followed him in his wars of conquest as far as Arabia, where they settled for a time;

- that from Arabia they were driven, on account of their practising their own form of worship, which was either paganism or more likely a corrupt form of Eastern Christianity.

Of course, when the Yoruba are said to be related to peoples of western Sudan, by implication it is also being claimed that they had their origin in Egypt or Nubia. Ultimately, Johnson (1921: 7) argues that "it might probably then be shown that the ancestors of the Yorubas, hailing from Upper Egypt, were either Coptic Christians, or at any rate that they had some knowledge of Christianity". Hence, in a few short pages Johnson was able to trace a rich swathe of classical and more importantly biblical associations in Yoruba history. Johnson's argument was so conclusive that Lucas (1970: 7) wrote,

> In a former work entitled *The Religion of the Yorubas* the theory of a close connection between Ancient Egyptian culture and Yoruba culture was proposed, demonstrated and proved. The evidence adduced showed, among other things, the survival of Ancient Egyptian Hieroglyphics and Emblems, and also of the worship of some of the Ancient Egyptian Deities in Yorubaland. A careful survey of the materials collected showed that Yoruba culture was not unique in this respect. There are other cultures in West Africa which stand in genetic relation to the Religion of Ancient Egypt; the impress of Ancient Egypt on them is clearly discernible.

He concluded that

> West African culture contains several elements which are similar to, or identical with,
> those of Ancient Egypt. These elements form the basic structure of West African
> Culture; they are so numerous and so important that if they are subtracted from the
> sum-total of the culture the remainder will be flimsy and insignificant.

(Lucas 1970: 391)

Biobaku's *The Origin of the Yoruba* (1971) was originally published in 1955, in the
period immediately prior to Nigerian Independence, and aimed to create a more
positive and unifying national history. Biobaku's concern was to prove that Nigerians
shared a common association with major developments in the classical world, but that
they had also subsequently developed their own history, on arrival in West Africa.
This allowed Nigeria to be proclaimed a part of world history, but also a nation apart,
and indeed within Nigeria this study allowed the Yoruba to be considered as a distinct
entity. He reviewed existing theories on the origin of the Yoruba and pointed out that
all of them agreed that the Yoruba had migrated into their present areas from the Near
East. He reasoned that "although there is much evidence that the Yoruba indigenous
religion incorporated Jewish stories, that fact mainly shows that the Yoruba were
subject to Jewish influence rather than that they were a Jewish people". He also
associated himself with what Frobenius had written on Ife with regard to the theory
of lost Atlantis and Etruscan civilization.

> Certainly there were striking points of resemblance between the Yoruba and the
> Etruscan culture … but the link between the Yoruba and the Etruscans is too tenuous.
> What was probable was that remnants of Tyrrhenian arts and beliefs filtered through
> the northeast by way of the Carthaginians who were closely allied to the Etruscans.
> Thus evidence of Etruscan influences suggests that the Yoruba came from the Near
> East where they were subject to those influences.

(Biobaku 1971: 9–10)

Biobaku (1971: 10) equated Yoruba culture with that of Ancient Egypt, even though
he did not accept that the modern Yoruba language is similar to ancient Egyptian. He
suggested that the Yoruba arrived with much of their culture intact from the "All-
Black Kingdom of Meroe" (Biobaku 1971: 20).

Obayemi (1985) reasoned that although immigration of the Yoruba from the
Middle East has *prima facie* plausibility, the main evidence depended "on relatively
late Islamicized Hausa-Fulani versions of Yoruba origins" (Obayemi 1985: 259). He
stressed that Islamic chroniclers often made "unwarranted assertions about [the]
trans-Saharan origins of African peoples" (Obayemi 1985: 259), and that "etymological
arguments conventionally used to back these assertions of Middle Eastern origins"
(Obayemi 1985: 259) were without substance. He (Obayemi 1985: 259–260) claimed
that linguistic evidence shows that the Yoruba and related groups had been in the area
for over 6,000 years, and that any reference to an eastern origin in Yoruba legends or
traditions "must refer to the Niger-Benue confluence area, rather than to Egypt"
(Obayemi 1985: 260). Subsequently archaeological research was conducted by
Oyelaran (1998) in north-east Yorubaland. A programme of survey and excavation
demonstrated an extensive cultural sequence. Most importantly Oyelaran interpreted
this sequence as demonstrating continuous occupation of the area back into the Late

Stone Age. There is no evidence of the influx of an exotic and supposedly superior population.

As Zachernuk (1994) has shown, many of these myths of external origins emerged under colonialism, and they served to proclaim a common origin for all the peoples and cultures of the sub-region as a rhetorical strategy for political unity. Accordingly, he claimed that the late colonial years, which evidently witnessed growing regional-ethnic antagonisms in Nigeria, led amateur local historians to adopt "the 'Hamitic Hypothesis' tradition in the search for historical primacy and cultural superiority over other Nigerian groups" (Zachernuk 1994: 451). But as Zachernuk demonstrates, the borrowing of the 'Hamitic Hypothesis' was done to benefit a wide range of explicitly African causes. Whilst local historians have not made the extreme claim for Hamitic or light-skinned people on civilizing missions into tropical Africa, intrusive 'Egyptian' elements were seen as part of a much broader cultural picture. Scholars such as Biobaku (1971) argued that until very recently the term Yoruba applied only to the Oyo Yoruba. If Lucas could reconstruct the word Yoruba from ancient Egyptian *rpa*, it would mean that a large portion of the modern Yoruba people, including Biobaku's Egba Yoruba, could not have had an Egyptian origin.

These theories of West African origins in Ancient Egypt have thus far been characterized by superficial comparisons between aspects of West African and ancient Egyptian culture. An altogether different approach was taken by Meyerowitz (1960), whose comparison of divine kingship amongst the Akan of Ghana and in Ancient Egypt was derived from her extensively published Akan ethnographies, based on work with the Bono-Takyiman. Her consideration of Akan and ancient Egyptian divine kingship is an extension of the work of Frankfort (1948), examining evidence for African elements of kingship in Ancient Egypt. However, Frankfort (1948), and Seligman (1913) before him, explicitly ruled out the relevance of West African ethnographies in understanding ancient Egyptian kingship. Rather it was Budge (1911) who had previously drawn on West African ethnography. However, Meyerowitz's approach was unique in that she was a specialist in African cultural anthropology, exploring connections using the ethnography as a starting point rather than Ancient Egypt. Also she generated a detailed consideration of the ethnography of a single society in comparison with ancient Egyptian practice, rather than the cross-cultural scattergun approach developed by earlier writers.

Meyerowitz considers in a succession of chapters the Divine King's various incarnations: the King's potency; the King's ancestors; rejuvenation ceremonies for the King (two chapters); the King's death; and the King's succession. In each of these chapters a detailed account is provided of a list of Akan features or rituals, before a comparable list of ancient Egyptian features or rituals are documented. This mode of presentation demonstrates that there are a large number of points of similarity, although also some significant differences. However, the style adopted by Meyerowitz is such that it is almost impossible to make use of this work. The information, rich as it undoubtedly is, is presented simply as description without discussion, with almost no comment and certainly with no conclusion. It is very difficult on this basis to evaluate the nature of the comparisons. On top of this rich detail with no comment, there is the added problem that Meyerowitz's eventual interpretation is based on a re-working of the 'Hamitic Hypothesis'. Thus, although

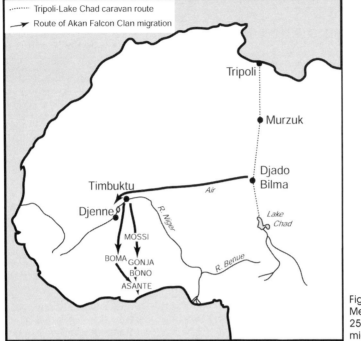

Figure 6:2
Meyerowitz's (1960:
25) proposed Akan
migration.

the work was not driven by Hamites, it was ultimately dependent on the 'Hamitic Hypothesis' for its interpretation (Figure 6:2). This interpretation appears in the final chapter, entitled 'Diffusion', taking up eight pages (out of a total volume length of 260). Meyerowitz (1960: 228) states that

> The matrilineal ancestors of the founders of the Bono and Asante kingdoms are believed by their descendants to have been a 'white people' who originally lived in the north in the 'country of the sand'. The 'white people', we may deduce, were predominantly Saharan Libyans and others descended from the Libyans of North Africa and the Fezzan.

In accepting this statement, based on fieldwork conducted mostly in the 1940s, Meyerowitz is clearly unaware of the processes by which West African historical traditions were generated since the early 19th century, emphasizing external origins (Zachernuk 1994). For Meyerowitz the connections with Ancient Egypt were already made clear in her introduction:

> The more I become acquainted with Akan beliefs and customs, the more I realized that they were not isolated phenomena. It became clear to me that they were ultimately based upon those of Ancient Egypt. Time and place and historical change had so modified these religious forms as to produce effects which made them not indeed repetitions of the Egyptian example but obvious deviations from it.

(Meyerowitz 1960: 16)

These points were reiterated in her conclusion. "Suffice it to say that the Akan state organization, religion, and much of the material culture is of non-negro African origin.

The Akan civilization, nevertheless, has an identity and a distinctive quality of its own" (Meyerowitz 1960: 235). The basis for this conclusion is never drawn out. As a result it becomes very difficult to judge the validity of Meyerowitz's conclusions. Whilst the Akan ethnography is apparently sound, her understanding of Egyptology was out of date, having a tendency to conflate ancient Egyptian history into a single, largely unchanging form. These weaknesses, and the date of publication shortly after Independence, may have encouraged rejection of the approach. Despite these problems, Meyerowitz shows that with the aid of a nuanced critique and a more critically aware interpretation, the kind of detailed comparative approach, searching for 'commonalities', which is advocated by Rowlands (Chapter 4, this volume), can bear considerable dividends.

Who were the Ancient Egyptians?

The current debate on the identity of the Ancient Egyptians seems to centre around Cheikh Anta Diop's (1981; and see MacDonald Chapter 7, this volume) argument that the Ancient Egyptians were black Africans. His argument was premised on the origin of early humans deriving from East Africa and, as such, being black Africans. From East Africa and through the Nile Valley these early humans would have spread to North Africa and other parts of the world. Diop used several lines of evidence to make his case for a Negro population for Ancient Egypt, among which were physical anthropology, human images, texts by classical authors, ancient Egyptian hieroglyphs, a biblical verse from the book of Genesis, and linguistic affinity. Howe (1998: 165) summarizes Diop's thesis as follows:

> Both the biological origin of humanity, and the emergence of civilization, took place in Africa. Egypt was the cradle of the latter, was specifically a black or Negro civilization, and was the fullest flowering of a cultural system unifying the whole African continent. That cultural system not only originated most important aspects of human social and intellectual development, but was distinct from Eurasian societies in its matriarchal, spiritual, peaceable and humanistic character. Ancient Greece – and hence all European civilization – took almost everything of value usually claimed to be theirs from this antecedent African-Egyptian culture.

Diagne (1981: 245), developing Diop's argument further, noted that

> Egypt was for a long time set on one side by comparison with the rest of the continent, or rejuvenated for the benefit of Mesopotamia or other centers of civilization which were assumed, on the basis of unsupported speculation, to be Indo-European or Semitic.

He argued that "the lexicon, the structure and the essential principles of written Ancient Egyptian … are closer to corresponding phenomena in languages such as Wolof or Hausa, or to the Dahomeyan graphic tradition, than to the Hamito-Semitic linguistic systems to which they had been incautiously assimilated" (Diagne 1981: 246). He argued further that "Egyptian writing and that of the Dahomey bas-reliefs or the Bambara, or Dogon ideograms" (Diagne 1981: 250) served similarly non-material needs. He posited that Egyptian, Dahomean, Bambara and Dogon writings were "used to glorify sovereigns" (Diagne 1981: 250) and linked Egyptian hieroglyphs to the writing systems of black Africa (Diagne 1981: 250–251).

Obenga (1981: 80) attempted to provide evidence to show similarities between African and ancient Egyptian cultures. It was argued that "the Egyptian language could not be isolated from its African context and its origin could not be fully explained in terms of Semitic; it was thus quite normal to expect to find related languages in Africa" (Devisse 1981: 75–76) and Obenga stressed that a fundamental problem "is to find appropriate techniques for comparing Ancient Egyptian with contemporary black African languages, in order, so far as possible, to reconstruct, on the basis of morphological, lexicological and phonetic analogies and affinities, their common ancestors" (Obenga 1981: 80).

Some scholars have started to read a mixed population from the ruins of Ancient Egypt so as to imply that the ancient Egyptian civilization could not have been the product of just a black race, no matter what their physical characteristics. Many of the current discussions appear to be characterized by abuse and by accusations of Afrocentrism (e.g. Fauvelle-Aymar *et al.* 2000). Obenga (2001), in his response to such attacks, demonstrates how science has been sacrificed to achieve preconceived objectives. He has consistently claimed that Semitic, Berber and Egyptian languages are not genetically related.

The work of Martin Bernal (1991; Chapter 2, this volume) has exposed the manner by which scholars sought to deny the contribution of ancient Egyptian civilization to the rise of Greek civilization. It seems that those rejecting the 'Ancient Model' – which accords pre-eminence to ancient Egyptian civilization – were also implying that Ancient Egypt could not be a significant civilization, African and black.

Egypt in Christian teaching in Nigeria

While there exists a raging (often both hot and vicious) scholarly debate concerning the true identity of the Ancient Egyptians, Christian teaching in Nigeria wants nothing to do with Ancient Egypt. Christian preachers, teachers and commentators do not debate what may have been the physical characteristics of the Ancient Egyptians mentioned in both the Old and New Testaments. Instead, they consider Egypt as a spiritual entity that is synonymous with sin. They maintain that the pharaohs of Egypt were great enemies of God who wanted to destroy God's chosen people. Indeed, the Bible tells the story of how God mightily delivered the Israelites from the land of Egypt and destroyed the pharaoh and his army in the Red Sea. Thus, Egypt has been used figuratively to describe anything that is unrighteous and sinful, and the Nigerian Christian is taught that Egypt was a land of sin where the children of God should not dwell. Christians are admonished concerning the sins of Egypt and when they are told "don't go back to Egypt" it means not going back to sin after redemption. Pharaoh symbolizes problems, illness, a barrier to progress, and misfortune generally. Christians therefore pray that God should destroy the pharaoh in their lives.

In a guide for daily Bible study the instruction for 1 October 2000 reads,

Today is Nigeria's Independence Day! Forty years ago, our Nigeria left the shores of our own "Egypt" on the journey to our promised land … The journey to Canaan, the promised land, which was to be a journey of forty days into a land flowing with milk and honey, turned into a journey of forty years on a hard and harsh terrain, moving round in circles most of the time! How true for Nigeria?

(Vine Branch Ministries 2000)

For 12 December 2000 the commentary reads,

All the congregation of the children of Israel wept, murmured and regretted leaving Egypt. Rather than face any difficulty, though for a while, they always resorted to asking Moses for their return to Egypt. For us as God's children, we must never forget that Egypt is the land of bondage [in spite] of the garlic, cucumber, fish etc. (Num 11: 5) that may be available there. No, we are resolved to follow Jesus. Egypt has lost its charm in us.

(Vine Branch Ministries 2000)

On 12 August 2001, it states,

Egypt for us is a type of the world and compromise of our faith. All that Abram experienced in Egypt was heartache but for God's intervention concerning Serah. Thank God that Abram came back home – to the place he built his tent at the beginning (Gen 13: 3). He was wise enough to realize that he should go back to where God's presence is. Have you moved away from God? Where God's presence is, is home.

(Vine Branch Ministries 2001)

Thus, a claim for an Egyptian origin in either the physical or spiritual sense is unthinkable for Nigerians who are truly in the Christian fold. There are active pressures on specific groups of West Africans not to identify with an Egyptian heritage. Such orthodoxy, however, does not apply to all, particularly outside the realms of active Christian worship. Some individual cultural revivalists exist, such as the late Nigerian musician Fela Anikulapo Kuti, whose perception of Egypt was different and radical. In the 1970s, his band was named 'Africa '70' and he changed the name to 'Egypt '80' in the 1980s, which it remained until his recent demise. For Kuti, Africa, particularly black Africa, was indeed synonymous with Ancient Egypt.

Conclusion

Ancient Egyptian civilization was founded on the continent of Africa and it was an African civilization. It would be odd indeed to imagine that a civilization such as that of the Ancient Egyptians lived in isolation and did not have relations with other groups. Ancient Egyptians should not be studied as if they lived on an island on the continent of Africa with the rest of Africa being a Dark Continent. They definitely shared some traits, such as language, beliefs, social organizations and technology, with their immediate neighbours. This chapter has demonstrated that Ancient Egypt has often been used as a means of denying Africans a significant past and that there are numerous methodological and theoretical pitfalls in drawing connections between West Africa and Ancient Egypt. Hopefully, however, it has also demonstrated that there are avenues of investigation which may still warrant further analysis. These avenues can be followed in a context which protects the sanctity of West African cultural development, whilst also enabling scholars to recognize Ancient Egypt as a truly African civilization.

Acknowledgments

I thank Mr Obare Bagodo with whom I had useful discussions on the subject of the chapter, and who provided some literature for its final version. Lastly, my participation in the conference on 'Encounters with Ancient Egypt' was made possible by the Leventis Foundation Research Co-operation Program.

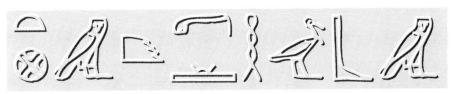

CHAPTER 7

CHEIKH ANTA DIOP AND ANCIENT EGYPT IN AFRICA

Kevin C. MacDonald

The majority of recent scholarship considering the Afrocentric ideas of the late Cheikh Anta Diop have been either hagiographies of his theories of a 'Black Egypt' or strident critiques of this same idea. It is not intended here to rehearse once more the question of Africa in Egypt, but rather to examine Diop's ideas on early migrations and the presence of Egypt in sub-Saharan Africa. In particular I will consider whether or not there is any archaeological basis for Diop's claims of Egyptian genetic, technological and ideological legacies in West Africa.

Introduction

Cheikh Anta Diop (1923–1986), physicist and archaeologist, was a path-breaking advocate for the (Black) African origin of Dynastic Egypt. Born in the coastal town of Diourbel during the French colonial occupation of Senegal, Diop's intellectual achievements as a young man led to graduate study at the University of Paris. Whilst in Paris he developed an aggressive programme of inquiry into cultural aspects of both Africa in Egypt, and Egypt in Africa. Although today he is perceived as having been a scholar-activist in the humanities, Diop was also a physical scientist, founding the first radiocarbon laboratory in Africa at Dakar during the 1960s. His impact at a national level is attested to by the fact that Senegal's primary university is now known as the *Institut Fondamental de l'Afrique Noire – Cheikh Anta Diop*. Globally, his ideas and writings have spawned many successors and were seminal to the academic paradigm of Afrocentrism (cf. Van Sertima and Williams 1989). At the heart of Afrocentrism is the notion that all civilization sprang from Africa, and more specifically from a Black Egypt.

A great deal of ink has been spilt debating the subject of a 'Black Egypt' (e.g. Asante 1992; Berlinerblau 1999; Bernal 1987, 1991; Howe 1998; Van Sertima 1995). Whatever position one chooses to take on the question of a 'white', 'black' or 'multi-racial' Egypt, one cannot deny the considerable impact of Diop on the literature of the African diaspora. Some have even seen fit to use Diop's ideas as a launch-pad for a hyper-diffusionistic Black Egypt, with cultural colonies in Europe, the Americas, and India (e.g. Rashidi 1992; Van Sertima 1985, 1987). It is thus surprising that so little has been written on a subject that Diop often dwelt upon – the connections of Egypt with a land far less distant than Peru – the impact of Egypt on 'Inner' Africa. Admittedly, there has been growing scholarly interest in the subject of Nubia as a sort of cultural bridge between Egypt and the rest of the continent (e.g. Davies 1991; O'Connor 1993), but there has been relatively little written on Egypt's influence beyond the Nile Valley. Here, I consider what role Diop saw 'Black Egypt' playing in the peopling and cultural formation of sub-Saharan Africa, and I compare them with data gleaned from the past century of archaeological inquiry. This examination will focus on those areas which Diop considered most closely, namely the Sahara and the Sahelo-Sudanic belt.

Diop on 'Egypt in Africa'

Establishing the racial composition of dynastic Egyptians, and subsequent shifts in that racial composition, is integral to most Afrocentric theses concerning a 'Black Egypt'. Thus, Afrocentrists have long held a two-staged hypothesis concerning the peopling of Africa: black Africans were indigenous to the Nile Valley before the dynastic period, and environmental shifts and foreign invasion led to several waves of dispersion of Nilotic black populations into the rest of Africa – and the consequent disappearance of most black peoples from the Lower Nile. Remarkably, there were few changes in Diop's hypothesis throughout his almost 30 years of publication on the subject. This thesis was present in his first major works: *Nations nègres et culture* (1955) and *Antériorité des civilisations nègres* (1967). These two volumes were then combined in the English translation *The African Origin of Civilization* (1974), which brought Diop to a global audience and had a profound impact on African American intellectual life. But there was little new from the pen of Diop in his later years. Although in 1960, with *l'Afrique noire précolonial* (first English translation: *Precolonial Black Africa,* 1987), he attempted to add more detailed linguistic evidence to support his arguments, the basic plot remained the same.

Diop begins with the supposition that at the end of the Pleistocene "tall Black Africans" were the sole inhabitants of the Nile Basin (Diop 1974: 181–182, 1987: 212–213). These "tall Black Africans" are claimed on the basis of Egyptian and Nubian oral traditions to have a more southerly origin, at the junction of the White Nile and the Blue Nile (Diop 1974: 180). Surrounding these Nilotic populations throughout the rest of the continent were pygmy peoples: "the Pygmies were probably the first to occupy the interior of the continent, at least at a certain period. They settled there prior to the arrival of larger Blacks" (Diop 1974: 182). The basis for this argument are references to "little people" in the African interior by Classical writers (namely Herodotus), and the widespread persistence of claims in West African oral traditions that current populations are not the first-comers, but were preceded by populations of "little people" (Diop 1974: 179–182, 1987: 212–213).

According to Diop the 'Supremacy of Blacks' in Egypt began with the Fayum Neolithic, continued through the predynastic period and then bloomed in the dynastic period, with the 'Decline of the Black World' beginning only with the sacking of Thebes by the Assyrians in 663 BC (Diop 1991: 23). At this time 'white' began to replace 'black' in the Egyptian world and the myth of a 'White Egypt' began to be perpetuated. The actual dispersion of black Nilotic peoples westward was seen to have begun before the civilization of Egypt was at its height, and to have continued well into the time of Dynastic Egypt:

> The idea of a center of dispersal located approximately in the Nile Valley is worth consideration. In all likelihood … [until ca. 7000 BC] … Black mankind first lived in bunches in the Nile basin, before swarming out in successive spurts towards the interior of the continent.
>
> (Diop 1987: 213)

Included in this dispersion from the Nile Valley are the ethnic groups of West Africa; the Yoruba, the Peul (Fulani), the Tucolor, the Serer (Soninke), and the Wolof being favourite examples for Diop (1974, 1987). Indeed, in his works, Diop spent a good deal of energy attempting to demonstrate the idea that these peoples were not indigenous to West Africa. This assertion he based on a miscellany of arguments drawn from colonial-era sources: word lists, oral histories, and comparisons of ritual, hairstyles, and physiques between Egypt and West Africa (Diop 1974, 1987). Some examples are instructive as to his style of argumentation:

> Like other West African populations, the Peul probably came from Egypt. This theory can be supported by perhaps the most important fact to date: the identity of the only two typical totemic proper names of the Peul with two equally typical notions of Egyptian metaphysical beliefs, the *Ka* and the *Ba*.
>
> (Diop 1974: 189)

> It may be pointed out that the 'pope' of the Yoruba, the Oni, has the same title as Osiris, the Egyptian God, [and] that there is a hill called Kuse near Ilé-Ifé [Nigeria], and another of the same name in Nubia, near ancient Meroë . . .
>
> (Diop 1987: 217)

> The Serer probably came to Senegal from the Nile basin; their route was said to be marked by the upright stones found at the same latitude from as far away as Ethiopia to Sine-Salum. This hypothesis can be supported by a series of facts taken from an article by Dr Joseph Maes on the upright stones in the 'French' Soudan village known as Tundi-Daro [today: Tondidarou, Mali].
>
> (Diop 1974: 192–193)

It would not be difficult to assail the grounds of Diop's tenuous ethnic linkages one by one, though that would require a work of book-length. Still, it is worth mentioning that the word *Ba* also means 'sheep' to the pastoral Peul (Fulbe) and appears to be an onomatopoeia. Thus a connection with local sheep herding rather than Egyptian metaphysics would appear the most likely origin for this family name. There is real danger in conducting amateur, non-statistical comparisons of languages by prehistorians. Indeed, this cavalier attitude shows a disrespect for the discipline and methodology of linguistics. Using phonetic similarities between isolated terms as signifiers of population origins – even when entire grammars are in utter discord – is nothing new for hyper-diffusionists (Howe 1998: 179; cf. MacDonald *et al.* 1995). Howe (1998: 167), in his critique of the logic of Afrocentrism, noted concerning Diop's scholarship that

> Much of Diop's work was evidently and badly flawed by its reliance on out-of-date sources, a tendency which deepened as he grew older. As Augustin Holl remarks, right up to his death Diop 'behaved as if nothing new had occurred in African archaeology in general, and especially in West African archaeology, history, linguistics, and social

anthropology' ... His enthusiasm for the work of Leo Frobenius is a striking case in point.

Despite these flaws, however, something important remains of Diop's assertions regarding the origins of West African populations and the role of Dynastic Egypt beyond the Nile Valley. What remains is that he asked appropriate and relevant questions – yet few have ventured to provide answers. Egyptologists believe they are reaching out to join hands with Africa, simply because they have grasped the hands of Nubianists. But they have ignored a virtually untried world beyond, to the south-west. Likewise, Africanists embarrassed by previous migration theories such as Sutton's (1974, 1977) 'Aqualithic' hypothesis have shied away from seriously considering population movements or connections with Egypt. This is a pity because much work could usefully be done on the topic of prehistoric drift in genes, language and/or cultures across Africa.

Evidence for Egypt in Africa: historical linguistics and prehistory

Historical linguistics has evolved rapidly over the past half-century and has furnished important fuel for modelling the prehistory of Africa (such as 'The Bantu Expansion', cf. Vansina 1995). In contemplating the ancient peopling of Egypt much can be gained by considering the linguistic homelands of the language phyla of Africa. It is asserted by historical linguists that at the beginning of the Holocene (ca. 12000 bp)[1] at least five major language phyla were extant on the African continent: Afro-Asiatic, Nilo-Saharan, Niger-Congo, Khoisan, and at least one 'lost' [extinct] language phylum (Blench 1993; MacDonald 1998a). It is also conjectured that Nilo-Saharan and Niger-Congo may have shared a common origin, once forming a macro-phylum, the 'Niger-Saharan' (Blench 1995).

The point of origin of Afro-Asiatic (formerly 'Hamito-Semitic') has been placed either in the Levant or the eastern Sudan/Horn of Africa (Blench 1993; Ehret 1982). Afro-Asiatic speakers include the Ancient Egyptians, and modern Berbers (North Africa), Omotic speakers (Ethiopia), Chadic speakers (Lake Chad Basin), Cushitic speakers (eastern Africa), as well as the Hebrew and Arabic languages.

As concerns the putative Niger-Saharan macrophylum, it is thought that Niger-Congo is a later split from the main trunk of Nilo-Saharan languages, with which it shares terms for wild, particularly riverine, resources. Blench (1995: 98) places the probable dispersion of this macrophylum, out of a North African homeland, some time after the end of the 'Ogolian' hyper-arid (ca. 20000–12000 bp); a climatic event which precluded communication between the North African littoral and 'Inner Africa' for at least eight millennia (Figure 7:1).

An explanatory model for the modern distribution of African language phyla could proceed as follows: the Ogolian hyper-arid would produce propitious conditions for the production of population isolates (and accelerated language diversification) throughout North Africa in the Terminal Pleistocene, leading to the diversification of Nilo-Saharan and Niger-Congo as these populations began to re-colonize the Sahara episodically during the early Holocene pluvial (ca. 12000–9000 bp). In the mid to recent Holocene, with increasing aridification, Niger-Congo and

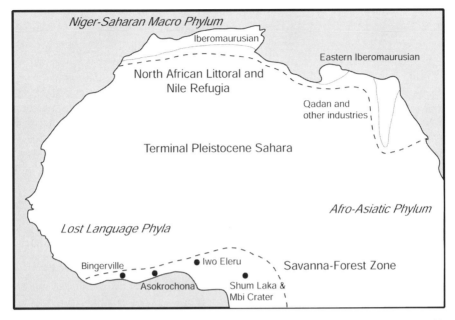

Figure 7:1 Africa north of the equator during the 'Ogolian' hyper-arid phase (20000–12000 bp). Dotted lines indicate boundaries of non-desertic areas during this period.

Nilo-Saharan speakers would have followed water sources southwards into West and Central Africa, gradually displacing or linguistically assimilating indigenous 'Lost Language' speakers (MacDonald 1998a). At the same time, during the Holocene optimum (ca. 7000–6000 bp), Afro-Asiatic speakers were probably entering the Lower Nile region from the south and the east, assimilating and displacing local speakers of Nilo-Saharan and Niger-Congo languages.

The mobility of languages and the ease of 'language death' (i.e. replacement) in regions is not surprising, indeed it is an ongoing process in Africa today (Sommer 1992). Modern language isolates in tropical Africa, and the loss of indigenous languages by distinct groups such as the 'pygmy' peoples of Central Africa point to the pre-existence of one or more language phyla in sub-Saharan Africa which have now been lost by processes of language death and acculturation (Blench 1993; cf. MacDonald 1998a). Archaeological evidence indicates that, during the Ogolian hyper-arid, sub-Saharan West Africa was occupied by mobile, isolated bands of hunter-gatherers sharing a technocomplex of quartz microlithic industries (MacDonald 1997). The languages which might have been spoken by these indigenous peoples are unknown. Likewise, the Egyptian language seems to have completely effaced indigenous tongues which were once spoken along the Lower Nile.

How do we make sense of all this in light of Diop's hypotheses? To begin with, there is some validity to Diop's 'little peoples' of extra-Nilotic Africa. Distinctive early Holocene sub-Saharan hunter-gatherer complexes are attested archaeologically (MacDonald 1997, 1998a), most West African oral traditions still do speak of autochthonous 'little peoples' who were displaced or replaced (e.g. Dieterlen and Sylla

1992: 65–67), and there is compelling linguistic evidence for a sub-Saharan language 'wipe-out' during the Holocene (Blench 1993; Sommer 1992). However, there is no real proof that all such peoples were pygmies, and Diop's simple cast of characters: tall Nilotic blacks, little peoples of Inner Africa, and Western Asiatic Caucasoids, is insufficient to account for a varied host of prehistorically attested peoples.

I have previously argued that the principal ancestral populations of modern West Africans were living in North Africa at the end of the Pleistocene (MacDonald 1998a). However, the study of modern African languages suggests that these populations were not Afro-Asiatic (e.g. Egyptian) speakers, but rather Niger-Congo and Nilo-Saharan speakers. Also, archaeological evidence indicates that Holocene colonists entered the Sahara from many points – including the Maghreb, Libya, and the Nile Valley – around 10000–7000 bp. Thus, whilst I would agree with Diop that there must have been 'black' peoples in North Africa at the beginning of the Holocene, and that they displaced or integrated the autochthonous populations of Inner Africa during the course of the Holocene, I would be less sanguine about associating such early colonists with Afro-Asiatic speakers of Egyptian origin. Indeed, in looking for southward and/or westward Afro-Asiatic language expansions into the interior of Africa we can discern only two discrete and comparatively recent prehistoric events: proto-Berber from the North African littoral into the Sahara by at least 4000 bp (or possibly a bit earlier, cf. Vernet and Onrubia-Pintado 1994) and proto-Chadic into the Lake Chad Basin from the Nile Basin at ca. 5000–4000 bp (MacDonald 1998a). Comparatively speaking then, linguistic evidence for the spread of Nilo-Saharan and Niger-Congo languages to northern and western Africa seems to be several thousand years in advance of Afro-Asiatic.

The ancient Egyptians, even before the dynastic period, were no doubt interacting with other African peoples and language groups. This might account for some of the Afro-Asiatic loan-words present in sub-Saharan Africa today – though they more probably derive from interactions between Berbers and diverse Niger-Congo/Nilo-Saharan peoples over the last millennium. A more remarkable phenomenon is the lack of Niger-Congo/Nilo-Saharan words or grammatical borrowings in Egyptian itself (cf. Greenberg 1955). This would seem to indicate minimal interaction of early Egyptians with speakers of these 'inner African' language phyla, and the rapid displacement and/or acculturation of speakers of these languages along the Lower Nile before Predynastic times.

Evidence for Egypt in Africa: direction of innovations

Despite a predilection of early Africanists to opt for *ex Oriente Lux* (eastern) solutions for early innovations in the African interior, current scholarship indicates a relative independence of 'Inner Africa' from Nilotic technological influence.

Ceramics

Africa is one of the three earliest world centres for the invention of pottery (the others being Anatolia and Japan). There are currently 21 African radiocarbon determinations on pottery (via associated charcoal) which place ceramics on the continent before 8500 bp (Close 1995; Roset 1987). Nine of these dates derive from the south-central Sahara, the earliest being 9370±130 bp from Tagalagal (Niger). The remaining 12 dates come from the eastern Sahara of Egypt, with the earliest determination being 9610±150 bp from Bir Kiseiba E-79–8. The directionality of the spread of this ceramic technology remains a matter for debate, although Close (1995: 32) states that "it was probably invented along the southern side of the Sahara".

The early ceramic-using cultures of the Sahara were without doubt early Holocene colonists from North Africa (the Maghreb, Libya, and the Nile). Relative stylistic similarity amongst early African ceramic assemblages suggests the maintenance of cultural contacts between the Nile and central Sahara (Niger/Chad) from ca. 9500 to 7000 bp. After this time considerable regional diversification in pottery, decorative motifs and technology begins, indicating the comparative isolation of Saharan and Nilotic populations from one another (Caneva and Marks 1990).

Cereal agriculture

Despite the presence of cereal agriculture (wheat and barley) in Egypt during the Fayum Neolithic by at least 6500 bp (Midant-Reynes 2000), there is no positive evidence for domesticated cereals in Africa outside the Nile Valley until ca. 4000 bp. After decades of archaeobotanical field research, it is becoming apparent that the Holocene colonists of the Sahara and its margins utilized abundant wild grains to supplement pastoral and/or aquatic resources, and did not resort to cultivation until after the current arid phase began around 4500 bp (Harlan 1989; MacDonald 2000; Neumann 1999). Subsequent domestication events were almost certainly multiple and independent of each other, some crops (e.g. millet and sorghum) probably being domesticated more than once in widely separated regions.

Metallurgy

Although iron metallurgy appears to have been present in Egypt by the end of the second millennium BC, there are no compelling technological similarities or patterns of date distribution to suggest connection with the first iron workers of West and Central Africa in the early first millennium BC (Woodhouse 1998). Increasingly, iron metallurgy seems, on the basis of dates, to have been an indigenous sub-Saharan invention (in part on the basis of seven furnace dates of greater than 800 BC from Cameroon, Rwanda, Burundi, and the Democratic Republic of Congo; cf. de Maret and Thiry 1996). Researchers, however, are having considerable difficulty explaining why sub-Saharan Africa's precocious iron smelting sites have no apparent local antecedent in copper or bronze technology.

Thus, on the basis of current evidence, it appears that the great techno-economic innovations of the Holocene did not flow from Egypt to the African interior, but rather that after a period of cultural contact (ca. 10000–7000 bp), 'Inner' Africa followed its own internal dynamic.

Evidence for Egypt in Africa: contacts with Dynastic Egypt?

In 1965, Egyptologist H. W. Fairman appealed for scholars to investigate Egypt as an integral part of greater Africa. He made tentative suggestions of possible socio-political commonalities including divine kingship or connections within the realms of myth (Fairman 1965). The possibilities for chance convergence in such areas of culture, particularly when separated by thousands of years of time in their occurrence, would seem to be high. But is there material evidence to support the hypotheses of scholars such as Diop and Fairman, positing past links between Dynastic Egypt and the African interior?

The notion that pharaonic Egypt might have had contact with civilizations in West Africa is really nothing new. In the 19th century, colonial European scholars such as Barth, Dubois and Delafosse made links between Egypt and the founding of the Songhai Dynasty (Masonen 2000). The origins of this assertion were Songhai traditions which claimed a visit from a pharaoh to their capital Kukiya (or Bourem, depending on the version), his interaction with local magicians, and with the biblical Moses and Aaron (Barth [1857–1858] 1965). It is ironic that the potential utility for this linkage for these early explorers of West African culture was to prove an external ('White') origin for West African civilization (cf. Delafosse 1900). Unfortunately for these theorists, archaeological and historical investigations have dated the origins of Songhai polities on the Niger bend to some time between the ninth and 11th centuries AD – long after the demise of Dynastic Egypt (Davidson 1977; Insoll 1996). It would seem that the origins of these Songhai traditions – along with many other claims for origins of West African royal lineages in strangers from 'Yemen' or 'Mecca' – probably have more to do with attempts at legitimation in the Islamic world than with historical veracity (Folorunso Chapter 6, this volume; Masonen 2000: 415–416).

On the other hand, early Egyptological writers such as Oric Bates pleaded a relatively insular worldview for Dynastic Egyptians:

> The whole of Africa west of the Nile was, to the Egyptian, a *terra incognita* which stretched away from the familiar haunts of men to the realms of the dead. To this unknown country the vague general term *imn-t*, 'the West' was applied, either to signify the country itself or the imagined soul-land beyond it. Within it, as the Nile dwellers came eventually to know, lay the oases and various tribes of foreign men … The oases [situated within the bounds of modern Egypt, Libya, and Sudan] were not subjected by the Egyptians until the time of the New Empire.

(Bates [1912] 1970: 48)

More recent scholars (e.g. Scham 2003; O'Connor and Quirke 2003b) have asserted geographical and political factors as reasons for Egypt's seeming isolation from much of the rest of the continent:

> Egyptian contact with and knowledge of Africa was relatively shallow, partly because of severe natural restrictions on access such as the Sahara and the difficulty of movement along the Upper Nile. A related and equally important factor was the comparatively unsophisticated Egyptian political and military organization, which never created an 'imperial' hegemony … Once territorial integrity was assured and

control over or access to relatively close trade routes and sources of raw materials was established the Egyptians seem to have had little impetus to advance further.

(O'Connor 1983: 252)

Furthermore, after decades of further research there is little epigraphic support for Egyptian contacts beyond modern Libya and Sudan. Most potential Egyptian long-distance contacts seem to have occurred during the Old Kingdom (2686–2181 BC) and New Kingdom (1152–1069 BC) voyages of exploration and trade into the land of Punt (i.e. modern eastern Sudan and Eritrea; Kemp 1983; O'Connor 1983, 1993 – but on the location of Punt, see Meeks 2003). As the kingdoms of Nubia usually blocked direct riverine routes of trading contact with Punt (for frankincense and myrrh), most of these sporadic journeys were made via the Red Sea, though some followed a tortuous desert route (Kemp 1983: 136; Yurco 2001). On one such sixth Dynasty desert trek, the expedition's leader Harkhuf "acquired a pygmy in Yam, said to be from the land of the Horizon Dwellers, one who could perform the 'dances of the god'" (Meeks 2003: 72; O'Connor and Quirke 2003b: 10; Snape 2003: 98; Yurco 2001: 40). The excitement created by this acquisition, evident in its recording in stone on Harkhuf's tomb chapel at Aswan, indicates the scarcity of Egyptian contact, even at one remove, with Central Africa.

Material culture evidence for contact between the Nile Valley and areas south of Meroe, or to the west of the great river, remain scant. One good example of what such contact might look like – at least in terms of trade – comes from the site of Jebel Moya in southern Sudan (Figure 7:2). Even there, however, scarabs and pendants of Egyptian provenance do not date any earlier than the New Kingdom and are probably all attributable to commerce during the Napatan period, ca. 1000–400 BC (Addison 1949). In a recent chronological re-evaluation of the Jebel Moya complex, Gerharz (1994: 330) noted that the high concentration of these goods in first millennium BC burials must have reflected a "great fascination" for locals with the Egypto-Kushitic civilization of that epoch, indicating links which might go beyond trade into ritual and religious spheres. However, such direct material culture evidence from Dynastic Egypt is, as yet, unknown to the west of the modern frontiers of Egypt and Sudan, or to the south of Jebel Moya.

Indeed, some long-held evidence for Dynastic Egyptian contacts reaching as far as the Algero-Libyan frontier has been decisively dismissed in recent years. In the first editions of Lhote's (1959) *Search for the Tassili Frescoes* much was made of Dynastic

Figure 7:2   Two Napatan period graves from Jebel Moya containing Egyptian imports (Graves 100/247 and 100/263; after Addison 1949: figs. 22, 23).

Egyptian 'influences'. In particular there were two famous scenes from Jabbaren which were thought to signify links with eighteenth Dynasty Egypt on stylistic grounds: the "Bird-Headed Goddesses" (Lhote 1959: col. pl. I; see also Figure 7:3) and

Figure 7:3   The (in)famous 'Egyptian Influence' Bird-Headed Goddesses of the Tassili – now thought to be a fake (after Lhote 1959: col. pl. I; Keenan 2002).

the "Scene of Offerings" (Lhote 1959: pl. 26). Interestingly, in the book's second edition, Lhote (1973) omitted all mention of these scenes and dropped all previously hypothesized Egyptian connections (save for the representation of an 'Egyptian' boat). As Muzzolini (1995: 240) notes, no photos have ever been published of the two famous 'Egyptian' scenes – only freehand drawings "too beautiful to be true". Muzzolini continues, "Egyptianized to the limit, they ring false, and nowhere else have such poses or hair-styles been recorded". The conclusion left to be drawn is that these 'Egyptian' drawings, which have never been re-located, were either overly-idealized in copying or were simply fakes. By the same token, Lhote's Egyptian boat, when viewed in context, is merely an arrow shot by an archer in an adjoining panel (Muzzolini 1995: 240). It seems that for some, the total absence of Egyptian cultural remains in central and western Sahara is so surprising that something must be invented to fill the void.

However, from the Lake Chad Basin and the Ennedi and Tibesti massifs there are some vestiges of possible contact with Nubia. Huard and Allard-Huard (1980) have argued for a zone of cultural contact with the Nubian C-group and central Sahara during the second millennium BC on the basis of similarities in the depiction of 'decorated' cattle in rock art. Their evidence is by no means definitive, but the similarity of this highly elaborate cattle motif distributed from the Nile Valley to the Tibesti is suggestive of a zone of interaction. As concerns ceramics, there is the striking early first millennium AD Haddadienne culture complex of northern Chad (Treinen-Claustre 1982). The highly burnished, red-slipped, painted conical pottery of the Haddadienne (Figure 7:4) has little in common with the traditional comb or roulette decorated globular pottery of central Sahara. As Treinen-Claustre notes, "the red and black 'Haddadienne' painted pottery … has incontestably, sooner or later, an Egypto-Nubian root". However, the only other such stylistic similarity of which I am aware comes from a few isolated sherds found in the lowest layer (ca. 1800 BC) of the mound site of Gajiganna (north Nigeria, Lake Chad Basin). These thin, highly burnished and slipped sherds, with incised designs, are very similar to their contemporary ceramics in Nubia (e.g. Kerma) and have no local parallels (Peter Wendt, pers. comm.). It is

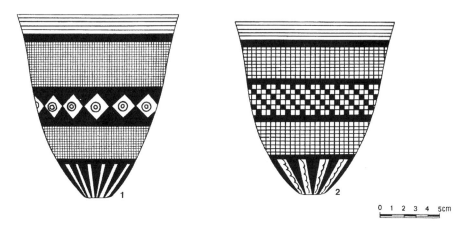

Figure 7:4   Conical painted 'Haddadienne' ceramics from the Borkou region of Chad (after Treinen-Claustre 1982: fig. 1).

tempting to connect these finds from the Chad Basin with the westward dispersion of the Chadic (Afro-Asiatic) languages ca. 4000–3000 BC.

Elsewhere (MacDonald 1998b), I have argued for a Trans-Saharan Pastoral Technocomplex dating to between 3800 and 1000 BC. Material support for this notion comes from a shared set of valued objects (notably small stone axes and stone rings), as well as a common pastoral economy and stylistically similar tumuli, which ultimately stretched from Kerma (Sudan) in the east to Dhar Tichitt (Mauritania) in the west. Such a technocomplex would not imply a common culture, nor even shared languages, but rather a shared economy (pastoralism), with comparable mortuary structures, and shared 'valued objects'. Again, this is a possible tenuous linkage between Inner Africa and Nubia, not Dynastic Egypt. It is worth noting that the monuments associated with this technocomplex (varied forms of dry stone tumuli dated from 3800 to 1000 BC) also have nothing to do with Diop's 'Egypt-influenced' phalliform stone circle of Tondidarou (Mali), which recent scholarship has dated to the early first millennium AD and placed within a local context (Person *et al.* 1991).

Compelling linguistic or material evidence of cultural contact with Dynastic Egypt has not yet been forthcoming from the African interior beyond Nubia. With the passage of time and the accumulation of research, the Nile Valley increasingly appears to have been more of a *cul de sac* than a corridor into 'Inner' Africa. The few exceptions mentioned above indicate only infrequent and weak interaction between the Lower Nile and the African interior after 7000 bp (ca. 6000 BC). Indeed, such contacts as can be documented are mostly between Egypt's rivals in Nubia (e.g. Kerma and Kush) and the interior. One is left to wonder why such plausibility has been given to cultural connections between the Egyptian state and Inner Africa, when (for example) Carthage – with apparent trade-links spanning the Sahara – has been almost ignored in this regard (cf. Bullard 2001).

Conclusions

I have attempted to expose the limitations of Diop's hypothetical connections between Egypt and the rest of Africa. It has been argued that there is little basis for strong cultural connections between Dynastic Egypt and the African interior. But, with all of their flaws, the works of Cheikh Anta Diop still raise some questions which are worthy of consideration concerning the peopling of Africa. These questions, which require utilization of data from historical linguistics and ethnography, have been conveniently ignored by past synthesizers of West African and Saharan prehistory. Despite late 20th century fashions to brush issues such as population movement and cultural influence under the carpet, they are still there and – however improperly addressed by early culture historians – will not go away. This is especially the case on the margins of the ever-changing Sahara, whose climatic cycles allow the periodic injection of populations in favourable periods, and demand their eventual expulsion at the next ecological collapse.

Finally, the works of Diop and other Afrocentrists have amply demonstrated the contemporary ideological importance of issues surrounding 'origins' and 'identities'.

It would be foolish for academics to abdicate responsibility for these issues on the African continent.

Note

1   Dates are expressed either as uncalibrated radiocarbon years before present (bp), or as calendar years (BC/AD).

CHAPTER 8

ANCIENT EGYPT, MISSIONARIES AND CHRISTIANITY IN SOUTHERN AFRICA

Bruce S. Bennett

This chapter discusses some of the ways in which Ancient Egypt informed the worldview of missionaries in southern Africa, arriving from the early 19th century, and the lasting effect this had on local Christian and secular thinking. Ancient Egypt was, for the missionaries, part of an ancient Near Eastern world which loomed large in their thoughts. It is most helpful to consider Egypt not in isolation but as part of this wider imagined place and time. This imagined world was centred upon the Old Testament, and supplemented by classical authors. These two sources were crucial not only to the missionaries but to most educated western Europeans of the time (Ucko and Champion 2003). The Old Testament included the record of the origins of humanity and the history of that part of it which had been central to the salvation history of the Christian religion. The Old Testament was crucial not only in its unique religious significance, but also as a detailed and coherent narrative history of an otherwise little-recorded past.

Classical learning comprised Greek and Latin writings, and such other parts of the knowledge of the ancient Mediterranean as had been preserved within them (such as, for example, the tantalizingly brief fragments attributed to Carthaginian sources). Western Europeans were acutely conscious of the fact that only parts of the original classical literature had survived. Whereas the Old Testament was, in a sense, complete (though not necessarily including everything one might have wished to know), classical literature was not: it was not a closed canon. The possibility of expanding or supplementing classical literature was an obvious and attractive idea. Such expansion, of course, happened with the rediscovery of ancient Egyptian history and other archaeological and philological advances of the 19th century.

Predominant missions in 19th century southern Africa were Protestant, and in particular associated with the British Free Churches and Independency (the theory of the right of the local church to interpret the Scriptures). Their focus was on individual salvation and they emphasized the reading of the Bible as indispensable, and although (where they made converts) the organization of a Church became important, their ecclesiology (theology of the Church) was weak. The missionaries were engaged in a project of seeking to understand the societies in which they were working. An understanding of the society would, they assumed, make it possible to communicate the Gospel. This interest developed over time and the earlier missionaries had relatively little appreciation of the cultural gap they were trying to bridge, but even for them the translation of the message required some attention to culture to be given. Later missionaries approached more explicitly the task of understanding the culture to which the Gospel was to be preached. Although this was the ultimate goal, missionaries seem seldom to have drawn close connections between their anthropological conclusions and any specific strategies of mission; that is, they treated their enquiries as pure research which would form the background to practise more than as applied research. Because of this, their ideas were influenced by their general missiological conceptions but not significantly by any connections with the specifics of preaching. The missionaries had a missiological model in Acts 17: 22–23: St Paul, entering Athens, had noted an altar to "an Unknown God", and used this as an introduction: "Men of Athens, I see that in everything that concerns religion you are uncommonly scrupulous … What you worship but do not know – this is what I now proclaim" (Acts 17: 22–23 NEB; AV has "ye are too superstitious"). The missionaries were, however, unable to apply this directly since they did not encounter 'idols' and indeed sometimes found difficulty recognizing a local concept of God, and though they could try to keep to the same spirit as St Paul, they seldom felt able to proceed as directly as the apostle from observation to preaching.

In the ancient world, classical writers routinely identified gods and demigods of one place with supposedly equivalent figures in another, noting differences in concept yet considering, for example, all sky gods to be in some sense the same. This is particularly the case in the Late Classical period when cross-cultural contacts were increasing, but even an early writer such as Herodotus followed the practice. Similarly, the idea that customs (especially religious rituals) had spread from place to place was commonplace among classical writers. Thus, ideas of comparative religion and cultural diffusion were part of the basic general knowledge of the educated western European (Harrison 2003; Tait 2003a).

In practice, the frontier missionaries were mainly interested in the dominant groups of existing states, even though they realized that these states were often multi-ethnic. If a missionary was allowed access, it would be to the capital, and to the ruling group. The groups concerned were Bantu-speakers, of two main linguistic groups, Nguni (including Xhosa, Zulu, and Ndebele) and Sotho-Tswana (including BaSotho, BaTswana, BaPedi and BaKhalagari). The speakers of the radically different Khoesan languages received considerably less attention.

Israelite parallels

Missionaries found interesting parallels between southern African societies and the world of the ancient Near East, and sometimes concluded that these parallels constituted evidence of linkages. The most frequently noted parallels were with the Old Testament Israelites, and with the Levitical code. A number of specific institutions could be cited. For example, both Nguni and Sotho-Tswana peoples practised circumcision and levirate marriage. Ideas about ritual pollution also had notable similarities, and the practice of naming children after some topical occurrence was also cited. In some cases even more striking parallels were locally observed, such as a version of the scapegoat ceremony found among the Zulu, and avoidance in some places of pig-meat (Tyler 1891: 182–183).[1] Other Near East parallels were less often noted, though it was suggested that cruel punishments among the Zulus were reminiscent of the Assyrians (Crabtree 1921: 27). The Sotho-Tswana had New Moon festivals that reminded some missionaries of ancient Israel, and apparently a lunar calendar.

Africans themselves were independently struck by some of these parallels. Perhaps more fundamentally, however, they recognized in the world of the early Old Testament a pastoral society more familiar and comprehensible to them than to the missionaries. It is possible that this awareness, which was expressed in an attention to the Old Testament that often surprised and discomfited missionaries, may have encouraged the missionaries' ideas about African-Israelite similarities.

Africans often responded to the Bible in ways not expected by the missionaries. As Hastings (1979: 71) points out, Protestant missionaries presented the Bible as *the* authority, and encouraged its reading, yet "had somehow overlooked, as essentially irrelevant, a great deal of what is actually in the Bible". This problem affected the Free Church Protestant missionaries of southern Africa more than many others, which indicates that, although such unexpected interpretations have often been presented in terms of cultural clash or accommodation, they also need to be seen in terms of the internal church dynamics of Independency. Catholic missionaries not only did not usually immediately present converts with the Bible, but also, and more fundamentally, clearly established the authority by which they interpreted the Bible in a particular way. The Free Church Protestant missionaries of southern Africa were often vague about this, and failed to recognize the extent to which they were merely *assuming* a uniformity derived from the more explicit ecclesiology of the Reformation. Thus, for example, they assumed that the polygamy and sacrificial laws in the Old Testament were not relevant to Christianity whereas the Ten Commandments were, but did not have a clear theology of why this should be. Coming from a background of Independency, they were not in a strong position to contest alternative interpretations. The missionaries were shocked by unexpected African readings of the Bible, but often failed to see that the Africans were as true as they to the Scripture: where they had parted company was over ecclesiology and the Tradition, which the Protestant missionary had thought was unnecessary. The unexpectedly significant texts were often, though by no means exclusively, in the Old Testament.

The Afrikaners, especially the frontier Boers, also developed a special interest in the Old Testament and in the books about the struggles of the Israelites to reach and occupy the Promised Land. There were several levels to this. It must first be noted that, as with the Africans, the setting of those books was simply more familiar to them than to western Europeans. A sympathetic Englishman who had mixed with the Boers in the years before World War I wrote later:

> These tough farmers of the northern plains … found in the scenes and atmosphere of Holy Writ the familiar pattern of their own lives. Utterly familiar to them were the sheep and the goats, the locusts and the wild honey, the ways of the serpent on the rock, the tactics and ruses of war with wild tribes … Far more than to the average European, the Bible spoke to the Boer in the trope and metaphor of his own daily life …

(Hastings 1947: 36)

However, according to many observers, the Boers tended to go beyond the finding of similarities to a form of identification. John Mackenzie wrote in 1871 that "no-one who has freely and for years mingled with these people can doubt that they have persuaded themselves by some marvellous process that they are God's chosen people, and that the blacks are the wicked and condemned Canaanites …" (Mackenzie [1871] 1971: 50). Mackenzie noted the constant reference to their enemies as "heathens". Later it was argued that this idea of a 'chosen people' was one of the roots of Afrikaner nationalism. In this view the 'Great Trek' of the Boers from the Cape into the interior equated to the Exodus, with the British as the pursuing Egyptians (Moodie 1975: ch. 1). However this view has been rebutted (Du Toit 1983: 920–952) and some have seen the image of Boer-as-Israelite as a British projection.

The Nile

Whether or not the frontier Boers' interest in the Israelites reached the point of identification, they naturally gave some thought to the physical location of the Promised Land and Egypt. (It has been noted that one result of the African interest in the Old Testament is the interest in the holy place, Zion.) Mackenzie noted that in conversation with frontier Boers he had often been questioned about these matters. 'Was Canaan near?' 'Where was Egypt?' Some of the northern Boers are said to have imagined that they might be approaching Egypt, and, for example, named a north-flowing river Nylstroom (Nile stream) in the belief that it would lead into Egypt (Chidester 1996: 174; Mackenzie [1871] 1971: 52). This was sometimes stated for the purpose of making the Boers appear ridiculous and ignorant, and it is uncertain how prevalent such ideas were in reality, but Mackenzie, although amused, pointed out that for someone with such limited formal education and understanding of geography it was not reasonable to expect a more accurate sense of relative distance (Mackenzie [1871] 1971: 52).

Such matters are in any case relative: at this very time David Livingstone was hoping to find the sources of the Nile in northern Zambia, a huge distance south of their actual location, and Mackenzie evidently thought Livingstone's geographical model probable (Mackenzie [1871] 1971: 486). Livingstone's theories about the Nile, which his last expedition was intended to test, proved to be mistaken in important respects. His theory was that Lake Tanganyika was connected to Lake Albert, that the Lualaba was the Upper Nile, and that Lake Bangweolo (Bangweulu, in northern Zambia) and the hypothetical Fountains of Herodotus were the sources of the Nile. In fact Lake Tanganyika is not connected to the Great Lakes north of it and the Lualaba is the upper Congo (Jeal 1985: 324–325, especially maps 5 and 6 which illustrate Livingstone's model and the actual geography). In his last days, Livingstone became fascinated by the idea that Moses might have travelled from Egypt far into Africa in his youth, an idea he connected with Meroe, and perhaps even to where Livingstone himself was then exploring. Jeal (1958: 328–329) suggests that this turn to fantasy may be explained by Livingstone's increasingly debilitating illness, with fever, loss of blood and extreme pain.

A search for origins

Where did the southern Africans come from? The question arose because both missionaries and secular scholars believed for different reasons that southern Africans must have come from somewhere else. Secular scholars at the time believed in cultural evolution often expressed in terms of diffusion, and in 'waves' of invading migrants populating the world. They had identified the Bantu language group, a large language family of relatively closely related languages spread over a wide area, and deduced a 'wave' of ancestral Bantu-speakers sweeping south through Africa. In fact this conclusion is still considered approximately valid (e.g. Phillipson 1993; Vansina 1994–1995); where modern archaeologists differ is in their assumption of a much longer time-scale allowing slow, undramatic change, rather than the waves of violent invaders required by the short time-scale of 19th century scholars, and perhaps preferred for other reasons as well.

Ideas of cultural diffusion, and of cultural links to be found by minutely examined examples, were current at this time. Missionaries, believing in a common human cultural origin, automatically looked for diffusion from the world of the early Old Testament. Folklorists in Europe looked for 'survivals' of ancient culture, in a way that may have influenced missionaries. Secular scholars of prehistory tended to perceive the human past in terms of waves, invasions, and diffusion of the culture of the most innovative 'races'. G. K. Chesterton satirized this sort of thinking in *The Flying Inn* (1914) in which a Muslim eccentric attempts to prove that English culture derives from the Islamic Middle East. Modern readers may not realize that the evidence he produces is hardly more far-fetched than that advanced in serious discussions of 'origins'.

Most missionaries, especially the earlier ones, either believed literally in the Genesis story of human origins, or assumed something fairly close to it.[2] It is worth noting the historical theory of religion held by early missionaries. Unlike secular scholars, missionaries tended not to believe in evolution, cultural or otherwise. These secular scholars could regard African religion as 'primitive', implying that religion followed a natural path of development from some basic starting-point and that African religion was 'primitive' in the sense of not having progressed much beyond this first stage. Other religions might be more 'advanced', to varying degrees. Such views were held by some later missionaries, but the early missionaries did *not* hold this view; rather they assumed that all peoples must have started out with some knowledge of God – being all the descendants of the sons of Noah – and that where this original knowledge was not found, it must have been *lost* or *corrupted*. Pagans were not 'primitive' people at a low level of progressive development, but people who had lost an earlier, fuller knowledge. Livingstone, for instance, who was not a literalist, did not regard Darwinism as a major problem (Jeal 1985: 329) but seems to have had similar ideas about the decay of an original religious knowledge (Livingstone and Livingstone [1865] 1971: 58). This theory of cultural deterioration was not only applied to religion, which was obviously the missionaries' first concern, but could also apply to other aspects of culture (Casalis [1859] 1997: 313; Crabtree 1921: 27). This made it quite easy for missionaries to postulate all sorts of cultural origins and linkages on the basis of apparently slight resemblances, since Africans (like Europeans) *must* have been descended from Middle Eastern peoples and any amount of knowledge could have been lost since the initial dispersal. The biblical Eden was somewhere in the Middle East (the rivers Tigris – Hiddekel – and Euphrates are mentioned; Gen 2: 10–14) and Noah's Ark came to rest on a mountain in Ararat (Gen 8: 4); the human race was therefore presumed to have spread out from this location.

The options for the origins of the southern African peoples seemed to be Palestine (or more broadly Arabia), Egypt or Ethiopia. Semitic origins were most widely favoured. Several missionaries tried to find linguistic evidence of Semitic origins for Bantu languages (e.g. Casalis [1859] 1997: 316–317). Much less attention was given to Khoesan languages but there were some suggestions of a link with Coptic (Ellenberger [1912] 1997: xxii). Ancient Egypt, though, also had its attractions. Notably, according to Herodotus (II.36.104), the Egyptians had also practised circumcision (Harrison 2003). Herodotus indeed implied that other countries which practised circumcision had adopted it from Egypt: the missionaries could not of course accept this as regards the Israelites, but the idea of Egypt spreading the custom elsewhere seemed plausible and would account for the differences between the Semitic and African practices which included, for example, circumcision at puberty instead of in infancy.

Suggestions of Egyptian origins

The idea of Egypt as a source of southern African origins received further encouragement with the discovery of the *diboko* (sacred animals or totems) of the Sotho-Tswana peoples.[3] Sotho-Tswana speakers were encountered by Europeans later than Nguni-speakers, and were perceived as being technologically and socially more advanced. Some early European visitors in fact declared that, unlike other peoples encountered in the region by Europeans, they qualified as "civilized" (Barrow [1801] 1975: 400). Furthermore, they seemed to have somewhat more definite religious ideas. Totems were (and are) inherited from one's father, although groups have sometimes changed their totem to mark a change of status, and it was generally held that the original and normative pattern was for the members of one *morafe* (tribe or polity) to share the same totem. By the mid-19th century this was far from the case, which could be explained by the processes of political upheaval and state-building in the recent past. The supposedly normative pattern, however, seemed to resemble the nomes of Ancient Egypt, with districts identified by animals. More generally, the reverence accorded to one's own totem was reminiscent of Egyptian veneration of certain animals such as cats. The widespread totem of the crocodile in southern Africa, and its status among groups where it is not actually the totem, was also interesting in view of Herodotus' (II.69) report that the Egyptians had venerated crocodiles. The parallel between Sotho-Tswana totems and Egyptian animal cults was one that seemed striking to Europeans, because in the ancient Mediterranean world the Egyptians' animal gods were noted as an unusual feature. Thus, in terms of the imagined ancient world that Europeans drew on for comparison, animal worship was an unusual feature regarded as *distinctively* Egyptian.

One study of the Bagananoa (a Sotho-Tswana group who have been classified as BaBirwa) suggested parallels between certain of their ceremonies and the Egyptian 'Book of the Dead' (Roberts 1915). Roberts, who was somewhat later than the early missionaries previously discussed, referred to a myth in which Horus defeats Seth, who tries to escape by transforming himself into a snake and disappearing into a hole in the ground. Other writers had already suggested that versions of this myth could be found in several parts of the world, and that characteristic signs of this myth were the snake, the hole, and footprints (possibly those of Horus – Roberts 1915–255). Roberts's publication, which is mainly about the male initiation ceremonies of the Bagananoa, describes rituals involving a symbolic elephant, which was the source of wisdom, and a carved wooden crocodile. During these rituals the wooden crocodile was placed on its back below the symbolic elephant. This, Roberts thought, constituted a version of the Seth-Horus myth, the snake having become a crocodile. He also mentioned sites of the 'Matsieng's hole' type. Such a site typically has a rock surface marked by carved footprints both human and animal, and is explained in Tswana tradition as being the place where a first-ancestor figure such as Matsieng emerged from the earth together with the animals (e.g. Walker 1997). Roberts found the combination of hole, footprints and (at least in the example reported to him) snake symbol clear evidence of the Seth-Horus myth (Roberts 1915: 256).

By no means all missionaries were convinced by such arguments, however. Whether or not they believed in a historical connection, many were struck by the differences, such as the fact that totem reverence applied only to the individual concerned. Whereas in Ancient Egypt cats were protected from everyone, a Motswana was concerned only that he himself did not kill or eat his own totem. This point might be considered as undermining the evidence for a historical connection, but could also be explained within the logic of cultural deterioration, whereby the modern Sotho-Tswana observed the restriction 'superstitiously', having lost the original religious meaning which made the avoidance more universal and significant.[4]

The general absence of ritual connected with totems among the main Tswana and Sotho groups is interesting in view of the usual expression for identifying a totem, "*go bina*", which literally means "to dance" in Setswana (thus, "*O binang?*" "What do you dance?" meaning "What is your totem?"). One possible explanation – that a ceremony once existed but had disappeared – was obviously satisfactory for missionaries with a theory of cultural deterioration, and could neatly explain both the similarities and differences with Egyptian animal cults. It must be noted, though, that this explanation was by no means restricted to missionaries and diffusionists. Isaac Schapera, regarded as the foremost authority on Tswana anthropology, wrote in 1937 that "There seems formerly to have been a fairly extensive ritual connected with the totem; but little of this now survives, even in the memory of the people" (Eiselen and Schapera 1937: 253).

Livingstone noted the parallels with Egyptian animal cults, but was also interested in more 'scientific' aspects of the possible connection. He was a qualified medical doctor and his work contains much scientific observation – he correctly identified the role of ticks in relapsing fever many years before it was confirmed in western publications (King and King 1992: 69). Livingstone noted that some aspects of the material culture he observed in southern and Central Africa seemed to resemble closely depictions in ancient Egyptian art – notably spinning and weaving. More remarkably, Livingstone hinted at a racial connection. Expressing a certain lack of confidence in the racial types described in contemporary scientific works, he noted that the heads of the inhabitants of Central Africa seemed to him to look remarkably like those in ancient Egyptian art. This struck him especially when he discovered some line drawings of faces carved on trees: "we meet with human faces cut in the bark of trees, the outlines of which, with the beards, closely resemble those seen on Egyptian monuments" (Livingstone 1857: 304). Livingstone's suggestion is in a way significant: despite his belief that African culture must give way to European "commerce and Christianity" he was constant in his rejection of any idea of African *racial* inferiority. Living away from Europeans for so long that his English became rusty, his knowledge of African languages was exceptional, and where some missionaries found Africans' resistance to the Gospel a sign of stupidity, Livingstone reported them engaging him in "remarkably acute" reasoning (Livingstone 1857: 25). For Livingstone, there was no reason in principle why these Africans' ancestors could not have been builders of pyramids.

One of the most thoroughly worked-out theories of southern African origins was that prepared by the missionary Frederick Ellenberger in Lesotho, in his monumental *History of the Basuto: Ancient and Modern* ([1912] 1997). Ellenberger was a member of a missionary family who settled in Lesotho in the 19th century. His children grew up speaking SeSotho as a first language and his account gives a central place to Sotho traditions. To think of Ellenberger simply as a missionary, in the sense of a man from outside, is perhaps misleading; his theories owe a great deal to a sort of Sotho patriotism as well as to his European education.

According to Ellenberger, the Bantu peoples of southern Africa had originated in Ancient Egypt, or possibly Ethiopia. However, he found cultural links (faint but detectable) not only with Egypt but also with Israel, which was of course only logical in view of the missionaries' belief in human diffusion from the single source described in Genesis. The New Moon festivities practised in southern Africa had similarities to both Jewish and Egyptian rites – Ellenberger referred to how Thoth was represented with a crescent on his head. Ellenberger thought that totems might have some link to Egyptian nomes and animal-worship, but he also thought that the totem animal symbolized God. Hence its worship constituted idolatry but not polytheism. Missionary opinion had by this time generally concluded that Sotho-Tswana religion was approximately monotheistic, believing in a remote High God who was, however, seldom if ever approached directly.

The ancestral groups of Bantu-speaking southern Africans were none other than the Bafokeng and Barolong, the oldest known Sotho-Tswana lineages. Of the two, the Bafokeng, the Lesotho branch, were (perhaps not surprisingly in view of Ellenberger's affinities) the more ancient. All southern and Central African Bantu-speaking groups except the Herero and Bavenda derived from the Barolong and Bafokeng (Ellenberger [1912] 1997: 333). Ellenberger believed that he could trace Bafokeng genealogical tradition back as far as 1,000 years. They had crossed the Equator in or after the 10th century AD (Ellenberger [1912] 1997: 356), and the Zambesi in the 11th or 12th (Ellenberger [1912] 1997: 333). Ellenberger did not discuss the 'Hottentots' in detail but quoted opinions that their language might have Coptic connections. They might therefore represent an earlier 'wave' of migration.

On the origins of circumcision, Ellenberger did not believe that the Bantu peoples had brought it from Egypt themselves, since he knew of various southern African traditions describing its adoption as a new custom. Such traditions placed the adoption before any clearly identifiable events, but in historical rather than mythical time. In particular, he cited traditions that it had been adopted from Khoesan speakers.[5] As he saw it, apart from the Israelites, who received circumcision by divine revelation, there were a few other possibilities for the origins of the practice. Herodotus (II.104) stated that the Egyptians practised circumcision, and that Ethiopia and Colchis learnt it from Egypt. However, Diodorus Siculus stated that the Troglodytes of Mount Seir also practised circumcision. Ellenberger therefore suggested that Bushmen were descended from the Troglodytes, and had brought circumcision with them. The Bantu peoples had then learnt it relatively recently from the Bushmen (Ellenberger [1912] 1997: 282).

Secular scholars were less inclined to see links between southern Africans and Egypt or the Near East, partly because of the Africans' perceived lower level of technology – especially in terms of monumental architecture, which tended to dominate European perceptions of cultural sophistication. Southern Africans, it was believed, did not build in stone. The stone constructions that were discovered, such as Great Zimbabwe, were assumed to be the work of other people. Insofar as the reasoning was not circular, it rested on the premise that there was no *contemporary* building in stone by southern Africans. However, missionary John Mackenzie had pointed out in 1871 that the stone ruins at Lobatse (southern Botswana) were obviously on the same pattern as contemporary Tswana villages, and that stone work had therefore been in use by local Africans quite recently. Mackenzie was attracted to the idea that the Ophir of "King Solomon's mines" (see I Kings 9: 28) might be in the region but he did not see any reason why Africans *could* not have built stone structures. Like Livingstone, Mackenzie repeatedly attacked supposedly scientific investigations and implications of African inferiority. In general, few missionaries intellectually accepted the ideas of inherent racial inferiority which were increasingly prevalent in late Victorian Britain, although many showed degrees of less conscious prejudice. On the subject of Ophir, Mackenzie pointed out in passing that the theory that Sofala in East Africa was the biblical Ophir had been current as far back as the 17th century, citing Milton (*Paradise Lost* XI 400; Mackenzie [1871] 1971: 485). Until the turn of the century, secular scholars argued that Great Zimbabwe was a non-African construction dating to before 1 BC, but in 1906 an archaeological study showed clear evidence that it was a local African construction of the early second millennium BC, a conclusion which all subsequent research has confirmed (Campbell 1998: 32–33; Hall 1990), although popular belief, particularly amongst European immigrant populations in southern Africa, has failed to observe these academic conclusions.

The basic reason why missionaries turned so readily to the ancient Near East for parallels to southern Africa is illustrated by a fictional graduate student in David Lodge's novel *The British Museum is Falling Down*:

'Would you say,' said the man at length, 'that [Kingsley Amis] is superior or inferior to C. P. Snow?'

'I don't think you can compare them,' said Adam wearily.

'I have to: they are the only British novelists I have read.'

(Lodge 1983: 119)

The data available to the normal educated western European was limited. To understand an unfamiliar society, the missionaries naturally turned to the examples of other civilizations known to them. Apart from their own, the ancient Mediterranean was the only one which had featured significantly in their education, and within this, the Near East was most familiar to men with a biblical education. A missionary would probably have read books about India (to take as an example another non-European civilization about which information was available) which were written or considered relevant by missionaries; whereas he would have had a much broader grounding in the ancient world. Mackenzie drew only limited comparisons with India, which tended to focus on aspects that related directly to mission work there (e.g. Mackenzie [1871] 1971: 488), whereas he could draw on much more various detail for ancient civilization or his own Scottish folk-culture.

Southern African Christianity and Egypt

The academic and religious ideas of the early 20th century filtered through to educated Africans, who, while not accepting blindly such ideas as the 'Hamitic Hypothesis' (Folorunso Chapter 6, Reid Chapter 5, Wengrow Chapter 9, all this volume), nevertheless naturally tended to fit their own theories into the received framework as expressed in their work. The theme of the Exodus appears in vernacular literature with the play *Puso ya ga Kgosi Faro* (The Reign of Chief Pharaoh) by Moroke (n.d.), a Methodist minister, which deals with the conflict between pharaoh and Moses in a moralistic vein (Maseia 1985: 645). Motsete (1899–1975), a versatile Motswana intellectual and politician now best remembered for writing the Botswanan National Anthem, apparently wrote a work on ancient Tswana customs, in which he argued that the Tswana or their Bantu ancestors had come from Ancient Egypt. His arguments apparently alluded to words or traditions which he thought referred to the Great Lakes, but his work seems to be lost and his theory is not now clear.[6]

More recently, connections and comparisons with Ancient Egypt tend to have been made more cautiously. In a 1986 study of Tswana physical cosmology, Clegg noted an Egyptian parallel with one belief about the sun. According to this Tswana theory, the sun is swallowed by a crocodile each night and excreted the next morning at the other end of the earth. This is reminiscent of the Egyptian myth in which Ra travels through a snake at night (Clegg 1986: 33–37). Clegg, however, did not suggest any actual connection between the two beliefs, and suggested rather that ideas about the physical universe may tend to develop along parallel lines in different places simply because they are economical explanations of commonly experienced observations.

In modern southern Africa, missionaries have given way to a localized Christianity, which is conventionally divided into the 'mainline' churches derived from the missions, and the 'African Independent Churches', which look to local founders and often attempt a greater degree of cultural synthesis. In the various Christian churches of southern Africa, several place names are used as significant references, including Zion, Ethiopia and Egypt. 'Zion', which often confuses visitors from abroad when they find that 'Zionists' may have no interest in Middle East politics, refers to "a Jerusalem somehow realized here in Africa" (Hastings 1979: 69) and is often associated with other aspects of the sense of a holy place such as a 'Jordan' of baptism (Hastings 1996: 499). 'Ethiopia' is associated with the Ethiopian movement, which arose in southern Africa in the late 19th century. The Ethiopian movement is usually seen as being about the Africanization of the Church in terms of leadership – accelerating a process which the missionaries approved in principle but seemed to delay and frustrate in practice – as opposed to Zionist and other movements which questioned more of what the missionaries regarded as core theology. This contrast is a useful starting point of analysis but is too neat; the usage of the two names, which evoke closely related visions, was not in practice as simple as this (Hastings 1979: 69). The reference to Ethiopia was, in origin, biblical: above all to the verse text "Ethiopia shall soon stretch out her hands unto God" (Psalm 68: 31 AV), with a further reference to Acts 8: 26–39, in which an Ethiopian eunuch responds readily to the Gospel, thus confirming the Psalm's prophecy about Africa's response (Boschman 1994: 2). These texts were popular with missionaries as well (Hastings 1996: 497); here again African readers perhaps read more than was expected. The victory of Ethiopia over Italy at Adowa in 1896 and its subsequent status as the only authentic independent black African state added an extra dimension to the concept of 'Ethiopia'. Thus, Ethiopia was mainly a biblical and symbolic Ethiopia, but with some reference to the historic kingdom. The image of Ethiopia has apparently declined in importance over time. James Amanze's *Botswana Handbook of Churches* (1994) shows no occurrence of the name in contemporary church titles, compared to numerous references to Zion, although 'Africa', which appears in many names, may be considered to have taken over some of the sense of 'Ethiopia'.

In Botswana, however, Egypt has been almost entirely a symbolic location, representing sin. "We must not go back to Egypt" will be said by a preacher with reference to sin or something that has rightly been left behind. The Israelites, in their periodic complaints during the Exodus, expressed the wish to go back to Egypt (Num 14: 3–4) and this subsequently became an image of backsliding in both the Old and New Testaments. The Old Testament prophets used Egypt especially to refer to the temptation of idolatry. The following example, in which "playing the whore" represents idolatry, illustrates the forceful condemnation of Egypt:

> She [Oholibah, representing Jerusalem] played the whore again and again, remembering how in her youth she had played the whore in Egypt. She was infatuated with their male prostitutes, whose members were like those of asses and whose seed came in floods like that of horses. So, Oholibah, you relived the lewdness of your girlhood in Egypt when you let your bosom be pressed and your breasts fondled.

> (Ezek 23: 19–21 NEB)

Such usage continues in the New Testament: in Revelation 11: 8, "Sodom and Egypt" is the symbolic name of the great city where the two witnesses are killed, which is the city "where also their Lord was crucified". Such allegorical usage originally took for granted the more literal meaning of Egypt as the land of slavery and bondage from which the Israelites had escaped, but for European Christians and hence missionaries this original political sense was less immediate. It is perhaps significant that southern Africans, despite their much greater interest in the Old Testament, did not in this case move beyond the missionaries' allegorical emphasis. This probably reflects the fact that while pastoral society was far more familiar to them than to Europeans, Egyptian bondage was somewhat remote for both.

In the 20th century, however, the political meaning of the Exodus from Egypt did take on much greater significance for Africans in South Africa. It was a popular text for the "Donkey Church" Methodists (so named for their emblem) who split from the white-led church among the BaRolong of Mafeking (Mafikeng) in the 1950s (Leloba Molema, pers. comm.). More recently, as apartheid intensified, Egypt became of significance to the liberation theologians. In free and independent Botswana, however, the meaning of Egypt in preaching remained spiritual. This may also reflect the fact that Botswana's African Independent Churches have been oriented to their members' immediate needs and problems, which have typically been expressed in less political terms than in South Africa.

Conclusion

Missionaries, in seeking to understand the populations they were evangelizing, made use of the sources most familiar to them – first the Bible, and of course their knowledge of their own societies, but also their knowledge of classical literature. Both missionaries and secular scholars viewed southern Africans as having migrated within the relatively recent past, and hence looked for cultural phenomena linking them to their supposed places of origin. Missionaries drew parallels both with Semitic cultures and with Ancient Egypt, the latter especially with reference to the Sotho-Tswana animal totems, but also sometimes with reference to circumcision. The missionaries, while agreeing with secular scholars on diffusion, diverged from them in some important respects: notably, they rejected ideas of inherent racial inferiority (although they were often personally prejudiced). Instead of the secular scholars' evolutionary model in which Africans had advanced only to a low stage because of their inferiority, the missionaries tended to a concept of cultural deterioration in which the peoples of the world – all of common origin – had lost the original knowledge of God due to various vicissitudes.

It is important to remember that the 19th century missionaries, while starting the process, account for only a relatively small number of conversions: the peak period of Christian expansion in Africa occurred in the 20th century. The missionaries occupy a pivotal point in history, and are thus important objects of study, as in this chapter, but this should not obscure the point that most African Christian converts were converted by other Africans. Partly as a result of this, African Christians do not necessarily read the Bible in the same way as European Christians, but they probably read it more. Understanding the ways in which African Christianity has developed requires knowledge both of African cultures and of the internal dynamics of Christianity.

The missionaries saw their ancient parallels and connections as historical and as helping them to understand their hosts, but not as relevant to the Christianity they had come to preach. Southern Africans, however, drew on these elements in constructing their own Christian identities. For them, 'Zion' and 'Ethiopia' had positive meanings, but 'Egypt', the enslaver of the Israelites, symbolized sin, or, later, political oppression. This symbolism, which has been especially prevalent in the popular African Independent Churches, may have made Ancient Egypt a less attractive image for southern Africans than might have been expected by an observer not aware of the importance of biblical and Christian discourse. These symbols derived initially from biblical usage, but in the case of Ethiopia a reference to the historical African kingdom (in its symbolic significance as the independent Christian African state, rather than in the detail of its culture or history) was also present.

Thus, while missionaries were interested in the idea of ancient Egyptian origins and connections for Africans, for the Africans themselves – who had internalized and appropriated the biblical references – the idea had less appeal, although it did interest some intellectuals. It is notable that BaTswana troops sent to the Middle East during World War II found great interest in the Holy Land, but apparently much less in Egypt (Jackson 1999: 94–95).

In explaining the relative lack of interest in Ancient Egypt, the key discourse to understand is a biblical and Christian one, operating according to its own internal dynamics. Although this cannot be understood without reference both to imperialism and to missionaries' theories, it cannot be explained simply in terms of them either. Missionaries introduced these biblical and other references but could not subsequently control their use.

Notes

1   The most striking parallels of all were in fact among the Lemba, who recent DNA evidence indicates actually may have a Semitic link (Parfitt 1997), but they had not been so much noticed at this time.

2   This was not, however, universal: David Livingstone, for example, had before becoming a missionary moved away from Calvinism and literal interpretation (Jeal 1985: 12–13) though he may have reverted to more literal belief in his last days (Jeal 1985: 328–329).

3   Actually, not all totems are animals, but the exceptions were considered to be special cases.

4   Chidester (1996) has analysed the reluctance of early missionaries to accord 'religious' status to African observances (see also Bennett 1997, 2001).

5   This is somewhat puzzling since circumcision is not a known feature of Khoesan culture and such traditions of circumcision being learnt from the Khoesan speakers do not appear among the Tswana. Sotho traditions are obscured by the fact that by Ellenberger's time the Baroa (Bushmen) of Lesotho had almost disappeared as a separate group, with the remnants of the "Mountain Bushmen" being absorbed into Sotho communities in the late 19th century (Gill 1993: 132–133).

6   Pers. comm. Kgalemang Tumedisco Motsete, 23 September 1969; pers. comm. Neil Parsons, 7 December 2001.

Acknowledgments

I thank Rev Dr Obed Kealotswe for his valuable assistance with the significance of 'Egypt' and 'Ethiopia' in southern African Christian thought, and Prof Neil Parsons and Dr Leloba Molema for their contributions. I am also grateful to Dr Karim Sadr, Dr R. G. T. Bennett, and Mrs H. G. Bennett for their assistance with sources not locally available.

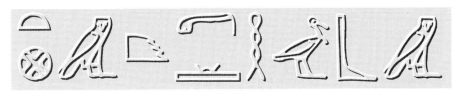

CHAPTER 9

LANDSCAPES OF KNOWLEDGE, IDIOMS OF POWER: THE AFRICAN FOUNDATIONS OF ANCIENT EGYPTIAN CIVILIZATION RECONSIDERED

David Wengrow

Introduction: archaeology, anthropology and colonialism in the Nile Valley

"Knowledge is power", wrote Wingate (1918: 1), in his preface to the first edition of *Sudan Notes and Records*, the official journal of the Anglo-Egyptian Condominium (1899–1956), of which he was then Governor General. This claim – now, ironically perhaps, a central tenet of postcolonial theory – would surely have held a particular resonance for the handful of British officials who then made up the government of Africa's largest country. While direct control over an area one million square miles in size was clearly a practical impossibility for the few hundred Oxbridge graduates who passed through its administrative service, a sense of intellectual and moral authority was at least possible, and perhaps psychologically necessary.

In a review of the *"Sudan Notes and Records* as a vehicle of research", Sanderson (1964: 164–165) observed a "strong bias" in the direction of colonial scholarship towards social anthropology in southern Sudan – notably among the Dinka, Nuer, Shilluk, and Azande – and an "even heavier emphasis" upon archaeology in the northern part of the country, with its "wealth of visible sites … [which] inspired many officials to become amateur field archaeologists". If knowledge is power, then the fact that these distinct forms of knowledge were consistently cultivated by the colonial government in the northern and southern parts of Sudan is of interest, both for modern perceptions of the region's past, and in understanding its politically divided, postcolonial present.

'Africa,' went the imperial slogan, 'begins at Malakal', in southern Sudan. To the north, from the Sixth to the First Cataracts, extended what were perceived as the outer margins of the ancient Oriental landscape, punctuated first by Meroitic temples and pyramids, and then by monuments of (ancient) Egyptian imperial domination. It was largely on the basis of such monuments that Sudan's distant past was defined by Reisner (1918a) in the first edition of *Notes and Records* (directly following Wingate's preface), in terms which draw a clear parallel between British and pharaonic domination of the land:

The country called by the Ancient Egyptians the 'Southern Lands' included all the vague region of Egyptian influence which lay to the south towards Central and Eastern Africa. Among its inhabitants, the inscriptions name the red men of the famous land of Punt which lay perhaps on the Somali coast, the black men of the southern districts, the Nubians of the Nile Valley, the Libyans of the western desert, and the nomads of the eastern desert. Thus the Anglo-Egyptian Sudan forms the greater part of the 'Southern Lands', and indeed much the same part with nearly the same races, which was administered by the Egyptian officials of the New Empire.

(Reisner 1918a: 3)

Mapped onto the physical landscape of the Nile Valley we therefore find a passage between two familiar subjects of the colonial imagination: the 'Orient', as a negative reflection of Europe's own monumental ambitions and destiny (Said 1978), and 'Africa', as a subject of "primordial colonialism, 'bound to violence' … a blank slate upon which the name of the firstcomer would be forever inscribed" (Miller 1985: 13).[1]

The image of Sudan as a place where oppression had been endemic since time immemorial was politically expedient for a British government seeking financial and moral support for its imperial venture. As Collins observes, the desire to quash the Nilotic slave trade, coupled with the martyrdom of Gordon, played a major role in mobilizing public opinion in favour of invasion (Collins 2000). The subsequent British decision to pursue the reconstitution of traditional, tribal frameworks of authority in southern Sudan, while encouraging the growth of a Western-style intelligentsia and administrative institutions in the north, is well documented, as is the role of ethnography in the service of government intelligence. By contrast, the distinct role played by archaeological knowledge and practice (or by its absence) in the development of colonial attitudes and policy has been little explored (cf. Rowlands 1998a).[2]

It was, in part, the activities of "amateur field archaeologists" in the colonial service, referred to by Sanderson (1964), that prompted a vociferous note to *Antiquity* by Crawford (1948) – professional archaeologist, pilot, and historian of the Funj – entitled 'People without a History'. Crawford contrasted the almost total lack of archaeological interest in the many mounds distributed across the Upper Nile region of southern Sudan (see Johnson 1990, and below) with the extensive fieldwork carried out in the north by Reisner and others. Aside from personal benefactions, of the kind which allowed Sir Henry Wellcome to dig at Jebel Moya (in reality more a philanthropic employment scheme than a scientific excavation; see Addison 1949), there appears, however, to have been little official support for archaeological research in southern Sudan during the Condominium (see Kleppe 1986). Crawford also criticized the conflation of Nilotic archaeology with Egyptology:

When I have told people that I once dug a site on the Blue Nile, almost invariably they have expressed surprise that there should be anything to find there. Many (to whom the Nile meant Egypt) have assumed that I must be looking for 'Egyptian' remains. My reply has always been that what I found was the remains of the ancient dwellers on the site …

(Crawford 1948: 8–9)

He concluded that

> the excavation of a Nilotic mound-site is more suitable to be undertaken at the present moment than that of yet another Egyptian temple. It will not add to the responsibilities of the Commissioner of Archaeology ... But it *will* probably provide the Sudan with a sequence of types by means of which future excavators will be able to date their finds and strata; and until they can do this, they had much better remain at home.

(Crawford 1948: 12)

During the early 20th century, the Anglo-Egyptian Sudan in fact lay on the cusp of a much wider division of European academic labour, which has been remarked upon by Rowlands (1994: 137–138):

> It is striking that archaeology was least developed in those parts of the colonized periphery where British anthropology was most powerful. We still know virtually nothing in fine-grain detail of the archaeology of vast tracts of west Central Africa, whereas ethnographically it formed the backbone for British structural functionalist anthropology.

The contribution of such disciplinary boundaries to wider colonial perceptions of peoples on the African continent, and hence to the formulation of policies on government and modernization, has not been sufficiently investigated (cf. Prakash 1995). As a perceived crossing-point between the 'Orient' and 'Africa', the Anglo-Egyptian Sudan would be a logical starting point for such an investigation in the future. The main concern of this chapter, however, is with the different forms of knowledge produced during the Condominium period, the way in which they have defined the parameters of more recent scholarship, and the possibilities and consequences of moving beyond them in the light of new research. In exploring these themes, I focus upon issues relating to the formation of dynastic civilization in the Nile Valley – a topic which has commanded undiminished scholarly and popular attention in Europe from colonial times to the present – and to the definition of an African context for this process.

The 'Hamitic Hypothesis'

The distinction between Nilotic peoples with, and without, history (to use Crawford's phrase; and see also Wolf 1982) was rationalized in early 20th century scholarship by what came to be known as the 'Hamitic Hypothesis' (Folorunso Chapter 6; O'Connor and Reid Chapter 1; Reid Chapter 5; all this volume). Its main contention was that dynastic civilization in Egypt had emerged out of a larger, 'Hamitic' cultural entity in North East Africa, remnants of which could still be observed among the living, cattle-keeping peoples of the Upper Nile region in southern Sudan. Although often characterized as part of an 'African substratum', the Hamites were in fact considered, on what now appear entirely spurious grounds, to be linguistically and racially affiliated to 'Mediterranean' rather than 'Negroid' peoples (see MacGaffey 1966), and scholars of the Vienna-based *Kulturkreislehre* (see Kluckhohn 1936) even considered possible a distant relationship with 'Indo-European' pastoralists of the inner Asiatic steppes (e.g. Schmidt 1935).

The 'Hamitic Hypothesis' incorporated the modern inhabitants of southern Sudan – as ethnographic subjects – into a remote past that was alien to them, and which was then being revealed by archaeological research in northern Sudan (Nubia) and Egypt. Its chief proponent was the founding father of Sudanese ethnography, Seligman, who contended that "among the cultural strata lying buried beneath the present day cultures of north-eastern and eastern Africa there are remains of one which presents such substantial affinities with that of Ancient Egypt that there can be no legitimate objection to speaking of it as Hamitic" (Seligman 1913: 596). Seligman's 'ethnographic excavation' of the Hamitic substratum involved comparisons of skull measurements taken from modern Sudanese subjects with prehistoric and ancient Egyptian specimens, and the identification of superficially common cultural traits, such as body mutilation, deformation of cattle horns, and divine kingship (Seligman 1934; Seligman and Seligman 1932).

In more or less attenuated forms, the 'Hamitic Hypothesis' remains a marginal feature of modern scholarship on the prehistoric and ancient Nile Valley, although the 'Hamites' are now more commonly portrayed as a purely African entity. Its ongoing influence is particularly clear in otherwise unsubstantiated claims for dating the vast corpus of North East African rock art featuring cattle to the period preceding state formation in Ancient Egypt (e.g. Červíček 1986). In some recent accounts, what began life as a primitivist and eurocentric discourse, locating the source of Ancient Egypt's development far outside the African continent (Folorunso Chapter 6, this volume), is turned on its head to support a case for the African origins of Egyptian civilization (e.g. Autuori 1996; Celenko 1996). However, in retaining an image of modern Sudanese peoples as living exemplars of a formative stage in the development of Egypt's ancient past, this new discourse serves only to reinforce the assumptions about African cultural dynamism (or lack thereof) which it purportedly seeks to undermine. In a peculiar trade-off, Ancient Egypt is rendered African at the price of Africa's more recent history.

The most sophisticated treatment of the 'Hamitic Hypothesis' undoubtedly remains that developed by Frankfort in his (1948) *Kingship and the Gods*, a comparative study of the relationship between cosmology and rulership in Ancient Egypt and Mesopotamia. While there is no doubt that Frankfort shared many of the racist assumptions of his time (see especially Frankfort 1950), he also laid the basis for a more reflexive approach to the use of ethnographic data in archaeological interpretation, which may owe much to Collingwood's (1946) philosophy of historical knowledge (see Wengrow 1999: 606). The 'main value of introducing anthropological material' was, for Frankfort, its potential to broaden the horizons of the modern interpreter in relation to archaeological material, rather than to act as a substitute for detailed analysis of that material on its own terms (Frankfort 1948: 382 n. 5). Rather than merely illustrating the diffusion of particular cultural traits over time and space, ethnographic accounts of societies in remote places could open avenues to an understanding of the past that remain otherwise hidden from view by the contingencies of our own, limited cultural experience.

Embodiment as an idiom of social power in Ancient Egypt

Of particular interest, in the light of more recent discussions of African political forms (e.g. Arens and Karp 1989; Argenti 1999; Rowlands 1998b, 1999), is Frankfort's characterization of Ancient Egyptian kingship as the embodiment of sacred power (see especially Frankfort 1948: 45). Although allied to what subsequent commentators have considered an exaggerated account of the king's divinity (Posener 1960; and see O'Connor and Silverman 1995), discussions of embodiment in *Kingship and the Gods* also focus to a considerable extent upon the concrete dimensions of experience and activity through which royal power was expressed in Egypt, rather than just its theoretical nature. In addition to archaeological and epigraphic data, Frankfort drew upon descriptions of Shilluk religion to exemplify how a society might recognize that "a succession of individuals embodies the same divine being, yet ... not disregard the individuality of each separate ruler" (Frankfort 1948: 199–200). His interpretation stresses the role of the king's body – and the objects, images and mythologies in which its force was localized, encoded, perpetuated and distributed – as the nexus, both of political power and of society's ongoing relationship with the cosmos. This aspect of Frankfort's account finds echoes in more recent studies, in the light of which its main tenets may be briefly reviewed.

Unlike that of Mesopotamia, Early Dynastic society in Egypt did not crystallize into a number of distinct, autonomous city-states, but rather "assumed the form of a single, united, but rural domain of an absolute monarch" (Frankfort 1948: 50; cf. Baines and Yoffee 1998: 208–209). Royal ceremony centred upon the body of the king, in which an immortal god was incarnated and personified. It consisted primarily in the erection and maintenance of permanent funerary monuments, and in a cycle of more ephemeral, revelatory displays, which celebrated his active role in binding the inhabited land to an ordered image of the cosmos (Frankfort 1948: 45, 79–139; cf. Baines 1995: 129–135, 1997). During the Old Kingdom, elite status was expressed in the idiom of proximity and access to the king's person, which provided the primary locus of political authority in the land (Helck 1954; cf. Baines 1999), and the transmission of landed property was regulated to a significant extent by participation in mortuary cults. These linked the ritual maintenance of a sensory life for the king and the elite to the dispensation of privileges and resources among their living dependants (Kemp 1983: 85–96; Roth 1991).

Increasing scholarly interest in developing or reviving accounts of Egyptian state formation based upon African models of political development constitutes more than an intellectual engagement with current social agendas. It also represents a frustration with the inability of existing models of social evolution, developed principally in relation to the archaeological record of South West Asia, to account for the distinguishing features of Egyptian political culture outlined above (cf. Fairservis 1989). In the remainder of this chapter, I highlight these shortcomings, and seek to outline the basis of an alternative account of early state formation, placing Egypt's development within the context of the Nile Valley as a whole, and drawing particularly upon recent archaeological discoveries in Central Sudan. Since it is generally accepted that the adoption of domesticated animals and plants during the neolithic period provided the material foundations for state formation, the focus of my discussion must be upon the particular form of neolithic society that emerged in the Nile Valley during the fifth millennium BC.

The inception of neolithic economy and society in the Nile Valley: an archaeological overview

By the late fifth millennium BC, there is clear evidence for domestic cattle, sheep and goats at early neolithic sites in both Egypt and Sudan (Chenal-Vélardé 1997; Gautier 1987). The adoption of domesticated animals in the Nile Valley is attested prior to that of cereal farming, although the precise route(s) through which they were introduced from South West Asia remains a subject of speculation. Neither domestic sheep nor goats have wild ancestors in Africa, and claims for the independent domestication of cattle in Egypt's Western Desert (Wendorf and Schild 1980: 277–278, 1998: 101) remain unconvincing, and have not been widely accepted (see Grigson 2000; MacDonald 2000; Smith 1986).

Early neolithic (Badarian) patterns of occupation in the Egyptian Nile Valley are known largely from fieldwork undertaken in the El-Badari region of Middle Egypt, ca. 30 km south east of Asyut (Brunton 1937, 1948; Brunton and Caton-Thompson 1928; Holmes and Friedman 1994). The original reports refer to the discovery of around 40 habitation sites located along the desert margins of the floodplain. Each comprised a series of midden deposits containing quantities of ash, charcoal and cultural debris, often reaching considerable heights and sometimes associated with hearths and storage pits. Traces of permanent architecture were largely absent, and thick layers of animal dung, as well as remnants of ephemeral enclosures, were reported from a number of sites (cf. Hassan 1988: 154; Krzyzaniak 1977: 70). Located ca. 150 km south of El-Badari, Maghara 2 is the only early neolithic site in the Egyptian Nile Valley to be excavated on a significant scale since the early 20th century. The economy of its inhabitants was based primarily upon fishing and herding, and a lack of stratified deposits indicates that the site was formed during a single, relatively brief episode of occupation (Hendrickx and Midant-Reynes 1988).

Over the last two decades, numerous contemporary (Khartoum Neolithic) sites and cemeteries have been excavated in Central Sudan, between the confluence of the White and Blue Niles and the Sixth Cataract. Building upon the pioneering but, until recently, isolated work of Arkell (1953), this fieldwork, which includes regional surveys, reveals for the first time the overall character of early neolithic society along the southern extent of the Nile Valley (Caneva 1988; Haaland 1987; Krzyzaniak 1991; and see also Mohammed-Ali 1982). The most striking point to emerge is the overall similarity of early neolithic developments in habitation, exchange, material culture and mortuary customs in the Khartoum region to those underway at the same time in the Egyptian Nile Valley, far to the north.

As in Middle and Upper Egypt, early neolithic habitation sites in Central Sudan comprise unstratified midden deposits, devoid of architectural features. A concentration of hearths found at El-Shaheinab by Arkell (1953: 79–81) constitutes the only evidence of fixed installations presently known. Throughout the Nile Valley, the poverty of early neolithic domestic remains contrasts with the rich material culture associated with contemporary burial grounds (Brunton 1937, 1948; Brunton and Caton-Thompson 1928 (Egypt); Geus 1986; Krzyzaniak 1991: 518–528; Lecointe 1987; Reinold 1991 (Sudan)). Cemeteries contained a cross-section of the living population, including adults of both sexes and infants. There are also marked similarities between the modes of burial observed at Badarian cemeteries in Middle Egypt and in the contemporary Khartoum Neolithic cemeteries of Central Sudan. While the contents of particular interments differed, all appear to represent variations within a shared form of mortuary practice, applied equally to adults and infants, the material characteristics of which may be broadly outlined.

The individual was laid within a roughly shaped pit in a supine position, knees contracted and hands often cupping the face. Prior to interment, the intact body was usually wrapped in animal skins or reed mats and decorated with ornaments made of coloured stone beads, pierced shells, worked bone, tooth and ivory. Many ornaments have survived *in situ*, indicating that they were worn over a wide range of body parts including the wrist, ankle, arm, leg, head, neck, and around the waist; nose and lip studs are also common. Body ornaments found in graves provide testimony to the procurement and circulation of an unprecedented range of materials originating between the Nile Valley and the Red Sea coast, such as marine shells, and beads of jasper, carnelian, alabaster, steatite, diorite and serpentine. This implies extensive prospection along the wadi routes of the Eastern Desert, through which small amounts of native copper were also acquired (cf. Majer 1992; Tutundzic 1989).

Similarities between early neolithic burials in Middle Egypt and Central Sudan extend beyond the treatment and ornamentation of the corpse to the deposition of functionally similar artefacts within graves: principally a range of cosmetic articles and implements, and small pottery vessels. Stone palettes, accompanied by grinding pebbles and pigments for the production of body paint, are typical grave goods in both regions. While Egyptian palettes of this period are usually made of siltstone and grooved for suspension (Baumgartel 1960: 55–57), those of Central Sudan are sandstone or porphyry, and are not grooved (Geus 1984: 30; Krzyzaniak 1991: 523; Lecointe 1987).

The suite of grave goods found in Badarian cemeteries also included cosmetic implements carved from bone and ivory. Combs make their first appearance at this time, as do spatulas, probably used with small ivory vessels and hollowed tusks for mixing and manipulating fluids. The distribution of these artefact types, including cosmetic palettes, within graves does not correspond with any obvious social grouping based upon age or sex (cf. Anderson 1992; Castillos 1982). Damp conditions in the Khartoum region have caused bone and ivory to decompose far more rapidly than on the desert fringes of Middle Egypt, a factor which must be taken into account in considering the apparent absence of similar objects in Khartoum Neolithic burials (see Geus 1984: 23, fig. 55; Lecointe 1987: 73). Stone mace-heads make their first appearance in Central Sudanese burials at this time (Krzyzaniak 1991: 523, fig. 11.4; Lecointe 1987: figs. 5, 7); they are not widely reported from contemporary cemeteries in Egypt, but were to become a standard grave good there during later neolithic (Naqada I–II) times (Cialowicz 1987).

In both Middle Egypt and Central Sudan, the early neolithic period also saw the introduction of polished ceramics, which were widely used as grave goods. They take the form of small, hemispherical or globular bowls, the outer surfaces of which were coated with a red ochre wash and burnished. On Badarian pottery, the burnishing overlies an earlier stage of decoration, in which the outer surface was combed to create a rippled texture. Finally, the vessel was fired to leave a distinct black band around the mouth of the pot (Adams 1988: 21). Polished bowls with round bases and red-coated surfaces are also typical of early neolithic pottery in the Khartoum region, and some vessels exhibit blackened rims. Unlike Badarian pottery, however, that of Central Sudan retained earlier (Early Holocene) forms of surface ornament, such as parallel dots, wavy lines and zigzags (Arkell 1953: 75–76; Chlodnicki 1984; and for an early consideration of the relationship between these wares, see Arkell and Ucko 1968: 149–151).

The interment of animals, whole or partial, within human cemeteries and burials constitutes another distinctive practice common to early neolithic societies in Middle Egypt and Central Sudan, although differences in detail between the two regions are again evident. At El-Badari, in Middle Egypt, animal burials formed a discrete concentration adjacent to two larger groups of human burials. They included a "large bovine ... covered in matting in exactly the same way as the human burials", as well as interments of caprines, and canids (Brunton and Caton-Thompson 1928: 6–7, 10–12, 18, pls. 4, 10: 6). At nearby Mostagedda, body parts of ruminants and complete animals were found within the graves of both adults and infants (Brunton 1937: 5–7, 33–34, 42, pl. 6: 8). Complete cattle burials within stone-covered tumuli are reported from Nabta Playa, in the south-western desert of Egypt (Wendorf and Schild 1998: 108). At El-Ghaba, in Central Sudan, cattle horns were found in an unspecified number of human burials, but isolated burials of animals are unknown (Lecointe 1987: 74, 77–78, fig. 5, pl. 1).

Approximately two millennia separate the inception of a neolithic economy in the Nile Valley from the period of state formation in Egypt and Lower Nubia. In characterizing this transition, archaeologists have tended to adopt the basic interpretative framework established by Childe (1936), according to which the establishment of a sedentary village economy, based on food production, sets in motion a process of urbanization and increasing social complexity (e.g. Hassan 1988; Kemp 1989; Wilkinson 1999). Political centralization is accordingly viewed as a conceptual and economic outgrowth of the settled way of life, as opposed to the mobile existence of hunter-gatherers. This view is maintained in spite of a lack of evidence for large, planned settlements in late prehistoric and Early Dynastic Egypt, which is often explained in terms of fieldwork bias or poor archaeological preservation (Kemp 1977).

An opposing view, most famously articulated by Wilson (1960), emphasizes the indigenous importance of mortuary culture and kingship as unifying social institutions in Egypt, by contrast with the central conceptual and political role of the city in Early Dynastic Mesopotamia (see, more recently, Baines and Yoffee 1998). Accordingly, the absence of an urban context for Egyptian state formation, and the prominence of funerary monuments in the archaeological record, is viewed as a positive indication of the "insignificant role played by the concept of the city in the political thought of the Egyptians" (Frankfort 1951: 83). In what follows, I extend the context of this debate both temporally, by placing it against the backdrop of neolithic economy and society, and spatially, by developing an integrated interpretation of early neolithic transformations in the Egyptian and Sudanese Nile Valley, based on the evidence outlined above.

Complexity without villages: the 'enigma' of early neolithic society in the Nile Valley

In Egypt, the only clear evidence for permanent village life during the early neolithic period derives from Merimda Beni Salama, on the fringes of the Nile Delta. The material culture of this site, and the burials found there, exhibit little sign of the technological innovations, circulation of exotic materials, and elaborate forms of personal display evident in contemporary cemeteries of the Nile Valley (cf. Hoffman 1979: 143, 181–189). Despite their original designation as "villages", the occupation middens associated with Badarian cemeteries in Middle Egypt exhibit no such evidence of a permanent constructed environment. The most carefully excavated of these sites, at Hammamiya, was in fact interpreted by Caton-Thompson as a "temporary camping ground" (Brunton and Caton-Thompson 1928: 74).

More recently, Butzer (1976: 14) has related the distribution of early neolithic (Badarian) sites along the outskirts of the Nile Valley to pastoral activity, while Midant-Reynes (2000: 160) sees them as "mainly … the result of pastoralism" and a "relatively mobile existence". Clark (1971: 36) similarly observed of Badarian sites that "the circle of grain pits surrounding a central area of ash and pottery suggests a plan similar to that of the Nilotic, cattle-herding Jie in Uganda, the Songhai south of the Niger bend and other Central African peoples where a central stock pen is surrounded by the grain stores and temporary or permanent dwellings of the inhabitants". The recent excavations at Maghara 2 support the view that the formation of early neolithic sites in the Nile Valley was generated through the seasonal sojourns of mobile herding groups, rather than the establishment of permanent farming villages (Wengrow 2001: 95, 99 n. 5).

Despite the lack of evidence for permanent dwellings or organized sedentary life, many commentators continue to describe early neolithic habitation sites in the Egyptian Nile Valley as "villages", "settlements", "homesteads", or even "hamlets" (e.g. Bard 1987: 86, 1994: 24; Hassan 1988: 154; Hendrickx and Vermeersch 2000: 40–42; Hoffman 1979; Krzyzaniak 1977: 81–82; Wetterstrom 1993: 215). It is often suggested that more substantial settlements were established close to the Nile floodplain, where horticulture was possible, and have therefore been destroyed or buried by the changing course of the river, or through the recent spread of irrigation (Bard 1994: 24; Hendrickx and Vermeersch 2000: 42–43; Midant-Reynes 2000: 160; Trigger 1983: 10). However, there remains little evidence that cereal production became an important economic pursuit in Egypt prior to late neolithic (Naqada I–II) times (Wetterstrom 1993). It cannot, therefore, be assumed on ecological grounds that early neolithic occupation of the landscape would have gravitated towards the floodplain.

Curiously, there have been no such efforts to explain away the lack of villages in neolithic Central Sudan. The adoption of domesticated animals in the latter region, where cereal farming played no known role in the neolithic economy, is in fact associated with a marked decline in the number of occupation sites adjacent to the floodplain:

Mesolithic gatherers and fishers were apparently more permanently attracted by riverine resources than neolithic pastoralists who probably came to the river only seasonally ... The complete transition to pastoralism seems to have led to the abandonment of permanent sites in favor of pastoral camps. The shift must have forced the inhabitants of the region to adopt a different life-style, consistent with the mobility required for stock breeding communities in arid climates. Therefore, although the region was probably just as intensively inhabited as before, as indicated by the numerous graveyards of this period, these seasonal sites have left few traces due to the ephemeral nature of the equipment used.

(Caneva 1991: 7)

Similarities in patterns of site formation, material culture, exchange, and mortuary practices, described above, suggest that this interpretation might be applied with equal validity to the Egyptian Nile Valley (*contra* Caneva 1991: 6). Its ongoing resistance can only be accounted for by the assumption that emergent cultural complexity, as documented in early neolithic burials, is "inconsistent with the small, poor camp sites and with the pastoral economy that seems to have been the sole support for these communities" (Caneva 1991: 7–8).

Constructions of prehistoric pastoralism

A nomad power is something inconceivable [for the Ancient Greeks]; if it is power, it cannot be nomad.

(Hartog 1988: 202)

The view that mobile, pastoral societies have poor material cultures and were marginal to the main stream of cultural development in the prehistoric and ancient world was a pervasive feature of late 20th century archaeological discourse (e.g. Bar-Yosef and Khazanov 1992; Chang and Koster 1986; Cribb 1991; Gifford 1978; Sadr 1991; Smith 1992; Zeuner 1954: 353, 374). While the economic foundations of early states have conventionally been sought in the development of agrarian production, the archaeological study of pastoralism has concentrated upon "inhospitable hinterlands" (Sadr 1991: 73; cf. Smith 1992: 17). The pastoralist, as Finkelstein (1995) puts it, is to be sought "living on the fringe", rather than at the hub of social change.

Ethnoarchaeological studies of modern pastoralists in Africa and the Middle East (see Finkelstein 1995: 23 for a survey) have contributed heavily to this image of pastoralism as an inherently marginal pursuit. Hole (1978: 131), for instance, proposed that in order "to gain some perspectives on pastoralism in prehistory", we must ignore those pastoral groups "whose exceptional exploits have affected history and become the elaborate stuff of myth and legend", and turn instead to "the tribes of the Zagros slopes, who missed most of the glorious episodes of the past just as they stand outside the course of history today". Cribb's (1991: 228) extensive study of pastoralism in modern Turkey leads him to a similar conclusion: "I am confident that nomadic campsites will continue to emerge as a minor component of the archaeological record of the Near East ... The significant finding which emerged from this research is that nomadic campsites are structured in a distinctive way that bears the imprint of an inherently unstable mode of subsistence." Smith (1992: 11), drawing upon descriptions of the Taureg, Nuer, Fulani and Khoikhoi, proposes that "pastoralism is a strategy of residential mobility designed to obtain minimum resources, such as pasture and water for the domestic herds, as well as access to markets where commodities not readily available can be produced by exchange".

It seems a curious strategy, however, to systematically pursue the minimum rewards, and there are surely echoes here, both of Crawford's "people without history", and of a puritanical view of pastoralism, rooted in the Old Testament narrative of pious, ascetic Israelites pitted against the "dark moral exemplar" of urban Canaan and Babylon (McIntosh 1999: 58).[3] Since the 1970s, anthropologists have increasingly argued that the widespread occurrence of impoverishment, instability and marginality amongst modern pastoralists is related to the impact of colonialism, urbanization, and the hostile expansion of agro-industrial nation states during the last two centuries (e.g. Asad 1973, 1979; Carr 1977; Comaroff and Comaroff 1992; Galaty and Salzmann 1981; Spencer 1998). The fact that these characteristics are widely present among pastoral populations says more about their resistance to today's dominant political and economic interests than it does about the inherent ability of pastoralists to alter the course of historical (or prehistorical) events.

This does not imply that archaeologists have nothing to learn from the study of modern pastoralists; rather, that the lesson has nothing to do with the potentialities of a given form of economy. Just as the existence of modern pastoralists is most clearly understood in terms of their relationships with the 'outside world' of today (Khazanov 1984), so that of prehistoric pastoralists needs to be understood in terms of the outside world of prehistory. The archaeological 'invisibility' of pastoralists may yet be overcome by questioning the arbitrary limits placed upon our vision through uncritical use of ethnographic models, and by critically adapting insights gained from ethnographic experience to meet the challenges posed by the archaeological record.

Pastoralism and political space: some examples

As Hartog has demonstrated in his study of Herodotus' portrayal of the Scythians, the conviction that mobile societies are incapable of generating distinct forms of social power has deep roots in western thought. As a people who were at once mobile herders and yet subject to royal power, the Scythians contravened a basic norm of ancient Greek political thought: the inseparability of political structures from the material framework of the town (*polis*) and from the practice of agriculture. Like other nomads, they were normally described as a negative reflection of Greek values and practices. In their exercise of military or royal power, however, they could only be represented in the idiom of a settled, 'domesticated' people, i.e. according to conventional understandings of the relationship between power, space and labour (Hartog 1988: 200–206; cf. Weissleder 1978).

Similarly, Burton (1980: 273) points out the strong tendency "to assume that a village is the primordial fully social arrangement and that the physical existence of clustered habitation sites imbues social relationships with a measure of permanence". As he demonstrates through a study of Atuot cattle-keepers in the Upper Nile region of southern Sudan, this point of view cannot be applied unquestioningly to mobile populations: "One observes a remarkably higher population in the cattle camps in contrast to the village areas, and, after a period of residence, a greater 'moral density' as well. It would perhaps make better sense to speak of cultivation camps and cattle villages" (Burton 1980: 273). Similar observations were made by Evans-Pritchard (1940: 116) in relation to the Nuer, and by Lienhardt with regard to the neighbouring Dinka:

> In view of the fact that the permanent settlements of the Dinka contain all their members at two seasons of the year only – for the sowing and around harvest time – it is understandable that political groups should be spoken of in the idiom of the cattle-herding group or cattle-camp (*wut*) and not of the homestead, village, or settlement (*baai*).
>
> (Lienhardt 1961: 7)

Historically, political and religious networks in the Upper Nile region have converged upon focal shrines which take the form of huge earthen mounds. "In a region where people must be continuously on the move, seasonally and periodically," writes Johnson (1990: 43), "such focal points are mediating centers, bringing together old and new members of the community". Luang Deng (The Cattle Byre of Deng) is among the oldest functioning mound-shrines in the Upper Nile region. Howell reported that some Dinka buried their dead facing towards it, and hung offerings of cattle-horns, iron bangles and tobacco on two sacred trees located at its summit. Representing the abode of the divinity Deng and his kin, the mound acted to fix "in one spot (rather than only in a succession of persons) the site where Divinity, or a divinity, could be approached" (Johnson 1990: 49; cf. Seligman and Seligman 1932: 180). Mawson (1991) has described events surrounding the construction of another mound-shrine, Luang Mayual of the Agar Dinka. In addition to reconstituting communal bonds through labour, the periodic rebuilding of Luang Mayual also provided an opportunity for the strategic negotiation of social influence. Animal sacrifices performed on the mound acquired a status which transcended immediate kinship relations, while heifers consecrated there acquired a special value in bride-wealth payments. Hence "access to cattle in this context was both a direct indication of relative politico-religious influence and an important way of reproducing influence in the future" (Mawson 1991: 361–362; cf. Johnson 1994: 106).

These modern Nilotic examples serve to illustrate how mobile pastoralists may generate idioms of political organization and practice that cannot be subsumed within models of social development based upon the metaphor of fixed, bounded structures (village, town, city/nation state). What they do *not* demonstrate is any form of direct relationship between modern and prehistoric peoples of the Nile Valley, beyond the fact that their respective social morphologies differ in similar ways from that of the largely urban intelligentsia which has made them an object of study.

Embodiment and domestication: the formation of the primary pastoral community in the Nile Valley

The preceding discussion has attempted to clear the way for an integrated interpretation of early neolithic society in the Nile Valley. As documented above, the poverty of domestic culture throughout this region contrasts with the richness of contemporary burial grounds. The similarity of funerary practices from Middle Egypt to modern Khartoum suggests a coherent and widely disseminated body of beliefs and practices, in which individuals, parted from the living group, were accompanied to the grave by those objects through which they had observed its self-imposed codes of consumption and presentation. These codes transcended differences of age and gender, encompassing the biological and social processes of reproduction and personal growth from infancy to adulthood. Rather than constituting merely a vehicle for ostentatious display (e.g. Hoffman 1979: 143, 181–189; Spencer 1993: 21, 24) or the temporary assertion of status (e.g. Anderson 1992; Wilkinson 1999: 29), the practice of body decoration in the early neolithic Nile Valley therefore exhibits the essential features of a *habitus* (Bourdieu 1977: 78), forming part of the objective conditions for experience of self and the development of personhood.

It is striking, in this context, that nearly all of the items interred with the dead were designed to be easily carried by, or wearable on, the individual person. Cosmetic implements were mostly provided with some means of suspension, either by perforation, incised grooves, or elaboration with decorative features, that would have allowed attachment by a string or cord. The mobile, body-centred *habitus* implied by this cultural assemblage is morphologically compatible with the everyday demands of a pastoral lifestyle, accounting for the concomitant lack of investment in static, bounded environments for dwelling and socialization.[4] The sustained mobility afforded by herding may also be related to the acquisition and circulation of materials which were integral to personal presentation, such as marine shells, coloured stone and pigments (e.g. malachite) derived from metallic ores originating in the Eastern Desert.

By contrast with those of South West Asia (Watkins 1990; Wright 2000), early neolithic habitation sites in the Nile Valley did not constitute the immovable centre of domestic space, but served as temporary loci of social activity. Accordingly, they should be thought of as marking out an arena for movement and periodic aggregation, rather than a series of bounded settlements and hiatuses in a static social landscape. Only in mortuary rites was the flux of geographical and social space suspended, and the body of the individual, together with the objects which formed the nexus of his/her relationships with other persons, withdrawn from circulation and laid to rest within a fixed, communal space. An idealized mortuary image of the deceased as a relational being was thereby inscribed onto the landscape of social history, creating what Battaglia (1990: 194–196) has termed a "positively valued negative space", to be filled by the living dependants. The subsequent development of this mode of social reproduction into a political economy of memory led, during the Old Kingdom, to the formation of a monumental landscape of commemoration (Wengrow forthcoming).

The integration of animals into mortuary rites – which was to become a lasting feature of ancient Egyptian and Sudanese culture – provides powerful testimony that, as in other parts of the Old World (Cauvin 2000; Hodder 1990), the inception of a neolithic economy in the Nile Valley was experienced through both objective and subjective processes of transformation. It formed part of a wider reconfiguration of human relationships with the landscape and its non-human inhabitants, which extended beyond the animated field of living relations into the material and conceptual space of death. Sherratt (1997: 359–361, 367) has coined the term "primary horticultural community" to describe the outcome of this process in South West Asia and temperate Europe, where early neolithic societies defined themselves, and their relations with the outside world, in terms of an ideal pattern of co-residence, embracing both the living and the dead within the physical community of house and village. The term "primary pastoral community" might be introduced in order to highlight the distinct character of early neolithic society in the Nile Valley, with its district configuration of herding, mobility, mortuary rites and the body as frameworks of social experience and reproduction. Just as the social morphology of early farming communities in Egypt and the Sudan was generated outside the physical confines of a constructed environment, so the cultural idiom in which they defined their changing relationships with the non-human world is best characterized, not in terms of 'domestication' (cf. Hodder 1990), but as a process of embodiment.

Conclusion

> Images of gaunt herders experiencing the double catastrophes of drought and famine reinforce distorted notions of the non-viability of a pastoral economy or of the failure of pastoral Africa to share the continent's expectations of and aspirations for development.

> (Galaty and Bonte 1991: 4)

The claim that Ancient Egypt arose upon 'African foundations' constitutes a powerful but vague rhetorical statement, which implies a historical relationship between what are, in reality, two relatively modern categories ('Africa' and 'Ancient Egypt'), both subject to a variety of possible understandings. The relativity of these categories, and hence of any perceived relationship between them, is highlighted by a consideration of their development in the context of colonial-era scholarship, with which this chapter began. To claim an African origin for Egyptian civilization did not then imply an 'Afrocentric' view of the past, of the kind later developed by Cheikh Anta Diop (MacDonald Chapter 7, this volume). Rather, the 'African' roots of Egyptian civilization were imagined by Seligman and others to extend far beyond the African continent, and were defined in opposition to an indigenous 'Negro' presence (Reid Chapter 5, this volume).

The comparative research on ancient and modern societies undertaken by scholars during the colonial period did, however, generate and record knowledge of African political forms, which today has a value beyond its original context in racial theory. Adherence by late 20th century scholars to models of ancient Egyptian state formation rooted in agrarian sociology may perhaps be seen in part as a counter-reaction to the racist implications of these earlier theories, which envisaged a pastoral 'substratum' to Dynastic civilization. By establishing a distance between the aims of colonial-period and current scholarship, intellectual history plays a constructive role in allowing ideas such as the latter, which are not in themselves racist, to be re-evaluated in the light of new evidence. Rather than simply reproducing past discourses, re-engagement with aspects of research undertaken during the colonial period can serve to question new myths, such as the non-viability of political systems founded upon pastoral economies, which are themselves rooted in the historical impact and experience of colonialism.

Notes

1   There is, perhaps, no more succinct vehicle for these linked constructions of the past than a rock carving of the early third millennium BC from the Second Cataract region of northern Sudan, showing a scene of subjugation presided over by an anonymous emblem of Egyptian royalty (Murnane 1987).

2   The title of Ward's (1905) *Our Sudan. Its Pyramids and Progress*, a treatise on the prospects of modernization in the Anglo-Egyptian Condominium, hints at a significant aspect of this relationship.

3   The pastoral societies of North East Africa were, in fact, regularly compared to the biblical Israelites by late 19th and early 20th century ethnographers interested in the origins of 'primitive monotheism' (see the historiographical essays by Pickering and James on this topic, in James and Allen 1998).

4   We might compare here Gell's (1995: 25) observations on the 'incarnate' character of Dinka art and material culture, "consisting of the bodies of the Dinka themselves and their cattle, and their expressive behaviour – their music singing, oratory, dance, body-decoration and so forth", or Klumpp and Kratz's (1993: 202–203) emphasis upon the role of the human body as a "primary medium of concrete aesthetic expression" for the pastoral Maasai and Okiek of East Africa.

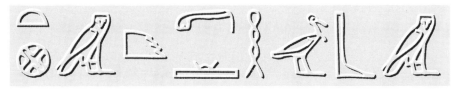

CHAPTER 10

ANCIENT EGYPT IN THE SUDANESE MIDDLE NILE: A CASE OF MISTAKEN IDENTITY?

David N. Edwards

The question of Ancient Egypt's relationship with, and significance in, Africa may draw us into many debates, ranging from the overtly political and polemic, often concerning representations of Africa's past and the politics of scholarship, to the more empirical, drawing on historical and especially archaeological studies. However, even a passing reflection on some of the common threads encountered in such debates, and their premises, may alert us to the fact that while they offer considerable opportunities for rhetoric, these are generally not matched by a significant archaeological contribution to the construction of debates and dialogue. This chapter examines some issues encountered when considering Ancient Egypt's place in Africa, and especially the influence of what can only be termed 'Egyptocentric' research traditions on the historiography of the Middle Nile/Sudan, the one region of sub-Saharan Africa most closely linked with Egypt. By contrast, in the second half of the chapter it is suggested that there are very different archaeologies and histories of the region still waiting to be written which do not need to look to Egypt and grand narratives of grand civilizations.

Ancient Egypt in Africa?

For the sceptical, doubts may be raised by some of the fundamental premises which often underpin these discussions. Egypt's location on the African continent is often cited as the point of departure in assertions of its significance and relevance for those concerned with Africa's past. That, however, such assertions are much less commonly made for equally 'African' countries such as Tunisia and Libya might alert us to the possibility that the self-evident truths of geographical location may not be entirely helpful. The extent to which Africa exists as a meaningful historical unit, rather than a political ideal of, for example, Pan-African movements and the Organization for African Unity, is of course highly debatable in itself. The character of Libya's role in, and claims on, sub-Saharan Africa over the last 30 years (St John 2000) can only remind us of the need to make clear the distinctions between political aspirations and rhetoric, in all their guises, and what we claim for historical scholarship.

The centrality of Egypt to certain types of Afrocentrist positions is discussed elsewhere (Bernal Chapter 2 and MacDonald Chapter 7, this volume). However, for many scholars working in sub-Saharan Africa, the perennial emphasis on, and fascination with, Ancient Egypt may seem mysterious and even perverse. Why look to Egypt? For earlier generations, one of its primary attractions would seem to lie in its conforming to the then current (western) notions of 'civilization' (with literacy, monumental architecture, cities, markets, 'art' etc.) – exactly what Africa was (all too commonly, and mistakenly) seen to be lacking, and something which could be reclaimed. However, the past 50 years of historical and archaeological research in Africa have quite transformed our understanding of its past. It has amply demonstrated to the wider world the originality, diversity and extraordinary achievements of a myriad of sub-Saharan cultures and the cities, kingdoms and art forms they brought forth (Connah 1987; Iliffe 1995; Shaw *et al.* 1993).

It is equally apparent that the history of African political development has had its own dynamics and that there are many trajectories followed by early African states which do not need to look to Egypt or beyond for their inspiration (McIntosh 1999a). The Eurocentric prescriptions of what constitutes 'civilization', produced by an earlier generation, are simply not sustainable and indeed we need to be far more self-critical in our deployment of the term and the oppositions between the 'civilized' and the 'uncivilized' which it constructs (Patterson 1997). That the ancient cultures and civilizations of sub-Saharan Africa are effectively ignored in prioritizing claims on an 'African' Egypt could well be seen to be doing African history a great disservice.

If political and ideological agendas are not hard to identify in such debates, the extent to which archaeological perspectives have made a contribution is not always apparent. Relatively few comparative studies exist which attempt to address questions surrounding the relationship of Egyptian cultural forms with those of other parts of the continent. One obvious focus for such studies is the Middle Nile, in modern Sudan, Egypt's southern neighbour in sub-Saharan Africa. It is only through the Lower Nubian corridor that Egypt has historically had access to Sudanic Africa, access which distinguished it from other parts of Africa north of the Sahara until the first millennium AD. Historically this is the region through which Egypt's relations with Africa have been mediated, and again, in recent years, it is especially through 'Nubian' evidence that many debates concerning Ancient Egypt in Africa have also been argued.

Ancient Egypt and the Middle Nile?

Narrowing our focus to the Middle Nile (Figure 10:1), the historical links between Ancient Egypt and the Sudanese Middle Nile would appear very considerable. Whether for an archaeologist or a visitor to the Sudan National Museum in Khartoum, the past in the Middle Nile looks to the north, with a special debt to Ancient Egypt. When archaeology was first taught in the post-Independence University of Khartoum in the 1960s, it was essentially a course in Egyptology which was provided. Similarly, within North America and much of Europe, Sudanese – if still largely represented as 'Nubian' – archaeology remains inextricably bound up with university and museum departments of Egyptology (Adams 1998).

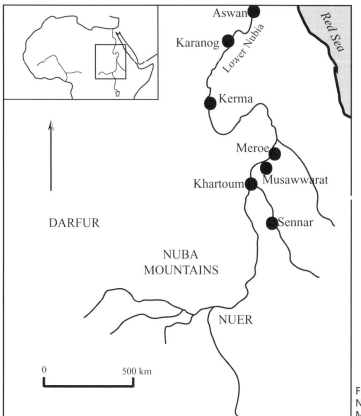

Figure 10:1
Nubia and the
Middle Nile.

The implications of these disciplinary links in the construction of the history of the Middle Nile and Nubia have been, and remain, by no means insignificant (Adams 1994). In terms of archaeological practice, a tradition of research in the Egyptian Lower Nile has certainly ensured a continued interest in monuments, art-objects and texts, and often introspective concerns of Egyptology (Trigger 1993: 1–2). Such foci have increasingly been displaced in many areas of archaeology, including Africanist research, by major theoretical and methodological developments over the last 50 years, particularly those which have sought to open dialogues with other areas of the historical and social sciences. More significantly, perhaps, Egyptological traditions have had very obvious, if understandable, influence in shaping *representations* of the ancient Middle Nile – framed around links to Egypt. As prominent in the archaeological literature as in the collections of the Sudan National Museum are the material remains of pharaonic imperialism and colonialism of the Middle and New Kingdoms, the temples and tomb contents of the twenty-fifth Dynasty and their Kushite/Meroitic successors. In later periods, the emphasis placed on churches and 'Christian' arts of the medieval Nubian kingdoms owes much to Coptic Studies.

As in Khartoum, similar representations and emphases are well reflected in many of the fine 'Nubian' collections and exhibitions around the world, not least in the

"Nubian Museum", set up under Unesco auspices, in Aswan. While a sense of national heritage is probably still poorly developed in Sudan, such influences have clearly been important in the development of what may be seen as 'national monuments', such as the pyramids of Meroe and the massive pharaonic statuary which adorn the Sudan National Museum. Such "symbols of transcendence … chosen from the rubble of cultural history" (Rowlands 1994: 134), have certainly acquired a sufficient resonance as symbols of a national heritage to warrant Presidential visits by heads of state of many political complexions. The extent to which such monuments are really adequate representations of Sudan's past is, however, by no means clear.

One of the most striking features of many current representations of the great 'civilizations' of the ancient Middle Nile, is the extent to which they conform, or appear to conform, to very familiar models, looking to Egypt and the north, and not to Sudanic Africa. As such they are placed very much within a core-periphery relationship, with an emphasis placed on cultural innovation coming from a dominant Egyptian culture. These are 'civilizations' which can very easily be interpreted and portrayed as such by foregrounding monumental architecture, literacy and a series of very familiar 'art' forms and crafts. They are highly visible – as currently represented they appear quite consistent with the models of what 'civilizations' ought to look like (Trigger 1993). However, if these are 'African civilizations', as we are often informed – *Africa in Antiquity* (Hintze 1978), *Meroe City: An Ancient African Capital* (Török 1997a) – explicit demonstration of what may be seen as distinctively 'African' traits tend to be lacking. Interpreted almost entirely through Egyptian parallels, paradoxically they are 'African' only in so far as Egypt is African.

So much of what we 'know' of the ancient Middle Nile and the way it is represented is mediated through essentially Egyptological discourses. Accessed through Egypt, rather than informing us about the 'African-ness' of Egypt, more commonly, oppositions are created between the known and an African 'other'. At one level, this may easily prompt both an examination and critique of Egyptology's relationship with a wider Orientalist paradigm (Said 1978) and its aspirations in establishing and maintaining certain power relations both within and beyond academia. Similar critiques may also be appropriate for those concerned with later periods where Orientalist traditions of historiography have done much to create very exclusive 'Arab' histories of the Sudan (Spaulding and Kapteijns 1991). A further consequence, however, is that with the historic role of Egyptology in forming our perceptions of the ancient Middle Nile, we are still poorly placed to compare and contrast the long-term histories of the Middle and Lower Niles. In attempting to address such problems we need to consider the possibility of alternative representations of the ancient Middle Nile.

Alternative pasts in the Middle Nile?

Sudan is the largest country in Africa and is located entirely within the tropics, occupying the eastern half of the Sahel and the great Sudanic belt. It clearly has an extraordinarily complex history, and in the present day is culturally diverse, with well over 100 languages spoken within its frontiers (Hurreiz and Bell 1975). Within this history, direct Egyptian engagement was limited in both its geographical extent and duration. Parts of Nubia, in the extreme north of the country, were conquered and occupied by pharaonic Egypt during the third and second millennia BC. For a brief period, in the eighth to seventh centuries BC, the roles were reversed when Kushite kings ruled most of Egypt as the twenty-fifth Dynasty, until expelled. It was some 2,000 years later that Egypt again moved south, when Ottoman Egypt extended its empire as far south as the Third Cataract in the late 16th century. Only in the 19th century do we see the expansion of Egyptian control far up the Niles, and to the east and west, with the carving out of what became the Egyptian (later Anglo-Egyptian) Sudan from the 1820s.

Against this backdrop, many modern popular representations of the Sudan need critical examination. The Middle Nile is all too often seen as separate from the rest of Sudanic Africa (Horowitz 1967), while the 'ethnographic present', of the late 19th and first half of the 20th centuries, is all too often mistaken for a timeless and 'traditional' world. This is most obviously seen in the oppositions created between a supposedly 'Arab/Muslim north' and an 'African south' (which also serve to promote perceptions of certain commonalities between Egypt and at least northern Sudan), oppositions fostered and codified during the Condominium by administrators doubling as historians, notably MacMichael (1922). The projection of such oppositions into the distant past is all too often implicit in much of the literature, although significant 'Arab' incursions into the region only began in the later medieval period. Prior to the medieval period, imposing any such divisions may be quite inappropriate.

The view from the south

As a point of departure, archaeologists and historians of the Middle Nile may be prompted to question not so much how Egypt became dislocated from Africa (O'Connor and Reid Chapter 1, this volume), but how the Middle Nile became disengaged from Sudanic Africa (Edwards 1996b, 1998a; Horowitz 1967). Many of the people of the Middle Nile are indeed "People without a History", as Crawford recognized more than 50 years ago in a prescient and provocative article. Following his lead, we might suggest that very different histories may be constructed and different research priorities developed: the "Sudanese … do not need to be told that there is such a thing as Sudanese, as distinct from Egyptian archaeology … to many others this is a new idea" (Crawford 1948: 8). As Crawford (1948: 12) went on to suggest, "the excavation of a Nilotic mound-site is more suitable to be undertaken at the present moment than that of yet another Egyptian temple". More than half a century later, no more than a few trial trenches have been excavated in such a mound (e.g. Kleppe 1982). However, in a search for different histories, we can already identify some lines of inquiry which may throw a very different light on the long-term history of the Middle Nile, as well as perhaps prompt reconsideration of some of the distinctiveness of Egypt.

I have suggested elsewhere (Edwards 1996b, 1998a) that it is possible to develop interpretations of the social, economic and political organization of the Kushite and later kingdoms of Sudan in which what may be termed 'Sudanic' models appear much more appropriate than those which have looked to the Egyptian Lower Nile.

These arguments would suggest that the very evident borrowings of some cultural forms (e.g. Kushite pyramids, monumental stone temples) from Egypt must not be equated with a slavish and wholesale adoption of a ('superior') culture. Rather, if we look behind the façades of the monuments we may begin to discern highly original imperial cultures being created and recreated within recognizably Sudanic idioms – fundamentally different from the pharaonic (Fuller Chapter 12, this volume). Such a model finds many resonances in other recent work on early African political formations in many parts of the continent (e.g. McIntosh 1999a).

To further develop such suggestions, it is also possible to follow very different lines of inquiry, social histories and social archaeologies far removed from more traditional 'state-centred' foci of research. Rather than beginning with histories of elite cultures and their monuments, we could profitably begin with 'subsistence' and more especially subsistence as manifested in the domain of culture (Sherratt 1999). The fundamental importance of food as a medium for initiating and maintaining social relations is well recognized in the anthropological and archaeological literature (e.g. Dietler and Hayden 2001; Douglas 1987; Douglas and Isherwood 1979; Farb and Armelagos 1980; Gosden and Hather 1999). Culinary culture may have powerful diacritical roles, as markers of identity, whether in overtly 'public' political arenas, in the definition of religious identities or in (commonly gendered) domestic contexts of production and consumption. Here we have the potential to learn much about how the ancient inhabitants of the Middle Nile lived and how they perceived themselves.

For such research, the Middle Nile would also seem to be a particularly interesting region, not least due to its location on the frontier between what seem to be two very distinct worlds, both environmentally and culturally (Alexander 1988; Goody 1971); the Eurasian world to the north and Sudanic Africa to the south. Whatever claims are made for Egypt's African heritage, notable differences between these two regions include very distinct traditions of farming and crop types, and as a consequence, different forms of food preparation and culinary culture, and potentially rather different relationships between subsistence and socio-political organization. Within the Nile Valley as a whole, apparently sharp contrasts may be identified between the tightly constrained agriculture of the Egyptian Lower Nile and the extensive and diverse mixed farming regimes of the Middle Nile basin, the former a world of irrigated wheat and barley, and the latter one of rainfed sorghum and millet cultivation, savannah grazing and hunting. Over the long term, this region, through the 'Nubian Corridor', has been an avenue for the exchange of crops and technologies, as one part of wider exchanges of cultural influences. Acknowledging that such differences may potentially be significant, they may also prompt us to look at more general patterns of consumption and linkages with other areas of material culture. Often highly elaborate pottery has been a particularly prominent feature of Nubian material culture over several millennia, a characteristic which interestingly contrasts markedly with the consistently unelaborated traditions of Egyptian pottery from the Early Dynastic period. That such pottery, and patterns of the consumption of food and drink which it relates to, was not simply concerned with 'mere subsistence' (Sherratt 1999) seems reasonably clear.

Linking food to material culture may also allow us to reassess some of our perceptions, and preconceptions, of cultural links, established over many millennia, between Egypt and the Middle Nile. The long history of trade and exchange between the two areas is well represented archaeologically in an often impressive range of imports of Egyptian or more exotic provenance into the Middle Nile, as well as the substantial cultural borrowings of religious cults and institutions, architectural forms and technologies. These are particularly visible during the Kushite period, when many aspects of Napatan and Meroitic elite and royal culture incorporated Egyptian and northern elements (Shinnie 1967; Welsby 1996). Much described in terms of known Egyptian aesthetics and iconographic traditions, interpreting their significance in their new contexts has remained far more problematic, not least in relegating indigenous traditions and contributions to a supposedly unknowable 'African' 'other'. To what extent does the rebuilding of an ancient shrine in stone, following Egyptian styles, transform an ancient Kushite royal cult? What were the indigenous value systems which determined which Egyptian items were valued and sought after in the Middle Nile? It may be that, in areas relating to the social world of food and culinary culture, we may begin to identify and appreciate the meeting of cultural traditions in the Middle Nile, and how we may begin to meaningfully compare and contrast them.

Outside the bread-eating world

Unlike Egypt, true domestication of indigenous grains appears to have been a relatively late phenomenon in the Middle Nile, probably not before the later first millennium BC. By contrast, in the Sahel and Sudanic Africa we are now beginning to appreciate something of the very long history of utilization of wild grains, and some of its possible social implications. There are suggestions that, from an early date, such cultivation may have been central in the development of new and highly gendered relations within a range of 'hearth-centred' female activities (Haaland 1995). At another level, the distinctive character of generally extensive farming regimes, resistant to state control, seems likely to have been a significant factor in determining the development of the more segmentary and heterogeneous state forms of the Sudanic belt (Edwards 1998a; McIntosh 1999a), very different from the homogenous and hierarchical pharaonic state and its successors.

While barley, and later wheat, seem to have penetrated into northern riverine areas of Nubia as early as the third millennium BC, any significant penetration further south is a much more recent phenomenon. One major consequence may be seen in the long history and remarkable diversity of different forms of sorghum-based foodstuffs in the Middle Nile (Dirar 1993), notably porridge/dumpling-type foods and fermented alcoholic beers (typically *merissa*). This may be compared with a very different bread-and-beer diet in Ancient Egypt (Samuel 1996, 2000).

These forms of food and drink are well documented historically and in ethnographic studies across the Middle Nile. As elsewhere in Africa, substantial proportions of grain crops may be consumed as beer; in Sudan we have estimates of 20–30 per cent of grain production being devoted to beer making (Barth 1967: 152–154; Iten 1979: 68). Historically, beers were widely brewed and consumed within riverine Central Sudan from the Blue Nile to northern Nubia (Burckhardt 1822; Cailliaud 1826) while the use of such beverages (commonly called *mizr*) by the inhabitants of the medieval Nubian kingdoms are recorded by a number of medieval Arabic sources (Edwards 1996b; Vantini 1975). The earliest evidence may be found in Strabo's record, drawing on Eratosthenes' account of the third century BC, of the Meroites' (*Aethiopians'*) preparation of a 'millet' beer, but a much longer history seems likely.

With the long history and great importance of beer in Egypt as well (Samuel 2000), foodstuff forms may not in themselves be particularly significant. However, important questions may be posed concerning their possible social, economic and indeed political roles. As is well recognized, drinking patterns are often intimately concerned not only with matters of hospitality, the promotion of social solidarity and the ceremonial life of communities, but may also play very active roles across the spectrum of social relations, in all their forms (Dietler 1990). Within the Middle Nile, historical and ethnographic accounts leave us in no doubt as to the social importance of beers, permeating all levels of social life (e.g. James 1971). If we may suspect that these roles may be long-established and deeply embedded in societies across the region, which may find resonances in many parts of sub-Saharan Africa, how these may be reflected in material culture, past as well as 'present', may be very informative. If we wish to understand social worlds of the Middle Nile, this may be a good place to start.

Working with beer

Most crucially, the brewing and consumption of beer in the Middle Nile has been strongly linked with work, and work parties. The potential 'economic' importance of drinking in the mobilization of labour cannot be overestimated. In many societies such parties are commonly the primary means for mobilizing labour beyond the core productive unit (Dietler 1996). Historically, such work parties, as part of a 'labour-for-beer' labour market, have remained the key to increasing agricultural production and organizing larger projects into modern times. Over the long term we may suggest that they have been a central factor in facilitating labour exchanges where agricultural production has, until recent times, commonly been organized at a household or indeed at an individual level (Barth 1967; Holy 1974), with a very limited engagement with the state. The tradition has remained strong, despite the appearance of wage labour within the increasingly monetized economy (Al-Bataal 1994: 235–237; El-Medani 1994).

Beer may also play an important role in other social and economic spheres, as part of the bride-price, or used in other forms of gift-exchange forming part of the marriage process, while economic manipulation of drink may be possible where differential access to grain may already exist. Beer may even provide a route to accumulating other forms of wealth, and examples are known from East Africa where beer-for-work parties may be used to collect iron ore, converted by the 'host' into valuable iron tools, in turn exchangeable for livestock or used directly in bridewealth payments for additional wives (Dietler 1990: 366). Such possibilities clearly have important consequences for the development of social stratification. In providing an opportunity to convert surplus agricultural produce into not only (productive) labour, but also into prestige, bridewealth, 'social credit' and political power (Dietler 1990: 369–370), many social dimensions may be added to the significance of grain beers and foodstuffs.

The 'economic' role of fermented beverages may be translated into more obviously political spheres concerned with power relations. Status differentiation may be marked in drinking practices, most basically with gender-based differentiation, but also in terms of age, or prestige. The importance of gender distinctions is also of particular interest in view of the prominence of women's labour in grain preparation (e.g. grinding and malting) and brewing activities, which represent an extension of a range of hearth-centred women's work of the kind discussed by Haaland (1995: 164–165). The common pattern which emphasizes its use in attracting male labour may alert us to the possibility that other social media may be used to attract additional female labour. Such questions are of considerable interest in relation to the widely encountered and persistent uses of specific drinking and culinary practices to distinguish certain classes or status groups (Goody 1982; Mandelbaum 1965).

The pervasive significance of sorghums and millets and their products, especially beers, is also found in their often intense ritual and ceremonial importance, reflecting both importance for subsistence and location within the domestic sphere. The remarkable resistance into recent times, to allowing either beer or labour to enter the cash economy in many areas is an interesting manifestation of such ideological constraints (Haaland 1998). *Merissa* beer plays, or has played, a central role in the ceremonies and festivals among a vast range of populations across the Middle Nile, festivals concerned with the rainy season and the harvests, at initiation and age-grade ceremonies and the installation of priests (Barth 1967; Dirar 1993, 1994; El-Medani 1994; Jedrej 1995; Kronenberg 1959). Even among cattle-oriented peoples such as the Nuer, the annual cycles of ceremonies have been structured around the availability of millet for providing both food and drink (Evans-Pritchard 1940: 84).

Forms of alcohol may also play roles in the maintenance of political authority, both through their use in the provision of hospitality, and also as forms of tribute, paid either as beer or grain. The reciprocal character of these transfers is of course very familiar within many African contexts where tribute obligations are matched by duties to provide hospitality in the form of food and drink. Interesting comparisons may be drawn with the connections between drink, generosity, patronage and wealth apparent in the use of palm wine in West Africa (Akyeampong 1996: 40–44). Again, the political significance of feasting, including drinking, is a much more widely recognized phenomenon, a prominent feature within studies of chiefdom-level societies (Dietler and Hayden 2001; Earle 1991, 1997).

Such examples, by no means exhausting the literature, serve to illustrate some of the possible social roles of sorghum/millet foods and particularly the alcoholic beverages prepared from them. The ubiquity of such practices cannot be doubted, and in the Middle Nile, as in so many areas of sub-Saharan Africa, the beers are a necessary feature of any ritual and/or status-enhancing event as well as fundamental to the mobilization of labour.

Beer, bread and changing identities

Within the long-term history of the Middle Nile, it is likely that many levels of socio-political relations were framed around traditions of community obligations within which food, drink and livestock were key foci. Such roles are likely to have been significant both in the core states of the Middle Nile as well as in the smaller-scale societies which existed at their peripheries. Prior to developing models of the activities of the state, evidenced in archaeologically prominent monuments, histories of 'subsistence' and the culture of foodstuffs may potentially illuminate many key social activities. Specific eating and drinking practices were closely bound up with definitions of identities, displays of status, as well as a range of more widespread social practices. These may be widely reflected in many areas of material culture, in the general character of ceramic culture, in burial assemblages and indeed in the repertoires of materials acquired in long-distance exchanges.

That the staple foodstuffs also occupied a central place in ritual activity seems very apparent in mortuary rites, probably used both for libations as well as in rituals of consumption. Changing patterns of usage may be traced over many centuries, and the social significance of such changes may have been considerable. While modestly marked in early Kushite graves, by the last centuries of the Meroitic period, very large quantities of vessels were being included in burials, having the capacity to contain several hundred litres of alcohol/beer. Functionally similar jar forms survived the end of the Meroitic Kingdom and remained a prominent feature of burials until the introduction of Christianity during the sixth century AD (Edwards 1996b: 71). Alcohol's role in other cultic contexts may also be traceable, as perhaps in massive deposits of pottery, including wine amphorae, encountered on hilltop sites, probably shrines of some form (Lenoble 1992). The considerable investment in fine and elaborate pottery during the Meroitic period may also be related to specific requirements of rituals of consumption, probably as alternatives to high-value metal vessels. The highly distinctive Meroitic finewares, largely drinking cups and goblets, appear closely linked with royal and cult centres, notably Meroe and the pilgrimage centre of Musawwarat es Sufra (Edwards 1999), but also in smaller quantities in burials. Over the long term, the unusual prominence of fine ceramics in Nubian material culture over millennia may be more generally explicable in terms of the particular emphasis placed on such social traditions.

A further status-related development of such practices may perhaps be seen in the elite use of imported wine, associated with both elite burials and other elite contexts such as the royal palaces and cult centres. The presence of imported wine amphorae in the elite graves marks them out by the special character of the alcohol used, but otherwise extends and amplifies far more widespread local practices. The importation of Egyptian and Mediterranean wines, as well as metal serving vessels, recall similar patterns in contemporary western Europe (Dietler 1996), perhaps relating to commensal feasting activities. It is not coincidental that forms of alcohol seem likely to be amongst the earliest imports from Egypt into Nubia and the Middle Nile, following widely seen patterns (Dietler 1990; Sherratt 1986) with the adoption of foreign alcoholic beverages by elites, and their assimilation into elite practices. The further adoption of drinking customs as well as forms of drink are also suggested by the use of imported bronze drinking sets.

This choice of imported metalwork may in turn alert us to further areas where the value systems of the Middle Nile may have been rather different from those of Egypt and the north. In particular, was there a preference for copper, even over gold? The historic role of copper in sub-Saharan Africa as a powerful and highly valued material is widespread and well documented (Herbert 1984). Interestingly, its high value in the Middle Nile is also explicitly noted in Herodotus' (III.23) account of the "Aethiopians". Bearing this in mind, the use of copper alloys for such drinking sets would be particularly appropriate in complementing the other diacritical associations of wine drinking among the elite. This potential importance of copper and bronze in the Middle Nile region has attracted little attention, not least because of what may prove to be an Egyptocentric focus on the gold resources of Kush; a focus and interest which may well not have been directly reflected in indigenous value systems.

The dominance of very different culinary traditions in the Middle Nile once again serves to emphasize the distinctiveness of its history when compared with Egypt. Bread may have acquired a limited role during the Kushite period, and perhaps earlier in religious contexts. However, the widespread appearance of bread foods seems to occur no earlier than the early medieval period, traceable in the spread of wheat from Egypt into Nubia (Rowley-Conwy 1989), as well as ceramic types (e.g. the *doka*) associated with the preparation of flat breads/pancakes, in more southerly areas, adapted for preparing sorghum breads. In the post-medieval period, such developments may be linked with major politico-religious changes within the Funj state during the 18th century, where traditional elites were challenged and ultimately displaced by new 'Islamicized' and 'Arabized' elites, whose identities were linked with, among other things, the rejection of alcohol and the traditional beers. An association with a culture of wheat (and bread) among a new emerging class of powerful Islamic teachers and holy men was explicitly noted by Burckhardt (1822) in the early 19th century. Similar patterns may also be seen elsewhere in Sudanic Africa where the spread of wheat and bread appears to be associated with Arab-Berber influences in the west, favoured by merchants and some local elites (Lewicki 1974: 39–41).

Over the long term, this expanding frontier of wheat and bread is one very central element in the history of the region. Spreading southwards and outwards from the riverine core, it has been slow, and is still an incomplete process. Where once reflecting linkages with Egypt and the north, new imperatives, often political, continue to drive this moving frontier and it remains closely linked to key social changes. Bread and wheat are promoted at the expense of indigenous Sudanic crops and foodstuffs; this shift is now a leitmotif of processes of 'development' and 'modernization' favoured notably by urbanized (and foreign) decision-makers. Prejudices against traditional foodstuffs, notably beers, have also come to be closely associated with the highly politicized 'Islamicization' of the modern Sudan in the 1990s.

Conclusions

Just as the post-medieval Funj elites of the Blue Nile may be identified as the "clothes-wearing" people (Spaulding 1985: 78–83), so another active element in the definition of earlier elites may lie in their food and drink as well as prestigious artefacts such as imported bronze vessels; in what they ate and how they ate it. Contrasts with the world of Egypt, the land of the 'bread-eaters', may reflect more fundamental distinctions than between modes of calorific intake. We might equally focus on livestock, especially cattle, the second pillar of 'subsistence' in the Middle Nile and the adjoining savannahs; peculiar objects of value, which may be accumulated and inherited, as well as consumed. As a medium for channelling the distribution of prestige, historically they seem likely to have been of crucial importance in the development of social hierarchies, especially so in societies lacking alternative sources of accumulable wealth, for example, through access to prestige goods acquired through long-distance exchanges.

Archaeologically, livestock are clearly of considerable significance over millennia. From their first limited appearance in the Middle Nile by ca. 4500 BC, their prominent cultural role is already apparent by the late Neolithic when livestock are becoming a major feature in burials across much of North and Central Sudan (Reinold 2000). Interesting parallels may be drawn with broadly contemporary developments in Egypt, and beyond, where cattle have long been recognized as enjoying a special cultural significance. In view of the considerable cultural similarities apparent between neolithic cultures along the Nile from Khartoum to Badari, their later divergence is especially interesting. The novelty and distinctiveness of new means of expressions of elite identities which were developing in Egypt from the protodynastic period (Wengrow 2001) is very marked. Such cultural patterns were maintained and developed in later centuries. That may again be glimpsed in the prominence of domestic livestock in prehistoric and later rock art of riverine Nubia (Figure 10:2), much of which seems likely to be of 'religious' significance. Livestock, and especially

Figure 10:2   Rock drawings from Lower Nubia.

cattle, continues to be prominent in mortuary offerings, especially in the emerging Bronze Age kingdom at Kerma. There, many hundreds, and ultimately thousands of cattle were incorporated into funerary rites of prominent individuals through the third and earlier second millennia BC (Bonnet 1999; Chaix and Grant 1987). These were only eclipsed by a shift to human sacrifice in the late 'royal' burials of the mid-second millennium BC at Kerma (Bonnet 1990; Reisner 1923).

Later developments of pastoral, and particularly cattle-oriented traditions of the Middle Nile remained relatively obscure until the relatively recent past, when the 'cattle cultures' of the Nilotic south entered the historical and ethnographic record. Representational evidence from Kushite reliefs give us some glimpses of the ritual and symbolic prominence of cattle and especially milk, in at least royal contexts. Like the queen of Punt depicted at Deir el-Bahri, Kushite royal women (Figure 10:3) are also depicted as unusually corpulent (Kendall 1989), as indeed were the royal women of Funj Sennar in more recent centuries. One link which may be made is with an abundant milk diet, a process which we may be seeing in an otherwise enigmatic scene depicted on a Meroitic bronze bowl from Karanog (Figure 10:4). While there may exist aesthetic associations between 'fatness' and beauty, such a representation

Figure 10:3   Kushite royal women, Meroe (after Kendall 1989: fig. 4).

Figure 10:4   Bringing milk to a Kushite royal woman (after Woolley and Randall-MacIver 1910: pl. 27).

may suggest other more general associations between power and the well-fed, and the distinctiveness of royal and/or elite women.

If archaeology chooses to look beyond the monuments and other more obvious manifestations of northern influences in the Middle Nile, the often fundamental distinctions which need to be drawn with regard to Egyptian cultural forms will, even at this superficial level, seem very apparent. However, if we may tentatively identify many ways in which Egyptian cultural traditions seem to diverge markedly from those which are still widespread in sub-Saharan Africa, clarifying what is really happening is a project of the future. It is only now that we can even begin to assess the apparently striking similarities between, for example, the Badarian Neolithic of Egypt and the neolithic traditions of the riverine Middle Nile (Wengrow Chapter 9, this volume). From a southern perspective, the novel cultural features which are increasingly evident in Egypt during the Naqada period would, in many ways, seem to mark a severance of links with cultural traditions which persisted and continued to develop in sub-Saharan Africa. It may be suggested that the adoption of wider perspectives which look to the south may ultimately prove invaluable in future research into predynastic Egypt. On the other hand, the assumed relevance of the Egyptian experience to understanding the ancient Middle Nile, an implicit assumption so deeply embedded in Sudanese archaeology, may not be our best point of departure.

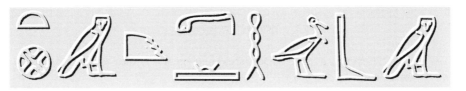

CHAPTER 11

ON THE PRIESTLY ORIGIN OF THE NAPATAN KINGS: THE ADAPTATION, DEMISE AND RESURRECTION OF IDEAS IN WRITING NUBIAN HISTORY

Robert G. Morkot

This chapter examines some issues around a very important aspect of Nubian history: the rise of an independent Kushite Kingdom following nearly 500 years of Egyptian domination of Nubia (from ca. 1550–1070 BC), the origins of its ruling family, and, most importantly, how Egyptologists have explained these changes. In Nubian studies this period (roughly 1070–600 BC) has become known as the 'Kingdom of Kush', the 'Kurru Kingdom', or the 'Napatan' period or Kingdom. The last, Napatan, is the term preferred in the older literature (along with the now obsolete 'Ethiopian'), and will be used here. These Kushite kings became powerful enough to conquer Egypt, where their rule is known as the twenty-fifth Dynasty (very broadly 750–650 BC). The twenty-fifth Dynasty is generally considered to be the last included in the Egyptian Third Intermediate Period (twenty-first to twenty-fifth Dynasties, broadly 1070–650 BC), a period of disunity in which dynasties of Libyan origin dominated much of the country.

The archaeological and textual evidence for the emergence of the Napatan Kingdom is actually quite limited. It comprises a few inscriptions, mostly from the temples dedicated to the god Amun at Gebel Barkal (Figure 11:1), and the archaeological evidence from the royal cemetery at el-Kurru (Dunham 1955; Kendall 1999; Reisner 1917, 1918b, 1919). A crucial factor is that since the excavation of the burials of the twenty-fifth Dynasty kings there, the el-Kurru cemetery has come to dominate the discussion of the origins of the Napatan Kingdom, and little other evidence has been considered, or even looked for.

Reviewing the literature that addresses the origins of the Napatan kings we see very clearly the importance of being aware of the context in which we order our evidence. Scholars have always explained Napatan origins within a framework of assumptions about specific details of archaeology, and chronology, and broader assumptions about Egypt, Nubia and Africa. As will be made clear below, no reconstruction of the evidence from the royal cemetery at el-Kurru has been made without prejudgment. The reason for this is the fact that the cemetery ends with the burials of four of the kings of the twenty-fifth Dynasty (Piye, Shabaqo, Shebitqo and Tanwetamani), who can be firmly dated, which circumstance meant that the normal

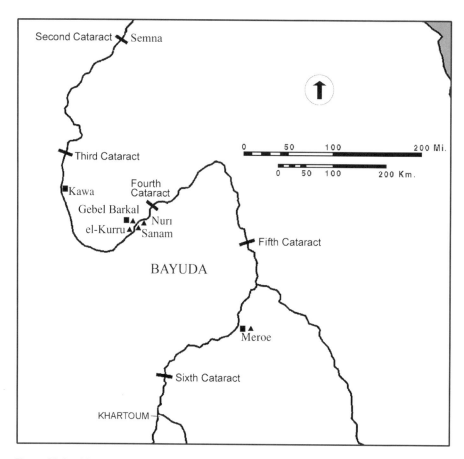

Figure 11:1   Map showing major Napatan sites.

process of dating a cemetery entirely by the types of object was thus prejudiced. Moreover, the earliest Egyptologists to consider Napatan origins did not have the evidence from the el-Kurru cemetery: they relied solely on textual material. This too was placed within a chronological framework which, ultimately, has been significant in the ordering of the el-Kurru material.

The context: general histories and the priestly origin of the Napatan kings

The way in which Nubian studies has developed, and the nature of much of the material, means that it is virtually inseparable from Egyptology. There are now, however, many working in the field who are not from a primarily Egyptological background. This is in many ways an asset. However, this lack of Egyptological background has generated problems, through the uncritical acceptance of Egyptological assumptions and their incorporation into new work.

There have been relatively few general histories devoted to Nubia. The first, by Hoskins (1835) was based largely on classical sources and the monumental record that he observed in his travels. The next major work was that of Budge (1907), which came in the wake of British imperial expansion into 'our' Sudan. Arkell's (1955) history was written following the first phase of archaeological work, and succeeding studies have increasingly adopted an archaeological, rather than text-based, perspective (Adams 1977; Emery 1965; Shinnie 1967, 1996; Trigger 1976a; Welsby 1996).

The issue of Napatan origins is important for Egypt as well as Nubia and the Sudan, and the general histories of Egypt usually have something to say on the subject. The mid-19th century saw a significant change in understanding of this historical phase through the discovery at Gebel Barkal of several well-preserved stelae including those recounting the conflicts of Piye and Tanwetamani with the Libyan dynasts of Lower Egypt (Morkot 2000: 17–18, 167–196, 294–296). At the same time Assyrian records relating to the same period were being published. Following an initial flurry of academic debate, the resulting ordering and interpretation of this material entered the public domain in Brugsch's *History of Egypt under the Pharaohs* (1877, 1879, 1891, 1902). Due in part to a similarity of names, Brugsch suggested that the Napatan kings were descended from the late twentieth Dynasty High Priests of Amun at Thebes.

Brugsch's account of the origins of the twenty-fifth Dynasty was accepted by Rawlinson (1881) and a majority of other late 19th and early 20th century writers, being perpetuated in a slightly modified form in the extremely influential *History of Egypt* (Breasted 1905). The general histories of Egypt written by Brugsch and Breasted were essentially text-based, and marked a new phase in the writing of Egyptian history. They followed the model of the ideal 18th to 19th century narrative chronicle form, particularly as it developed in Germany, and exemplified in the works of Gibbon, Grote, Ranke and Mommsen. For Egyptology, this chronicle style only became possible at this date because of the enormous advances made in the understanding of Egyptian language, and the publication of 'historical' 'texts', in the preceding decades (the concept of both historicity and 'text' in this context could be lengthily debated). The narrative chronicle largely superseded the key early works on Egypt, notably Rosellini's (1833, 1841), which combined the classical and biblical sources with the Egyptian monumental record. Rosellini's approach was, however, developed by Wiedemann (1884), and by Petrie (1905). Petrie's volumes actually take a step further towards the empirical, and monument-based, studies of specific reigns that have appeared more recently. Petrie largely rejected the classical and biblical sources, cataloguing the monumental record, using texts and presenting a historical conclusion with hardly any theory: "Facts are what we alone consider in this History, without giving weight to the opinions that may have been based on those facts", as Petrie (1905: 283) himself, rather optimistically, put it.

Although Brugsch proclaimed in his title that his work was a *History of Egypt under the Pharaohs* derived entirely from the monuments, this is transparently not the case, and he was clearly influenced by more general academic theories about race, language and culture. A mass of material published in the 1860s and 1870s, including the stela found at Gebel Barkal in 1862 and the Assyrian annals and archives, had radically rewritten the history of the twenty-fifth Dynasty. Brugsch's work brought this into the public sphere in a digested, synthesized form. However, alongside his undoubted achievements, Brugsch shows the Egyptological reaction to the classical, and perhaps to a lesser extent biblical, sources which had formed the backbone to Rosellini's synthesis and the very positive views of 'Ethiopia' in the first accounts of Nubia, such as that of Hoskins (1835).

A brief survey of the literature shows some radical changes in European ideas about Nubia in the 19th and 20th centuries (Morkot 2000: chs. 2–3; Morkot and Quirke 2001). They derive not only from the 'discovery' of new textual, and later archaeological, material, but also the more general academic trends that influenced the development of the disciplines of Ancient History, Egyptology, and Archaeology. Bernal (1987) has discussed many of these ideas in his highly controversial *Black Athena*. In the subsequent debate (Lefkowitz and Rogers 1996; Bernal Chapter 2 and North Chapter 3, both this volume), there has been a largely sympathetic attitude to Bernal's aims, if not to specific aspects of his methodology and conclusions. Bernal's study is more about Greece than Egypt, and not about Nubia at all. The many issues raised by it are, however, fundamental to any analysis of writing on Egyptian and Nubian history.

Brugsch argued for the priestly origin of the Napatan kings by claiming they were direct lineal descendants of the Theban High Priests of Amun, Herihor and Piankh. So, after the death of the last pharaoh of the twentieth Dynasty, Ramesses XI:

> The whole South … recovered its freedom, and the Ethiopians began to enjoy a state of independence. Meanwhile, if the power of Egypt was no longer felt, Egyptian civilization had survived. All that was wanting was a leader. Nothing could have appeared as more opportune for the priests of Amen than this state of things in Nubia and Ethiopia where the minds of an imperfectly developed people must needs, under skillful guidance, soon show themselves pliable and submissive to the dominant priestly caste.

(Brugsch 1891: 387)

This is clearly the product of northern Europe in its imperial heyday. Brugsch's views of racial differences between Egyptians and Nubians were made clear at the beginning of his work. Hoskins (1835) and other early writers (such as Russell, see Morkot 2000: 12–13), basing their syntheses on the classical authors, understood southern Nubia – *Aethiopia* – to be the source of Egyptian civilization. Brugsch, at the beginning of his *History of Egypt under the Pharaohs*, rejects this. He invokes the monumental record, and the newly read inscriptions, and categorically denies the classical tradition. At the same time, he brings in a racist note: "[the Egyptians] ascended the river to found in Ethiopia temples, cities, and fortified places, and to diffuse the blessings of a civilized state among the rude dark-coloured population" (Brugsch 1891: 3).

Brugsch's (1891: 2) Egyptians are "a branch of the Caucasian race" and hence related, even if remotely, to the Indo-Europeans. In Brugsch's mind (conscious or subconscious), Nubia, and its population, is in need of civilizing. This happens when the Egyptians conquer, and occurs again with the development of the Napatan state under the rule of émigré Theban priests. (It was also of great importance, of course, at the time of the English translations of Brugsch, when the British were most active in Sudan.) The broader 19th century academic influences on Brugsch are quite clear and these render his claim that he wrote history "entirely from the monuments" (Brugsch 1891) deeply suspect, although he no doubt did believe that he was writing empirically and had confidence that his racial assumptions were true (for similar assumptions current at this time see Reid Chapter 5 and Wengrow Chapter 9, both this volume). Breasted's modification of the émigré priest idea rids it of its overtly racist elements and provides a new historical context: the conflict in Thebes in the reign of the Libyan pharaoh, Takelot II. The principle, however, remains: the Nubians were incapable of creating a state without external stimulus. This idea was abandoned in the 1970s, although the problem of the origins of the state was left unresolved. Indeed, a more dramatic division opened. The end of the New Kingdom served as an appropriate chapter-break, and the archaeology of the el-Kurru cemetery (in the Reisner-Dunham version) was viewed as the beginning of a new phase. A 'Dark Age' thus descended on Nubia for the intervening period (James *et al.* 1991a; Morkot 1994a, 1994b, 1995, 2000, 2001).

Brugsch (1877) was translated into English by Seymour in 1879 a new edition, condensed and translated by Brodrick appeared in 1891, and another in 1902. The continued reprinting of general histories, such as those of Brugsch and Breasted, raises further important factors. Brugsch's history was reprinted and translated over a period of some 30 years; Breasted's for nearly half a century. Although Brugsch's edition produced by Brodrick in 1891 claimed to have been revised, in the chapter on the twenty-fifth Dynasty it clearly was not, and consequently perpetuated errors which had been rectified in academic literature (see Morkot 2000: 18–19). Breasted's 'revised' editions similarly failed to include new material relating to the issue of Kushite origins.

Breasted had studied at Berlin with Adolf Erman, and his own *A History of Egypt from the Earliest Times to the Persian Conquest* (Breasted 1905) follows Brugsch's model in many ways, particularly the emphasis on text, and later editions were referenced to Breasted's own important series of volumes, *Ancient Records of Egypt* (1906–1907). Breasted (1905) has certainly been one of the most influential English language contributions to the genre; with a second revised edition in 1924, it continued to be translated and reprinted until 1948. The context of Breasted's émigré-priest theory (from the second edition, 1924: 537–538) is an interpretation based on texts. The notes, which are omitted from the following extract, are all brief references to Breasted's *Ancient Records of Egypt* …

… after the Theban hierarchy had been maintaining a strong hold upon Nubia for over a hundred years from the end of the 13th century, their control had strengthened into full possession for two hundred and fifty years more. When we recollect that the Tanites of the XXI Dynasty had banished to the oases the turbulent families of Thebes, who had opposed their suzerainty; and that they were later obliged to recall the exiles; when we remember the long and dangerous revolt of Thebes under Takelot II, and the pardon of the rebellious city by oracle of Amon, it will be evident that under such conditions the priestly families at Thebes may easily have been obliged on some occasion to flee from the vengeance of the northern Dynasty and seek safety among the remote Nubian cataracts, which would effectively cut off pursuit. Such a flight would not be likely to find record, and hence we have no direct documentary evidence that it took place; but by the middle of the eighth century BC a fully developed Nubian kingdom emerges upon our view, with its seat of government at Napata, just below the fourth cataract. Napata had been an Egyptian frontier station from the days of Amenhotep II, seven hundred years earlier; and long before it was held by Egypt, it had doubtless been an important trading station on the route between Egypt and the Sudan. It was, moreover, the remotest point in Egyptian Nubia, and hence safe from attack from the North.

> The state which arose here was, in accordance with our explanation of its origin, a reproduction of the Amonite theocracy at Thebes. The state god was Amon, and he continually intervened directly in the affairs of government by specific oracles. [Breasted follows with a summary of kingship as it appears in Hellenistic sources on Meroe.]

(Breasted 1924: 537–538)

In this passage Breasted appears to reject the idea of direct lineal descent from the High Priest Piankh which is found in Brugsch, although he acknowledges an important Theban model, and perhaps presence of Theban priests. Nor do we find any of the overt racial comments which Brugsch uses to explain the formation of the state, although they do seem to be implicit. There is no reference in text or notes to the excavations of Reisner at Barkal or el-Kurru, and the historical reconstructions based upon them. In this section, Breasted's edition is not, therefore, "fully revised" as it claims and in fact is little different from the first edition of 20 years earlier.

Reisner's excavations opened up an entirely new perspective on Napatan origins. Reisner who, like Breasted and Gardiner, had studied in Berlin with Erman, began his excavations in the temples at Gebel Barkal. Reisner (1917: 26) summarized the history of Kushite origins following the generally accepted view as found in the work of Breasted. Although he acknowledges "an obscurity lasting three centuries", Reisner assumes that "there must always have existed a certain sympathy and intercourse between the priests of Amon-Ra of Napata and the priests of Amon-Ra of Thebes" (Reisner 1917: 26). When he discusses Kushite expansion he states that the "military leaders and the priests who controlled the oracles were no doubt of largely Egyptian descent" even if "the mass of the levies must have been Nubians or negroes" (Reisner 1917: 26). This idea was developed further in the report on the excavations of the cemetery at Nuri, where Reisner identified the pyramid tombs of Taharqo and many of his successors. In his historical summary Reisner (1918b: 80–81) expresses a number of racial views that had already been important in his interpretation of early Nubian cultures based on his work in 1907. These ideas, essentially those found in Brugsch, had been elaborated by anatomists such as Smith (1923) and Derry (1956) who had worked on the Egyptian and Nubian archaeological material. In addition to emphasizing the lack of any indigenous contribution, Reisner introduces the possibility of a Libyan ("Lybian") element as well:

> The native negroid race had never developed either its trade or any industry worthy of mention and owed their cultural position to the Egyptian immigrants and to the imported Egyptian civilization. The early kings sprang certainly from the Egyptianized ruling class and had without doubt a large proportion of Lybian or Egyptian blood in their veins. ... The Egypto-Lybian elements in the royal family and in the ruling class were gradually replaced by the native negroid elements, probably through climatic influences and intermarriage. The deadening effects of this racial change appear in the gradual decline of all the arts and crafts.

(Reisner 1918b: 80–81)

Based on the evidence of an alabaster vessel with the name of Pashedenbast, son of a Pharaoh Sheshonq, Reisner (1919) proposed that the prince was a governor for the twenty-second Dynasty and ancestor of the family.

The series of excavations directed by Reisner (1921: 22) ended with the "miserable little heaps of ruins" at el-Kurru, where Reisner was surprised to find the graves of the twenty-fifth Dynasty pharaohs Piye, Shabaqo, Shebitqo, and Tanwetamani (Figures 11:2 and 11:3). Because of their position in the cemetery, Reisner (1921: 24) concluded that these burials were the latest, and immediately began to hypothesize. On the evidence from the cemetery at Nuri (Figure 11:1), Reisner proposed, quite reasonably, that the earliest burial was that in the "primary site in the field" (Reisner 1921: 24), which in this case was a simple tumulus situated on the top of a low knoll, with the other graves apparently placed in front of it. However, Reisner introduced another very important, and quite unjustifiable, interpretation. Rather than attributing the burials to a single line of rulers, Reisner ordered the graves into six 'generations' preceding Piye, with two or three burials a generation. These "generations" comprised a 'chief', his wife, and sometimes a predeceased 'heir'. Reisner assigned 30 years per generation, giving an approximate date of 920–890 BC for the lifetime of the

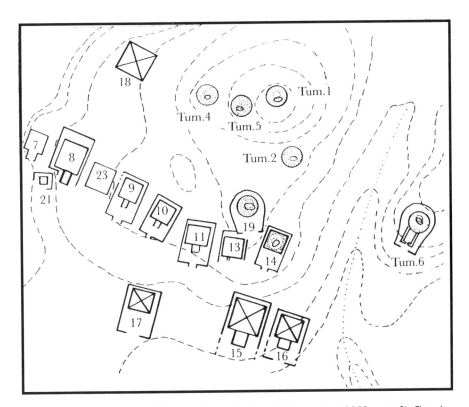

Figure 11:2 The main part of the cemetery at el-Kurru (after Dunham 1950: map 2). The plan omits the large later pyramid "Kurru 1" and the separate group of burials belonging to the queens. The contours indicate the gently rising ground with the presumed earliest burials (Tum. 1–6) on the highest point and the latest, possibly pyramid burials, of Piye (17), Shabaqo (15), and Tanwetamani (16) in a row in front, with that of Shebitqo (18) tucked in at the back.

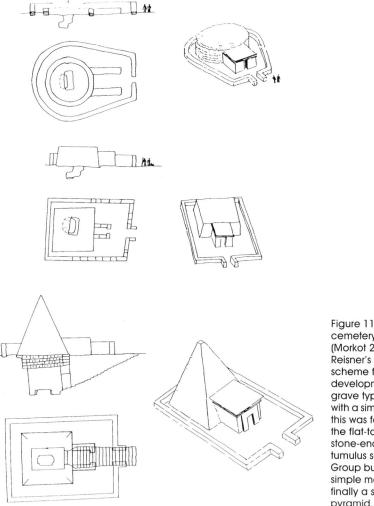

Figure 11:3   The cemetery at el-Kurru (Morkot 2000). Reisner's proposed scheme for the development of grave types began with a simple tumulus; this was followed by the flat-topped, stone-encased tumulus similar to C-Group burials; then a simple mastaba and finally a steep-sided pyramid.

'founder'. The question Reisner (1921: 26) immediately posed was: "Who was this man who founded a family of kings, and what was his race?" He clearly presumed that the person was not indigenous. Although there were no inscriptions, the evidence of large numbers of arrowheads of a Libyan type led Reisner to conclude that "The first ancestor came, therefore, from a more primitive condition of life than prevailed in Egypt, and from an area under the influence of Libyan forms" (Reisner 1921: 26). This Libyan association was apparently confirmed by the stela of Queen Tabiry, a wife of Piye, on which Reisner read (incorrectly) the title "great chieftainess of the Temehuw" who he understood to be the "southern Lybians". Reisner (1921: 31) concluded that it "was probably the old story, often repeated in the histories of the great world empires, of a fresh and vigorous tribe from the outer wilderness forcing its way to the enjoyment of the resources of an ancient empire which had become softened by centuries of prosperity". This idea was a main theme of the late 19th century decadence (and of course was central to Gibbon's *Decline and Fall of the Roman Empire*).

In the middle of the 20th century the Libyan 'tribal' origin was gradually discarded, although the idea of direct influence from Thebes and lineal descent from Theban priests, essentially in Breasted's rather than Brugsch's formulation, was still widely accepted (Hall 1925). For Zeissl (1944: 10), citing the 1936 German translation of Breasted, the idea that the Napatan state was the result of Theban influence was 'generally accepted'. Later, Kees (1953: 264, 265), incorporating some of Reisner's arguments, acknowledged both Theban and Libyan backgrounds. Although by the late 1950s and early 1960s some Egyptologists and Sudanese archaeologists were beginning to argue against the old idea of a priestly origin of, or stimulus to, the nascent Napatan state, there were still some who favoured it: both Arkell (1955) and Emery (1965) maintained the idea of a priestly 'government in exile' as a stimulus to the Napatan Kingdom, as did the influential history of Drioton (1962: 524, 537–538).

The 'noble savage' and the 'frontier barbarian'

The general histories of Egypt which succeeded Breasted's in the middle of the 20th century reveal a new prejudice against the later periods. Wilson's *The Culture of Ancient Egypt* (1956), originally published as *The Burden of Egypt*, dismisses the thousand years of post-New Kingdom Egypt along with any Egyptian cultural legacy in 29 pages (less than one-tenth of his entire work), the 500 years from the Persian conquest receiving two paragraphs. Wilson therefore has little space to account for the origin of the Napatan state. He does, however, comment that Piye (Pi-ankhi)'s "culture was a provincial imitation of earlier Egypt, fanatical in its retention of religious form … The story of Pi-ankhi's conquest of Egypt is an extraordinarily interesting human document, particularly in the contrast between this backwater puritan and the effete and sophisticated Egyptians" (Wilson 1956: 292–293). Wilson (1956: 293) then recounts the installation of the God's Wife of Amun and concludes, "Thus Egypt fell under the nominal rule of an Ethiopian from the despised provinces and under the effectual rule of a woman". With Egypt reduced to such appalling circumstances, perhaps we can hardly blame Wilson for wishing to wash his hands of it!

In the 1950s and 1960s, the theory that the Napatan Kingdom owed its origins to direct external stimulus was gradually rejected in favour of an indigenous origin, and perhaps direct relationship with the much earlier Kingdom of Kerma. This view received some support in the most influential English-language general history since Breasted (and dedicated to his memory), that of Gardiner (1961) who had also studied in Berlin with Erman. Gardiner was rather more generous to the whole of the Third Intermediate Period and Late Period (two chapters, about one-sixth of the text) than Wilson, and devoted several enthusiastic pages to the narrative of the Victory Stela of Piye. Gardiner begins by noting the importance of Napata and Gebel Barkal from the time of Tuthmosis III, and continues, "… we may be sure that Egyptian culture still persisted there in a dormant condition coupled with a passionate devotion to Amen-Ra, the god of the mother-city Thebes. It was probably that devotion which actuated

Piankhy's sudden incursion into the troubled land of his Libyan adversaries …"
(Gardiner 1961: 335).

Gardiner recounts the conflict in Egypt before addressing the issue of Napatan
origins and rejecting Breasted's and Reisner's theories. Of Piye, Gardiner says,

> … behind the verbal expression we cannot fail to discern the fiery temperament of the
> Nubian ruler, a temperament which had also as ingredients a fanatical piety and a real
> generosity. His racial antecedents are obscure, the view that he came from Libyan stock
> resting on very slender evidence. The vigour and individuality shared with him by his
> successors makes it equally unlikely, however, that they were simple descendants of
> emigrant Theban priests, as some have supposed; their names are outlandish and non-
> Egyptian, and fresh blood must have come in from somewhere to give them such energy.

(Gardiner 1961: 340)

Gardiner makes no disparaging comments about 'provincials' or their culture; there
are no 'veneers' of Egyptian civilization (a term still found in some current writers).
He apparently accepts that a deep cultural and religious legacy lies behind an
otherwise undocumented process. Yet, Gardiner's analysis is not totally devoid of
broader theoretical residues. We have vestiges of the 19th century scientific theories of
cultural decadence in the idea of vigorous "fresh blood" contrasted with the notion of
tired blood (an important theme in 19th century literature), paralleling Wilson's
"effete and sophisticated Egyptians". The ground is laid for the appearance of the
'frontier barbarians'. The collapse of old 'exhausted' and sophisticated civilizations to
vigorous barbarians is an important theme of 19th century history and fiction.

In the academic (as opposed to synthetic/popular) literature, a significant
contribution was that of Dixon (1964) who followed Thabit's (1959) and Dunham's
(1947) argument that the Dynasty was indigenous, and descendants of the much earlier
Kerma rulers "overlaid with a rather thick veneer of Egyptian civilization" (Dunham
1947: 3). Dixon's summary paraphrases Gardiner: "The vigour and individuality
displayed by Pi'ankhi and, in varying degrees, by his successors, make it unlikely they
were merely descendants of emigrant Theban priests" (Dixon 1964: 130). But the choice
of "merely" over Gardiner's "simple" seems to introduce a contemptuous tone,
perhaps reflecting the anti-clerical bias found in some other literature of the period.

The "vigour and individuality" of Piye/Piankhi brings us to the alternative
visions of Nubia which adopt the 'noble savage' and 'frontier barbarian' themes. In
contradistinction to inept Nubians incapable of producing a kingdom without outside
help, the noble savage theme gained favour amongst a more recent generation. The
image of 'priest-ridden' Thebes that emerges also has late 19th, early 20th century
origins (and can probably be traced back to the 18th century). It relates to another
important anti-clerical theme in the writing of Egyptian history.

Returning to the origin of the Napatan state, Adams gives some of the clearest
analyses of the various theories and the historiography in his articles (1964) and book
(1977). He (Adams 1977: 257) rejects the theory of a priestly origin although he
acknowledges the importance of Egyptian religion as a legitimizing force in Nubia
and Egypt. Generally in his work, Adams prefers a cool archaeological interpretation
to a theoretical approach, but in this section uncharacteristically moves into a more
colourful mode. It may be the language and discussion of Piye's Victory Stela which

stimulates this. Perhaps he, like Gardiner, felt that for the first time, a Kushite voice really speaks to us. Adams finds the generalized historical theory of Toynbee (1934–1961) most suited to his purpose. He therefore characterizes the emergent Napatan state as "a classic example of a barbarian people turning the tables on its former overlords and oppressors", the Nubians are Egypt's "external proletariat" and finally we become witnesses to "the spectacle of an ancient civilization delivered into the hands of a barbarian upstart" (Adams 1977: 261). Adams' interpretation only works within a context of presumptions (most, I believe, demonstrably wrong) about the Egyptian-Nubian relationship in the New Kingdom, and the history and archaeology of post-New Kingdom Nubia.

Since the 1970s, Nubian Studies has largely followed the path, also preferred by Egyptology, of rejecting narrative history. Unlike some other areas of Ancient History, or Classics, theoretical approaches have found relatively little favour. The approach generally preferred is the development of the empirical Petrie method, with an emphasis on the description of archaeological phenomena. One writer who has adopted broader, anthropological approaches to ancient Nubia is Bruce Trigger. His (1976a) popular account of Nubia rejects the idea of a priestly origin for the Napatan kings, but highlights the possibility of a 'residue' of Egyptian culture. Trigger also rejects the association with, or descent from, the Kerma Kingdom argued by Thabit and advocated by Dixon. He prefers to address the origin of the Napatan state through the archaeology of el-Kurru (at the time of writing still dependent on Reisner's and Dunham's analyses), pointing out the similarities with Kerma, but also Priese's suggestion of a stimulus from the Meroe region. Shinnie (1967), concentrating on the later Meroitic Kingdom, confines himself to rejecting Reisner's theory of Libyan, in favour of indigenous, origins. But that Shinnie needed to do this emphasizes the persistence of old ideas and the difficulties in eradicating them.

The context: the current debate on the origins of the 'Napatan' state

Since 1990, the origins (genealogical, political and cultural) of the 'twenty-fifth Dynasty' have again become a centre of controversy, sometimes heated, amongst a small group of Nubiologists. Although the public airing of the controversy was at the Meroitic Conference in Berlin in 1992 and the Nubian Conference in Lille in 1994, the debate originated in ideas first proposed by Kendall in 1982. In these later discussions there has been an attempt to revive, in a considerably modified form, the idea of direct Theban priestly influence on the early Napatan Kingdom. Although the idea found in some older literature that the Napatan royal house was lineally descended from the Theban high priests of the late twentieth and twenty-first Dynasties appears to have been abandoned, the germ of the idea has been adapted, and archaeological evidence invoked to support it. Here we consider a number of issues rising from this 'revised model', particularly the transmission and adaptation of ideas within Nubian Studies, and what that reveals about the attitudes of Egyptologists towards Nubia, and Egypt itself. Most notably this consideration focuses on what is 'African' about these cultures, societies and states, and also issues of the 'Africanness' of Nubia contrasted with the 'non-Africanness' of Egypt.

The process of reassessment began with Kendall's catalogue for an exhibition of material from Reisner's excavations held in Brockton, Massachusetts. In his brief overview of the el-Kurru cemetery, Kendall (1982: 22–23) noted that some of the objects, particularly decorated faience vessels, were of a typically late New Kingdom type. He tentatively suggested that it might be possible to re-date the graves in the cemetery, and that they might extend from the late New Kingdom through the centuries to the twenty-fifth Dynasty. Within the context of the catalogue Kendall had insufficient space to expand on his ideas, but his continued work on the museum material, and his renewal of excavations at Gebel Barkal, culminated in a paper presented at the 7th International Meroitic Conference in 1992.

There was not much immediate academic response to Kendall's (1982) ideas, perhaps because of the limited distribution of the Brockton catalogue. It was, however, of significance to my own doctoral thesis, which considered the historical and cultural relationship between the Egyptian domination of Nubia in the New Kingdom and the Kingdom of Kush (Morkot 1994a). What actually interested me was the end of the Egyptian empire, the post-imperial period and formation of a new state, and the failure of Egyptologists and Nubiologists to adequately address these issues.

Kendall's suggestion that some of the material from el-Kurru might be late New Kingdom opened up intriguing possibilities for some continuity, rather than the yawning void that was invoked in most discussions. At the same time, another, even more radical, possibility was being considered by James *et al.* (1991a, 1991b), examining the controversial issue of lowering the accepted dates for the Egyptian New Kingdom. The archaeological evidence from a range of sites in Western Asia and the east Mediterranean suggests that it would be possible to lower the generally accepted date for the end of the Egyptian New Kingdom by some 230 years, from around 1070 BC to 840 BC (Table 11:1). This would effectively shorten the Third Intermediate Period in Egypt, but would make it a far more dynamic period of change. The possible effects of this alternative chronology on our understanding of the history and archaeology of Nubia were first outlined in a chapter in the collaborative volume *Centuries of Darkness* (James *et al.* 1991a), and at the Nubian Conference in Geneva in 1990 (Morkot 1994b). Egyptological responses to *Centuries of Darkness* when it appeared in 1991 were generally hostile (James *et al.* 1991b, 1992). Nevertheless, the subject of Napatan origins was back on the table and addressed by Kendall in his 'The Origin of the Napatan State' presented at the 7th International Meroitic Conference in 1992.

Kendall's paper consisted very largely of a reassessment of the archaeological material from the cemetery at el-Kurru, which had been excavated by Reisner and published by Dunham (1955). The value of Kendall's work lay in the presentation of much material that had not been fully published in Dunham's account of the excavations, and had not been examined for many years. Kendall supplemented his presentation of the archaeological material with a historical interpretation of its significance. The published version of the paper (Kendall 1999) is considerably more elaborate than that actually circulated before, and delivered at, the conference. The contributing papers presented at the Conference (e.g. Morkot 1999a; Török 1999a) and those subsequently published, responded to Kendall's original circulated paper, and not the version which has now been published.

Conventional dates   Alternative dates

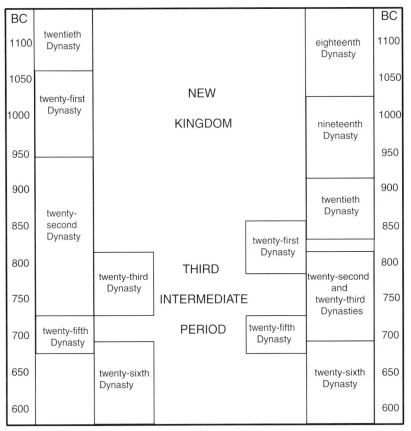

Table 11.1   Comparison of the conventional dates for the later Egyptian New Kingdom and Third Intermediate Period with the alternative scheme proposed by James *et al.* (1991a: table 10:4).

In his historical interpretation, as we shall see, Kendall revived the issue of Theban priestly influence on the nascent Napatan Kingdom. Kendall's paper also rather forcefully rejected the ideas and interpretations that he had proposed in the Brockton catalogue, preferring to return to a modified form of Reisner's original chronology of the cemetery. Török had taken up some of the ideas in Kendall's earlier work and proposed a long chronology for el-Kurru. The resulting debate became extremely heated (see Kendall 1999: 165).

At the same conference the present writer's 'Kingship and Kinship in the Empire of Kush' (Morkot 1999b) discussed the inscriptional and genealogical material relating to the Napatan kings, and the theories of royal succession, particularly matrilineal and fraternal, that had been argued by scholars such as Dunham, Laming Macadam, and Priese. The paper did not address the theory of a Theban priestly origin for the Napatan kings: I thought that as this was now totally rejected in favour of indigenous origins, it was not an issue worth resurrecting. One issue that was raised in the paper, and which has some broader relevance to the issues under consideration here, is that of matrilineal and 'brother' succession. Of the contributing papers, only that of Török (1999b) has any bearing on the issues raised here. Although written independently, Kendall's paper and my own were complementary in that they dealt with two major aspects of the origins of the Napatan state. It could be said that Kendall's approach was archaeological (being site and artefact based) and my own historical (being based on text, anthropology and theory).

In his conclusion, Kendall supports Reisner and Dunham's chronology of the el-Kurru cemetery, with a few, relatively minor, revisions (the minutiae of which have no relevance to the theme of this chapter). Reisner and Dunham's estimated date for the beginning of the cemetery, in the early–mid ninth century BC, was based on allocation of the graves to six or seven 'generations', at 20–30 years per generation, and calculated back from the 'known' dates of the twenty-fifth Dynasty kings. Reisner's reconstruction totally ignored the objects associated with the graves as a possible dating criterion. Kendall re-examined and published many objects from the graves, and Lisa Heidorn made a study of the pottery (Heidorn 1994). Kendall attributed significant numbers of objects to the late New Kingdom, but interpreted them as 'heirlooms'. For a variety of reasons, it proved more difficult to give precise dates to the pottery, and Heidorn's *published* analysis generally prefers to follow the lower possible dates within the ranges for various types. Despite the apparently early objects, Kendall (1999: 50) proposes lowering Reisner's date for the earliest graves by half a century, stating that "Evaluation of the evidence in light of contemporary Egyptian history may actually suggest that the cemetery was founded as late as 850–830 BC".

Kendall (1999: 57) proceeds to revise the dating of the cemetery, not on archaeological grounds, but by a proposed association of the earliest rulers with events following the appointment of Crown Prince Osorkon as High Priest of Amun at Thebes, which is dated by most Egyptologists to the period ca. 839 or 827/822 BC, when Crown Prince Osorkon was faced with a series of 'rebellions' in Thebes, which were suppressed. Kendall (1999: 57) states,

> It is of the greatest interest that these events seem almost exactly to coincide in our chronology with the sudden infusion of Egyptian ritual influences at Kurru during Generations A through C. One is thus drawn to the highly intriguing possibility, over eighty years ago proposed by Breasted (1905: 538), that the Kurru rulers had received a band – or intermittent bands – of Theban priestly personnel who had fled to Nubia in order to escape persecution from the royal faction.

Egyptian artefacts are common in the early graves, but the appearance of an Egyptian ritual does indicate a significant change, which Kendall is trying to explain. But associating the change in ritual with the pontificate of Crown Prince Osorkon requires (1) the internal ordering of the graves and their relative chronology to be correct, and (2) the dates ascribed to the pontificate of the Crown Prince to be correct. A small degree of flexibility is possible, but it is small.

Kendall has used the theory of Theban priests to explain the cultural phenomena of certain burial practices, notably the "breaking of the red pots". An external influence on the nascent Napatan state is therefore implicit. At the same time, the chronology of the cemetery has been tied very closely to events in Egypt. From the perspective of archaeology this is dangerous. The relationship between the graves and the reign of Takelot II is not based on object types or inscriptional material, it is based solely on the *possibility* that this was the *most likely* time when priests may have fled from Thebes to Nubia. Kendall follows the dates for Takelot II and the Theban revolt as given by Kitchen (1973) in his fundamental study of the Third Intermediate Period, and he does not address any of the more recent reassessments of late Libyan chronology which affect the date. Aston (1989) proposed that the reign of Takelot II should be lowered by 25 years. Furthermore, working with Taylor (Aston and Taylor 1990), Aston has shown that there are other problems with the late Libyan material that *could* indicate a lowering of the reign of Osorkon III by a further 20 or more years (something they choose not to do) which would have as a repercussion a further lowering of Takelot II's reign. If Kitchen's date for the Theban revolt is significantly altered, the chronology of the el-Kurru cemetery must be too. Kendall's tightly honed chronology for el-Kurru cannot easily absorb a reduction of 25 years, let alone one of 50.

Normally the subjects selected for main papers at Meroitic and Nubian conferences vanish into oblivion until the next generation chooses to reconsider them, but unusually the origin of the Napatan state immediately reappeared as a main session at the Nubian Conference in Lille in 1994. There, the main paper was presented by Török (1995a), with additional contributions from Yellin, Zibelius-Chen, and the present writer (Morkot 1995). Török's paper (and its expanded version, Török 1995b) discusses the archaeology of el-Kurru and devotes itself even more to the ideology of the state. Török's work deals primarily with the textual, archaeological and iconographic material. He discusses the ideas of some (selected) recent writers, but largely avoids reference to older sources (except, for archaeological reasons, Reisner) and historiography.

Kendall's paper concentrated on the artefacts from the early graves at el-Kurru, and in that lay its strength. Török's paper was more theoretical. Török argued a long chronology in which the cemetery contained only the graves of rulers. There was, therefore, only one burial per generation, rather than the clusters that Reisner (followed by Dunham and Kendall) presumed. On Török's estimate, the cemetery began around 1000 BC. However, the dates of the earliest graves did not accord with the late New Kingdom suggested by Kendall for some types of objects. Török therefore suggested lowering the date for the twentieth Dynasty, but even this does not align the suggested dates of the object types with the dates of the graves. Table 11:2 shows the 'long' and 'short' chronologies of the el-Kurru cemetery set against the conventionally accepted dates for the Egyptian New Kingdom and Third Intermediate Period, and against the lower dates suggested by James *et al.* (1991a, 1991b).

One striking feature of all interpretations of the chronology of the cemetery of el-Kurru is the cavalier attitude displayed by writers to the artefacts as dating criteria. It is usual in archaeology, when confronted with artefacts without textual material to establish a date, to date the objects by reference to parallel material, and then to date the graves and cemetery accordingly. This has never happened at el-Kurru. In all reconstructions, the dating of the objects has been subordinated to preconceived notions about the internal chronology of the cemetery. So, rather than using them as dating criteria, as he suggested doing in the Brockton catalogue, Kendall now dismisses the majority of objects that he dated to the "late New Kingdom" (generally

Conventional dates		Kendall 1999		Török 1999a		Alternative dates			
Dates BC	Dynasty					James et al 1991a		Dynasty and Ruler	Dates BC
1020-1000	twenty-first Dynasty			Gen a	Tum 1	1	Tum 1	nineteenth Dynasty	Ramesses II	1020-1000
1000-980				Gen b	Tum 5	2	Tum 5			1000-980
908-960				Gen c	Tum 4	3	Tum 4		Merneptah	980-960
960-940				Gen d	Tum 2	4	Tum 2		Siptah	960-940
940-920	twenty-second Dynasty			Gen e	Tum 6	5	Tum 6	twentieth Dynasty	Ramesses III	940-920
920-900				Gen f	Ku 19	6	Ku 19		Ramesses IV	920-900
900-880				Gen g	Ku 14	7	Ku 14		Ramesses IX	900-880
880-860		"Lord A"	Tum 1, 5	Gen h	Ku 13	8	Ku 13		Ramesses XI	880-860
860-840		"Lord B"	Tum 2, 4	Gen i	Ku 11	9	Ku 11			860-840
840-820		"Lord C"	Tum 6, Ku 19	Gen k	Ku 10	10	Ku 10	twenty-second Dynasty	Sheshonq I	840-820
820-800	twenty-third Dynasty	"Lord D"	Ku 14,13	Gen 1	Ku 9	11	Ku 9		Osorkon I	820-800
800-780		"Lord E"	Ku 11, 10	Gen-1	Ku 23	12	Ku 23		Osorkon II	800-780
780-760		Alara	Ku 21			13	Ku 21	twenty-third	Sheshonq III	780-760
760-747		Kashta	Ku 8						Kashta	760-735
747-716	twenty-fifth Dynasty	Piye	Ku					twenty-fifth Dynasty	Piye	735-710
716-700		Shabaqo	Ku						Shabaqo	710-695
700-690		Shebitqo	Ku						Shebitqo	695-690
690-664		Taharqo	Nuri 1						Taharqo	690-664
664-656		Tanwetamani	Ku						Tanwetamani	664-656

Table 11:2   The 'long' and 'short' chronologies of the cemetery at el-Kurru set against the conventional chronology and dynasties on the left, with the tentative allocation to reigns in the alternative chronology proposed by James et al. (1991a; and see Table 11.1). The graves are indicated as "Tum" (Tumulus) and "Ku" (mastaba or pyramid graves). The dates BC are given in notional twenty-year generations.

late eighteenth to twentieth Dynasties) as either 'heirlooms', pillage from earlier graves, or objects manufactured in an antique style specifically for a Nubian market.

The key group of objects at the centre of Kendall's theory (and also important in Török's arguments) is a type of pottery vessel with painted decoration. These vessels were ritually broken at the funerary ceremonies, perhaps after a funerary banquet (Kendall 1999: 22 n. 28). Many of the vessels (recognized as very similar to New Kingdom types) were decorated with strikingly late New Kingdom Egyptian funerary images in white. Kendall associates this with the Egyptian ritual of 'breaking the red pots', also noted at the Lower Nubian site of Debeira. The ritual continues until Kurru 13 (and possibly Kurru 11), but probably stops then (there is some uncertainty as to which is the latest burial to have broken pots). Both Kendall and Török attempt to explain away the ritual as an indigenous custom and not the well-documented Egyptian rite, Kendall attributing it to the appearance of his Theban émigré priests at Napata. They are both forced into this explanation as an indigenous, even if Egyptian-inspired, ritual on chronological grounds because, in Egypt, the ritual is not attested after the New Kingdom.

There is an obvious danger in trying to attach imprecisely dateable archaeology to equally imprecisely dated historical events. The equation of destruction levels in Western Asiatic tells (e.g. Lachish) to textually documented attacks on the same city is an understandable element of archaeological interpretation. But it is a different matter to try to attribute a change in funerary practice to an entirely hypothetical, and undocumented, migration linked with an imprecisely dated historical event in a neighbouring country. The site of el-Kurru may be one of the most important for this phase, but it is not the only one (Morkot 2000: 145–166). The archaeology of el-Kurru needs to be examined as other sites would be, without prejudice, and its internal chronology determined by the artefacts. The true development and significance of the site might then become clearer.

Egypt, Nubia, and Africanness

There are undoubted problems with reconstructing the archaeology of a cemetery in the light of assumptions rather than artefacts, but it is the specific historical context that Kendall imposes on his model that raises questions about the transmission of ideas within the discipline, and broader ones about the subconscious or inherent attitudes of the discipline to cultural processes in Nubia. Most writing, as we have seen, acknowledges that there was some sort of Egyptian stimulus to the culture, if not actually a causative element in the process of state formation. Whether this was a 'residue' from the period of Egyptian New Kingdom domination (e.g. Gardiner 1961; Trigger 1976a) or a new stimulus (as in the form of émigré priests) has been more contentious. 'Residue' can imply a time lag between the initial influence and its result, unfortunately voiced by Adams (1977: 244–245) as "it took some time for the lesson of the pharaohs to sink in". This comment was, in many ways, forced upon Adams, because, as an anthropologist and archaeologist, rather than an Egyptologist, he was not in a position to argue some fundamental concerns which seem implicit in his study. Rather remarkably, the Napatan Kingdom has not been widely studied within the context of post-imperial or postcolonial models. Apart from reviving Breasted's suggestion of Theban influence, Kendall (1999) says little about the broader historical context, and does not address more theoretical questions of economy and processes of state formation. Török (1995a, 1995b, 1999a) has little to say on historical context. It was the issue of broader historical context, and particularly post-imperial situations, that I attempted to address in my thesis and related papers (Morkot 1994a, 1994b, 1999a, 2001) and which led me to question some basic chronological assumptions (in James *et al.* 1991a; Morkot 1994b).

The émigré-priest theory is itself clearly a relative of 'diffusionism' which played a major role in Reisner's interpretations of Nubian history and archaeology from 1906 onwards. Arkell (1955) modified the diffusion idea, arguing that with the end of the centralized Meroitic Kingdom in the fourth century AD, there had been a (largely elite) movement westward through Chad which provided the stimulus to medieval African kingdoms of West Africa. A similar diffusion theory underlies Diop's work (MacDonald Chapter 7, this volume). No archaeological evidence is available for either migration (Folorunso Chapter 6, this volume).

As Bernal (Chapter 2, this volume) has clearly shown, there have been ambivalence and changes in European attitudes towards Egypt since the 18th century. In the late 19th century, as shown by Brugsch's *History of Egypt under the Pharaohs*, this resulted in the Egyptians being described as 'Caucasians' and hence distinct from the African Nubians. Reisner's fundamental interpretation of Nubian cultures expanded considerably on this, with the rise and fall of the different Nubian cultures being attributed to influxes of peoples from Egypt and 'negroid' elements from further south, respectively. It also manifested itself in Reisner's assumption (followed by many archaeologists) that a 'cultural lag' was typical of Nubia (also in the distinction he made between 'Nubians' and 'negroes'). Bernal, Adams and others have acknowledged that the racism which is implicit (and at times explicit) in the writing of the later 19th and early 20th centuries is more often the result of institutionalized academic racism (backed up by scientific 'proof') than individuals who were following their own agenda. The legacy of these attitudes has deeply affected perceptions of Nubia and its cultures and, even with some radical challenges to those interpretations (e.g. O'Connor 1993), is still apparent in many publications.

This legacy reveals itself in many important issues regarding the de-Africanizing of Egypt and its culture, and the marginalization of Nubia, which fall outside the scope of this chapter. One issue, which does relate closely to the origin of the Napatan state, is the idea that the Kushite royal succession passed through the female line. This has been widely accepted, as has the idea of 'brother succession', even though the evidence for either is extremely thin. Having argued against both (Morkot 1999b), I concluded that the idea of matrilineal succession had become important less because there was any actual evidence for it, but at least in part because matriliny was thought of as an 'African' phenomenon. This has parallels in the references to female rulers and succession in "Aethiopia" found in Greek and Roman historians, which may relate to a classical (at least Greek) *topos* of powerful women (such as the Amazons, Cleopatra, and the Meroitic 'Kandake' system of government with central Queen Mother) as an inversion of the ideal norm. Classical writers have themselves had considerable influence on the reconstructions of the Nubian past, from Hoskins (1835) to Breasted (1905) and beyond, as Török (1989) has detailed. Some modern Afrocentrist writing idealizes the concepts of matrilineage and the importance of women (two different, if connected, issues) as a particularly African phenomenon, contrasting with white European male-dominated aggression. However, African monarchies are as likely, if not more so, to have patrilineal as matrilineal, and vertical as horizontal, succession (Morkot 1999b: 214–218).

We all have acquired views of what Egypt and Nubia were like, and how they functioned; however, the historiography of the subject is not generally considered to be important. We still think that we can adopt an empirical approach to the material, unaware of the ways in which ideas of an earlier generation are still influencing our interpretations. The literature about the priestly origin of the Napatan kings demonstrates this quite clearly. Kendall has consciously chosen to revive Breasted's idea of émigré Theban priests in a slightly modified form, in order to explain a specific archaeological phenomenon. Kendall's interpretation of the chronology of the el-Kurru cemetery has been supported in more 'popular' literature, as has his idea that there *may* have been direct Egyptian cultural stimulus from Theban priests (Shinnie 1996: 99; Welsby 1996: 14). The result is that, after three decades in which lineal descent, or direct external influence, had generally been discredited as factors in the emergence of the Kushite Kingdom, we have returned to an explanation of Kushite origins hardly different from that of our predecessors at the beginning of the 20th century.

The one issue examined here, Napatan origins, shows how ideas based upon dubious historical and racist assumptions can be adapted and modified, abandoned, then resurrected and reapplied to explain the archaeology of a site. In order to achieve a better understanding of ancient Nubia, and of Ancient Egypt, we need to be aware of what our predecessors wrote, and, as important, how and within what context they formulated their ideas.

CHAPTER 12

PHARAONIC OR SUDANIC? MODELS FOR MEROITIC SOCIETY AND CHANGE

Dorian Q. Fuller

Introduction: pharaonic and Sudanic models

In the eighth century BC a new kingdom emerged onto the historical scene, when its ruler led his military forces to the conquest of Egypt. This was the king Piye, known to later Egyptian historians as the founder of the twenty-fifth Dynasty of Egypt (which lasted roughly 80 years). He came to Egypt, and ruled Egypt, from far to the south at ancient Napata (modern Gebel Barkal). This remained the centre of a kingdom even after his successors lost control of Egypt to the Assyrians (for a discussion of the still enigmatic process of the emergence of this kingdom see Morkot Chapter 11, this volume). This Kingdom of Napata, generally known as the Meroitic Kingdom in its later phases (fourth century BC to fourth century AD) when its capital was located at the city of Meroe, was an important regional power, often referred to as an empire, for more than a thousand years. The core region of this kingdom was focused along the Middle and Upper Nile from the Khartoum area, where the Blue and White Niles merge, to the Third Cataract of the Nile (Figure 12:1). In this region a number of important temple and city sites are known from this kingdom. Further north, beyond the Third Cataract, Meroitic control of the region was not continuous, and particularly north of the Second Cataract there is evidence that Persian rulers of Egypt and the Ptolemaic (Greek) rulers of Egypt controlled the region for at least some periods, interspersed with periods of Meroitic dominance, indicated by temple inscriptions and building in the region, especially at the important fortress and temple site of Qasr Ibrim. After the Romans had established control of Egypt and failed in a conquest attempt of Nubia in 23 BC, an official frontier of Roman control was established at Maharaqqa, with the region to the north, under Roman control, known as the Dodekaschoenos, whereas south of this frontier was acknowledged as Meroitic (or 'Aithiopian' in the ancient classical sources).

The wealth of evidence on the archaeology and history of the Meroitic Kingdom provides a unique opportunity to examine the interactions, cultural similarities and differences between Egypt and another region of the African continent. As an adjacent region to Egypt, Nubia has long been discussed as an 'African' hinterland of Egypt. It has been variously termed a "corridor to Africa" (Adams 1977) or an African "rival" (O'Connor 1993). The Meroitic Kingdom has been credited as a land in which ancient

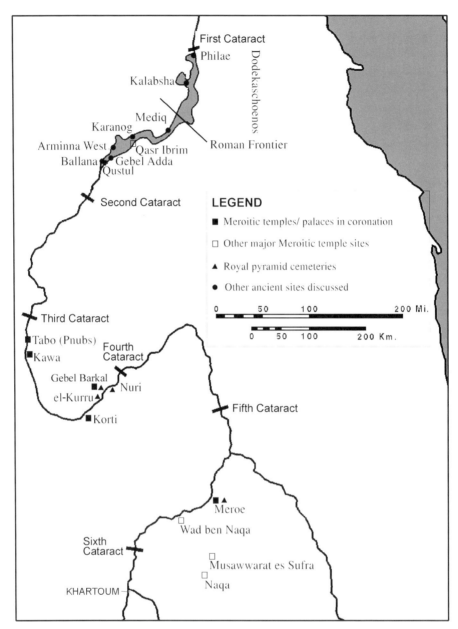

Figure 12:1   Map of greater Nubia including sites mentioned in the text, and the ancient frontier between the Roman and Meroitic empires.

Egyptian artistic forms and religious beliefs persisted after they had been largely eradicated in Egypt through Romanization and eventual Christianization (e.g. Edwards 1961; Shinnie 1967; Smith and Simpson 1981),[1] and the use of Egyptian iconographic elements (see Figure 12:2), including Egyptian deities and a script derived from Egyptian hieroglyphics, attests to the importance of borrowings of

Figure 12:2   Sandstone lintel and door jamb from Arminna West, Cemetery B, Tomb 23, with representations of goddess Nephthys, winged sundisk and uraei (Fuller forthcoming, Pennsylvania Yale Expedition to Egypt 1963).

Egyptian culture in Meroitic Nubia. In this chapter, I move beyond cataloguing Egyptian borrowings in terms of material styles and motifs, and focus instead on the issues of the underlying social and political organization of the Meroitic Kingdom, and how it may have been quite different from that of Ancient Egypt. Indeed, I suggest that because of its closeness to Ancient Egypt, and obvious interaction and borrowings, Nubia's divergent system of social organization has often been overlooked in favour of viewing it as essentially an Egyptian society (Edwards Chapter 10, this volume). The conventional Egyptian model for the organization of the Meroitic state and its society is in part responsible for debates about apparently contradictory historical and archaeological evidence about control of northern Nubia. In addition, this understanding of Meroitic political power is linked to a broader misconception of the organization of Nubian communities. I argue for an alternative perspective, which I term Sudanic, of political and social organization at the regional, interregional and community levels. I discuss some historical and archaeological evidence from the northern Meroitic region and adjacent Roman Dodekaschoenos. Also, I consider how the Sudanic model is demonstrated in the archaeological evidence of a particular community, that of Arminna West, from which I have been studying the excavated material in recent years (Fuller 1997, 1999). This perspective provides us with new insights into the processes of social change in the fourth century AD, when the Meroitic Kingdom is conventionally seen as ending.

The history of archaeological research in Nubia is inextricably linked to that of Egypt, with many of the same prominent figures carrying out archaeology in both regions (Adams 1977; Morkot 2000; Trigger 1982). Thus, understandably, concepts employed in interpreting Ancient Egypt have also been found useful in discussing ancient Nubia, and among them has been the assumption that the Meroitic Kingdom was a pharaonic state, organized like that in Ancient Egypt. I suggest that accompanying this pharaonic model are simplistic assumptions about the nature of trade, mortuary ritual and social identity which fail to provide an understanding of how human communities in ancient Nubia were structured and how they changed, especially during the crucial historical juncture that has been termed the "fall of Meroe" (e.g. Kirwan 1960; Shinnie 1967; Welsby 1996). In recent years, a growing body of archaeological and historical research, and models drawn from African ethnography and history, favour an alternative 'Sudanic' model (especially Edwards 1996a, 1996b, 1998a). This latter model provides an insight into some of the nuances of late Meroitic archaeology and the nature of social changes which have proved problematic within a pharaonic framework of analysis.

The pharaonic model of sociopolitical organization represents the classic definition of the state in anthropological evolutionism and comparative sociology. The state has a centralized power structure deployed across a boundary-delimited territory by means of a bureaucratic infrastructure and with significant state control in the economy (Edwards 1996b: 8 ff; in general see Earle 1994; Mann 1986, 1988; Trigger 1993). The development of this classic state model of the Meroitic Kingdom may seem the obvious extension of two observations in Nubian history. First, there is a long-recognized influence of Egyptian institutions on the symbolic expression (both monumental and textual) produced by the earliest documented Kushite rulers, the founders of Egypt's twenty-fifth Dynasty, Kashta, Piye and their successors (e.g. Shinnie 1996: 100–101; Török 1997b: 131 ff; Trigger 1976a). The twenty-fifth Dynasty is conventionally seen as taking over and implementing the Egyptian state apparatus, as exemplified in the following synopsis:

> This period saw the development of a state-controlled economy modeled along Egyptian lines and no doubt administered by Egyptian or Egyptian-trained bureaucrats. Similar craftsman produced luxury goods for the enjoyment of the upper classes, while large amounts of standardized wheel-made pottery suggest that centralized control was exercised over the surpluses of many basic commodities … The Kushite rulers succeeded in imposing significant elements of Egyptian style political organization upon their homeland by implanting there the religious cults and other cultural values of Dynastic Egypt.

(Trigger 1978a: 226–227)

The means by which Egyptian institutions were transferred more or less wholesale to Nubia has been assumed to have been a top-down imposition by local rulers (the rulers buried at el-Kurru who founded the Napatan Kingdom), and is generally connected to concepts of a territorial state with a centrally controlled economy.[2] This view tends to see the pharaonic institutions in an essentialist fashion rather than as symbols that might be employed and reinterpreted by Nubian agents. A second observation, although less explicitly discussed, seems to underlie the assumption that an Egyptian-style state apparatus continued until the end of the Meroitic Kingdom: in Meroitic texts of the late period (i.e. 100 BC–350 AD) numerous titles of state 'officials' are recorded which can be translated because they are borrowings from ancient Egyptian titles (known especially from demotic, the late period Egyptian script). This latter observation is particularly problematic as our very incomplete understanding of the Meroitic language relies on loanwords from Egyptian and guesswork on other terms for titles and affiliation (see Griffith 1911, 1912; Haycock 1976; Millet 1968, 1981; Török 1979; Trigger and Heyler 1970). In the case of both of these observations the similarity with ancient Egyptian state structures may be more apparent than real. As others have noted in the realm of iconography, Egyptian symbols provided a "vocabulary through which Nubians could express their world view" (O'Connor 1993: 83). As I argue below, the Sudanic state model entails that these Egyptian adoptions became Nubianized through their use within the very different organization of the Meroitic Kingdom.

The Sudanic model has been proposed as an alternative system for understanding the Meroitic Kingdom (Edwards 1996a, b, 1998a), deriving in large part from Southall's (1956, 1988) concept of a segmentary state, together with reference to later historic kingdoms of the Sudan, such as the Funj sultanate. The segmentary state is defined by four key aspects (Southall 1956: 248–249; Stein 1998: 20). First, it is made up of numerous centres of political power. Second, political power is differentiated between royal suzerainty (held by a single king and recognized by all, often through ritual form) and practical power held by local elites, which we might term local sovereignty. The power of the king shades off as one moves away from his centre. Third, while the royal centre is organized through an administrative system and coercive (military) force, other locales of power repeat such administrative capabilities backed up by force, normally on a reduced scale. Thus, political centres reflect the same model as the central power and may be further divided into more local power foci. Finally, the segmentary state is prone to fluctuation in size, especially at its spatial extremes because "the more peripheral a subordinate authority is the more chance it has to change its allegiance from one power pyramid to another" (Southall 1956: 249). These features together differentiate the segmentary state from ancient territorial states, of which pharaonic Egypt was one, and ancient city states, such as Old Babylonia or the Yoruba civilization of West Africa, as defined by Trigger (1993). While city-state systems share some characteristics with the segmentary state, such as multiple local centres of administration and military power, the segmentary state clearly differs in the wide spatial reach of ritual power of the king, as well as tendencies towards more dispersed agrarian and pastoral settlement with less importance given to any central city.

The importance of the segmentary state model lies in the processes it envisions. It must be noted that the segmentary state is a controversial category, and one that was rejected outright by one recent conference on the archaeology of early states (Marcus and Feinman 1998), but which has gained currency within African archaeological circles (e.g. McIntosh 1999b) in addition to other historical contexts such as South Asia (Stein 1998; Southall 1988, 1999). While it certainly is the case that Alur society described by Southall (1956) was nothing like a state in terms of hierarchical complexity, this defining example nevertheless highlights recurrent patterns that fit predictions of the segmentary state model (Edwards 1996a, b, 1998a), most particularly, that territorial sovereignty (direct control through military and/or bureaucracy) is limited while suzerainty (symbolic authority) is more extensive, and central government has reduced control over the peripheries of suzerainty. The use of armed force may have been equally limited, with local 'officials' with military-like titles representing local warlords. Most of the time force may be used for raiding, a source for acquiring wealth in such things as cattle and slaves, rather than for territorial acquisition. Within this model, legitimation is achieved through religious symbols and through the redistribution of prestige goods to local elites. Edwards (1996a, b: 12–13) combined the segmentary state with Mann's (1986: 22–28) idea of four different, and potentially not unified, sources of social power: political, economic, ideological and military (see also Earle 1994). While the pharaonic model had generally assumed these sources of power to be largely coterminous, the Sudanic model allowed for these sources to be overlapping but differing in their territorial extent and their degree of intensiveness at a distance from centralized authority.

The most archaeologically evident implication of the Sudanic model is the interpretation of Nubian trade as part of a prestige goods economy that played a crucial role in the creation and maintenance of Meroitic ideological power. While the evidence for long-distance trade with Egypt and elsewhere has long been obvious, it has often been conceived in a fairly simplistic and capitalist vein, in which the economic benefits of trade were implicitly self-evident (cf. W. Y. Adams 1977, 1981, 1988; Török 1984). Edwards' (1996b: chs. 3 and 4) analysis of the distribution of imported trade goods indicate that most were limited in quantity and focused on regional centres of elites, with most rare exotic items being focused in the royal cemetery at Meroe, implying that the exchange of these items was likely a royal monopoly. Some of the luxury goods, as well as centralized manufactures (probably including some Meroitic fine wares) were then distributed to local elites, who in turn gave tribute and showed allegiance to the Meroitic king through the giving of local wealth objects and probably some services in warfare or raiding. A similar pattern of tribute and elite gift-giving may have been carried out between regional elites and more local elites on an increasingly restricted scale. This form of maintaining relationships of power through exchange can be considered through the broader anthropology of gift-giving (Gregory 1982; Mauss [1950] 1990) and substantivist views of the economy as inherently embedded within social systems in pre-modern times (Polanyi 1968). To quote from Guyer (1995: 87): "the history of exchange and the history of relationships must permeate one another." And indeed the prestige-goods economy and Meroitic trade can be understood as an example of a phenomenon well documented in African history and ethnography, in which material wealth is exchanged for social influence or 'wealth-in-people' (Guyer 1995; Guyer and Eno Belinga 1995; McIntosh 1999b). Our very ethnocentric conception of wealth as material goes hand-in-hand with seeing states as territorial (i.e. possessing strictly defined lands), whereas if we accept that the Meroitic Kingdom worked within a different framework in which the brokering of influence and social power were primary, it becomes necessary to re-conceive a number of issues and debates in Meroitic studies.

The power of the Sudanic model: dissolving debates

The conceptualization of power in the Sudanic model is fundamentally different from that of the centralized pharaonic state, and this alternative understanding of authority and sovereignty is a powerful tool for understanding the archaeological and historical evidence available for the Meroitic Kingdom (cf. Edwards 1996b; Fuller 1997). A key difference in the segmentary Sudanic model is that power focuses on the gaining of influence over people, for example, through the formation of alliances and situations of social debt, rather than on the absolute rulership over territory, administered through bureaucratic officials, and ownership of material goods (McIntosh 1999b: 16; and see also Guyer 1995; Guyer and Eno Belinga 1995; Southall 1999). This notion of 'wealth-in-people' and indeed power in terms of influence through social networks provides an important contrast with our conventional notion of the centralized nation state with territorial hegemony (see e.g. Mann 1986, 1988; and for Egypt, Kemp 1989). In the context of the Meroitic Kingdom therefore we might ask whether conceptions of state boundaries are of particular relevance and need have any correlation with power networks defined on the basis of honourific titles.

Considering the Meroitic evidence in terms of Mann's dimensions of social power makes it clear that we are dealing with networks of differing extents. As argued by Edwards (1996b), central control of subsistence produce was probably limited to river basin agriculture near Meroe and surrounding savannah agro-pastoral production in the Western Butana which could have been 'taxed' through the temple and reservoir complexes in that region (cf Török 1997a: 470). Within this region fairly intensive economic power, presumably backed up by intensive military power, and the ideological power expressed in temple monuments formed the basis of political authority. It is also likely that agricultural produce was obtained by other royal palace-temple establishments from local basin agriculture in such regions as Napata, Kawa and Pnubs (in the basins of the Fourth to Third Cataracts), but the generally low agricultural productivity that is likely to have been the case during this period would have prevented the kind of large scale centralized storage of agricultural surpluses which characterized Ancient Egypt (and can be attributed more generally to many Eurasian complex societies, cf. Goody 1976; McIntosh 1999b; Southall 1999). A measure of centralized control at these centres would seem to be implied by textual evidence, all from the earlier Napatan period (up to ca. 315 BC), for successive enthronement ceremonies carried out at each of these places as part of what Török (1992, 1997b) has referred to as "ambulatory kingship". As discussed by Török, these ceremonies imply a tradition in which these separate centres of ideological power (and perhaps previously separate political powers) are symbolically unified by the accession of the Meroitic king, but they may also imply that some ideological power remained focused on the temple at each of these locales. This need for sequential movement of the king to legitimate his authority has parallels in the later Funj sultanate (cf. Edwards 1998a; Spaulding 1979).

That this itinerary did not include regions further north, such as Lower Nubia, suggests that it lay outside the regions of direct sovereignty united under the king. Certainly evidence from further north (and the later Meroitic period) implies that ideological power associated with other temples was drawn upon by Meroitic kings and other elites for legitimation but that the influence of these temples was extensive, perhaps diffuse, and extended across territorial boundaries. Thus Philae, a site for which there is no reason to believe it was ever not part of Roman Egypt, contains numerous inscriptions of Meroitic Nubian elites, and some Meroitic kings, implying that visits to this temple and participation in its rituals aided legitimation in terms of ideological power at a place where actual military or political control was clearly held by others (i.e. the Roman Empire). In addition, within Lower Nubia, the temple site of Qasr Ibrim provides ample evidence for Meroites (i.e. individuals fluent in the Meroitic script) and Egyptians (leaving inscriptions in demotic) actually making pilgrimages to the site (as attested by their inscribed footprints of pilgrimage – Wilson 1996), as well as apparently epistle-like ostraca and dockets that may have been addressed to oracles from Meroitic as well as Egyptian individuals (Edwards and Fuller 2000; Rilly 2000; Zauzich 1999). This evidence clearly attests to the cross-cutting extent of ritual (ideological) powers at these temples and indicates the non-equivalence of the different sources of power in the Middle Nile region.

By seeing the Meroitic Kingdom as a segmentary state with differing degrees of involvement in the sources of power in different regions, it is possible to dissolve some areas of long-standing debate in Meroitic studies. Three particular areas of controversy can be seen to be unproblematic, perhaps even predictable, when all of the implications of the Sudanic model are taken on board: the issue of a Meroitic-Ptolemaic 'condominium' in the Dodekaschoenos, the involvement of the Meroitic Wayekiye clan in the Dodekaschoenos in the third century AD prior to Roman withdrawal from Nubia, and the issue of Meroitic north–south contrasts as well as northern 'autonomy'. Of crucial importance is to assess these issues in terms of the political worldview implied by the Sudanic model, in which social power predicated on ritual legitimation and reinforced through sumptuary gift-giving was primarily to do with influencing people rather than controlling territory. This provides an important contrast with the pharaonic situation, or that of imperial Roman Egypt, in which centralized military control of territory was paramount.

The possibility of a joint rulership of the Dodekaschoenos between Ptolemy IV and Arqamani during the third century BC becomes something of a non-issue within a Sudanic view of the Meroitic Kingdom. The coexistence of temple inscriptions and evidence for building activity sponsored by both Ptolemy from Egypt and the Meroitic king Arqamani at Pselchis and Philae (and similar evidence for Ptolemy VII and Adkeramon) has often been interpreted as a form of condominium or joint rule of Lower Nubia, or at least the northern part (Dodekaschoenos) by Ptolemies and Meroites (e.g. Adams 1977: 334–335; Shinnie 1967: 41). Interestingly, the motive for Meroitic involvement suggested by Adams (1977) is purely commercial, namely the control of the northern access to Wadi Allaqi gold mines. As discussed by Török (1997b: 427–430), it makes far more sense to see these building activities as sequential during periods of Ptolemaic followed by Meroitic and then again Ptolemaic control of the region, with the Meroitic interlude perhaps relating to an Upper Egyptian revolt by Hor-wenefer. Nevertheless, the sequentiality of these building episodes and their correlation with absolute chronology remains guesswork predicated on the assumption that both the Ptolemies and the Arqamani were after the same thing: territorial control. In contrast, we can suggest that the building activities by Arqamani (and the problematic Adkeramon) need not be seen as territorial claims but only as efforts at ritual legitimation, especially amongst populations within Lower Nubia, through giving architectural gifts to the local temples. While the Ptolemaic building was doubtless directed towards asserting sovereignty over the region, the Meroitic building should be seen perhaps through a rather different worldview, even if facilitated by a period of weak Ptolemaic defence of the region.

A similar perspective makes sense of the activities of the Wayekiye family in Meroitic Lower Nubia, the Roman Egyptian Dodekaschoenos and at Philae. This family is attested by funerary inscriptions from Gebel Adda, Madiq near the southern border of the Dodekaschoenos (the historically attested southern Roman frontier) and from inscriptions at the temple at Philae (clearly within Roman Egyptian territory) dating in general to the mid-third century AD. This family included title-holding elites within the Meroitic 'officer' system of Lower Nubia, as well as the title *Pelmos* which has been connected to the Ptolemaic Greek title *strategos*, or "general" (Griffith 1912: 18; Haycock 1976; Millet 1968: 43–45, *passim*, 1981; Török 1979: 93 ff, 1980, 1987: 172–174). This family was clearly active within officially Roman territory, possessing titles referring to Philae, and probably were also active within the Dodekaschoenos, such as at Kalabsha (cf. Fuller 1997: 117, based on AW4 of Trigger and Heyler 1970) while also being prominent figures at the Meroitic Nubian site of Gebel Adda and clearly being well intermarried with elite families in Lower Nubia (Millet 1968, 1981), including those of Arminna West (Fuller 1997; Trigger and Heyler 1970), as well as apparent relatives of the central Meroitic royalty. The apparently elite status enjoyed by this family within the Meroitic domain as well as within the Dodekaschoenos need not imply weak Roman control of the latter territory as some have assumed (Török 1988: 26), but only that the Wayekiyes and indeed other Lower Nubian elites were focused on ritual legitimation and social relationships within Roman territory, rather than territorial control as such. While numerous Meroitic Nubians presented themselves in the Philae temple as envoys of the Meroitic king to the Roman world (Griffith 1912; Török 1978, 1979, 1980), the suggestion that these pilgrimages were "nothing else than embassies" (Török 1989: 63) must surely downplay the importance of their ritual legitimation both of their own elite status and of their role in both recognizing and maintaining the symbolic hegemony of the central Meroitic king. That their power within Lower Nubia may have been facilitated by some weakening of Roman authority, or indeed of Meroitic authority (cf. Fuller 1997, 1999), does not escape the likelihood that their trans-territorial power derived from the active pursuit of ritual legitimation and social influence without clear military or territorial control.

The power of the Wayekiye family is often discussed in relation to the contentious issue of the extent of integration of the Lower Nubian province, known as *Akin*, and the central Meroitic monarchy during the later period. As suggested by Millet (1968) on the basis of texts such as those of the Wayekiye family, and as argued by Adams (1976, 1977) on the basis of archaeological contrasts between the archaeologically 'secular' North and 'sacred' South, the Lower Nubian province may have been largely autonomous from the central Meroitic monarchy. The problematic secular-sacred distinction aside, this separation has been critiqued largely on the basis of the presence of Meroitic officials in Lower Nubia attested to by funerary inscriptions with references to the Meroitic royal family (but not to specific kings) (e.g. Haycock 1976; Török 1976, 1979, 1987). The close integration of Lower Nubia with Central Sudan makes sense if we assume that the Meroitic titles indeed represent economic officers on the pharaonic model. But if we see these titles as honorific epithets that were employed by regional elites for their legitimation by reference to the symbolic central authority, then their use implies strategies for coping with circumstances of local power negotiation (Fuller 1997). During the late to terminal Meroitic period (third to earlier fourth century AD) Meroitic office holders in Lower Nubia proliferate, with a greater range of office titles and a greater number of individual office holders named in funerary inscriptions (Fuller 1997; Trigger and Heyler 1970). Given that there is no equivalent evidence from Central Sudan and that evidence for active involvement of Meroitic kings in Lower Nubia (e.g. through monumental building and inscriptions) is extremely limited during this late period, the proliferation of Meroitic title-holders in Lower Nubia is perhaps best understood within its own regional context of power and legitimation. Archaeological evidence for trade in Lower Nubia (Edwards 1996b) contrasts with that elsewhere in the Meroitic domain, indicating some distinct economic connection between the northern province and Roman Egypt that was not part of the central Meroitic prestige goods economy. This raises the clear possibility that elites in Lower Nubia participated in different networks of economic power, while at the same time acknowledging the ritual hegemony (ideological power) of the Meroitic monarchy.

Substantive practices: material culture and ritual in a segmentary world

As the economics of Meroitic trade have been recast as playing a role in the maintenance of power, burial rituals too and the use of material culture need to be considered within a context of social relations and local power networks. While conventional analysis of Meroitic funerary inscriptions has focused on their content, especially in terms of translatable office titles and kin relationships, their occurrence in the funerary context must be considered alongside other deposits and erections. The occurrence of these stelae generally accompanied other sandstone monuments, including ba-statues and figural or inscribed offering tables, placed outside small pyramidal burial monuments containing the burial (Adams 1977; Geus 1991). While this monument type has been found in central Meroitic Sudan, where it appears to be in the small minority (Edwards 1998b), it dominates cemeteries of northern Nubia. What is interesting about this is that while the pyramidal tomb structure clearly mimics in miniature the royal pyramids of Meroe (Figures 12:3, 12:4 and 12:5; and as noted by Woolley and Randall-MacIver 1910), this referencing of royal practices was more important at the distant periphery of suzerainty than within the region of clear sovereignty. This state of affairs implies that local legitimation through connection with the ideological power of the Meroitic royalty played an important role in the social relations of northern Nubia. This evidence further implies that essentialist understandings of burial customs in terms of Meroitic or non-Meroitic identity are flawed and that social identities must instead be seen as representations in the context of local power dynamics.

Figure 12:3   Royal pyramids and chapel at Meroe (© Dorian Fuller).

Within northern Nubia inscriptions proliferate in the late to terminal Meroitic period. They are found at a range of smaller sites, and contain increasingly long sections referring to kin and their honorific titles, implying an increased emphasis on legitimation through established networks of social power, and Meroitic means of memorialization. This proliferation of conventions, which symbolically at least indicates connections with the central Meroitic royalty, and burial customs, are transformed in the late third to early fourth century, which is before the historically attested 'fall' of Meroe. Analysis of the small cemetery at Arminna West suggests that while kinship remains important, as indicated by the continuing re-use of individual tombs and burial clusters that probably represent kin groups (Figure 12:6), the actual practices of burial, some of the grave goods and the practice of erecting stelae, statues and offering tables undergo progressive change and experimentation (Fuller 1997, 1999). While some of the new burial customs appear to be inspired by elite burial monuments in the Dodekaschoenos, such as those at Kalabsha which might be attributed to an emergent elite deriving from populations of the Red Sea Hills (Williams 1991), other changes in the burials appear to be purely local developments. This implies that the existing social order in which the symbolism of the older pyramid-statue-stela-offering table practice, which probably referred to royal Meroitic practices, lost its symbolic currency, and local communities began to work within different frameworks of legitimation. Thus a detailed consideration of burial customs, and indeed other aspects of life such as pottery production and agriculture, promises to provide glimpses of the dynamics of social change during the post-Meroitic period.

Figure 12:4   Excavated pyramidal tombs at Arminna West, Cemetery B. Note small chapel on tomb in background (Fuller forthcoming, Pennsylvania Yale Expedition to Egypt 1963).

The terminal Meroitic transition: rephrasing the questions

Conventional accounts of the end of the Meroitic Kingdom have tended to imply passive local communities in receipt of change, while the alternative approach promoted by the Sudanic model of Meroitic society examines local communities as actively engaged with social and political change. This model clearly implies a substantivist view of a socially embedded economics, but I have suggested that it should also include an understanding of the manipulation and creation of material culture and ritual in the context of social relations. While older models of the emergence of the post-Meroitic X-Group by ethnic migration have been criticized (Adams 1977; Trigger 1965, 1982), a model of transformation that addresses local social dynamics has remained elusive. Adams (1977: 413–416) once proffered the alternative theory that linguistically Nubian underclasses threw off the yoke of their Meroitic overlords to establish the post-Meroitic Ballana culture and its Qustul-

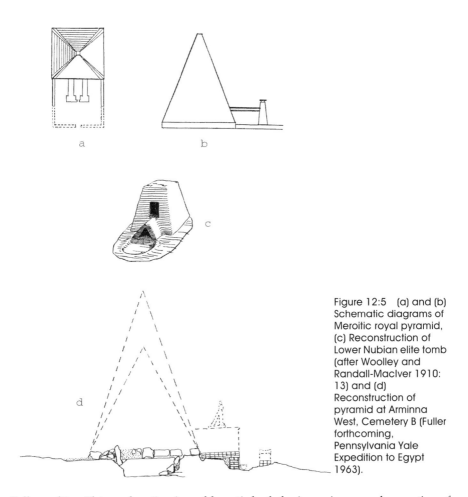

Figure 12:5   (a) and (b) Schematic diagrams of Meroitic royal pyramid, (c) Reconstruction of Lower Nubian elite tomb (after Woolley and Randall-MacIver 1910: 13) and (d) Reconstruction of pyramid at Arminna West, Cemetery B (Fuller forthcoming, Pennsylvania Yale Expedition to Egypt 1963).

Ballana elites. This explanation is problematic both for imposing a modern notion of a class system (which may not be relevant in a Sudanic context, cf. Goody 1976; McIntosh 1999b) and because it replaces the totality of ethnic groups with the totality of classes. These explanations seem to derive from asking questions in terms of what the differences are between the 'Meroitic' culture and 'post-Meroitic' culture and then interpreting these cultural historical abstractions in terms of generalized human groups, whether ethnic groups, states or social classes. Instead we need to ask how individuals and communities drew upon existing practices, beliefs and material culture to perpetuate or change aspects of their social life. Changes in material culture need to be seen in terms of their reflection of the dynamic, and often very local, processes of communication and agency in the past (see theoretical works such as Barrett 1994; Chapman 2000; Dobres 2000; Schiffer and Miller 1999). While Török's (1988, 1997) view on this transition accepts population continuity and social change within Lower Nubia by-and-large, accompanied by an unprovable northward movement of elite who establish themselves at Qustul, an understanding of the

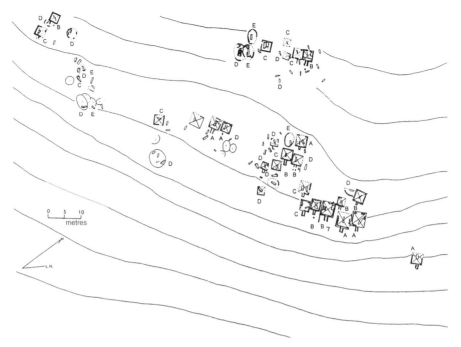

Figure 12:6   Plan of Arminna West, Cemetery B. Note that the tombs group into five clusters, each with a range of superstructure types. Letters near tombs indicate probable period of earliest interments: A = Classic/Late Meroitic (late second century – ca. 240 AD); B = Late Meroitic (ca. 240–300 AD); C = Terminal Meroitic (ca. 300–340? AD); D = Kalabasha Phase post-Meroitic (ca. 330–380 AD); E = Qustul Phase post-Meroitic (ca. 370–420 AD).

transformation in local terms, and in terms of Lower Nubian archaeological evidence, remains to be developed.

    As outlined briefly above, the archaeological record from Arminna suggests local reinterpretation of and innovation within late Meroitic rituals which was probably responding to changed political circumstances. This suggestion for Lower Nubian change should be seen as parallel to the reconsideration of the 'fall' of Meroe, which has conventionally been attributed to an invasion of 'Noba' tribesman followed by conquest by Aksum (e.g. Shinnie 1967; Török 1988, 1997b). As later fourth century tumulus burials from El Hobagi containing some 'royal' grave goods suggest, the fourth century needs to be seen in terms of a transformation of Central Sudanese political power and associated symbolism of burial rites (Edwards 1996b; Lenoble 1999; Lenoble and Sharif 1992). While the terms we use to describe and comprehend this change remain controversial, it is clear that simplistic reference to invasions and the 'fall' of the state is not enough.

    The straight-jacket (or 'state-jacket') of the pharaonic model for Meroitic society fails to makes sense of nuances in the archaeology of Nubia. Indeed Nubia, over many periods, seems to have challenged aspects of our conventional tribe to chiefdom to state typology of social evolution (Fuller 1996; cf. O'Connor 1993). By seeing the Meroitic kingdom as a totality, with causes of change predicated on invasion or collapse, individuals and local communities of ancient Nubia are relegated to passive roles. As argued in general terms by Trigger (1978b), communities are an appropriate scale for archaeological analysis of social processes, and it is at this scale that local social relations can be seen to interact with broader networks of power and shared symbols. As the archaeological evidence from Arminna West attests, particular communities followed their own historical trajectories, responding in unique but not incomprehensible ways to the changing context of power networks and political authority.

Conclusion

The relationships between the cultural traditions of the societies in Meroitic Nubia and those in Egypt were clearly complex, involving different levels of interaction and inspiration. In the broader context of Africa, Nubia certainly served as a corridor of transmission in terms of trade between the Lower Nile (Egypt) and the savannahs beyond the Middle Nile (Central Sudan). Egyptian products, such as ceramics, glass vessels, wine and perhaps some copper vessels, moved south in the Meroitic period while cotton cloth, gold, ivory, tropical hardwoods and fauna moved north. In the long term it also served as a conduit for the diffusion of crops, with sub-Saharan crops like sorghum and cowpea moving north, whereas horses (in the Egyptian New Kingdom) and at much earlier prehistoric periods wheat, barley and other winter crops moved south. Diffusion of articles of this kind, however, even when incorporated into local practices, may carry with them little in terms of cultural understandings, and indeed there is reason to believe that Nubia and Egypt maintained different food traditions over a long period (Edwards Chapter 10, this volume). In the realm of ritual and political culture there was also much inspiration from Egypt in Nubia, but in this case Egyptian symbols and practices were construed in terms of the social behaviours and political intrigues of Nubia. As such, Egyptian iconography and religious motifs ceased to be Egyptian and became Meroitic, and were utilized by elites and communities in Nubia as potent symbols in maintaining and modifying Nubian power relationships. Thus, at the most visual level of Egyptian inspiration in Nubia, such as pyramidal tombs and temple iconography, the 'Egyptian' elements bore Meroitic meanings and in terms of these cultural symbols Nubia served less as a corridor between Egypt and the rest of Africa and more as a rival in generating symbols and practices of legitimation, which in turn would have been available for selective reinterpretation by other societies further south. Thus Nubia must not be seen as passively receiving culture from Egypt, as many older narratives of Egyptian cultural survival in Nubia imply, but rather as actively borrowing and reordering symbols as part of it own distinctive Sudanic system of power. In understanding Nubian society of the past, therefore, we must be wary of interpreting apparently Egyptian symbols in Egyptian terms, and attempt instead to understand the traditional dynamics of Nubia in Nubian terms.

Notes

1   One wonders to what extent the modern Egyptological interest in Kush as a late preserver of Egyptian tradition has been influenced by references in this vein found in Late Period Egyptian literature (such as Manetho) and some classical sources in which deposed Egyptian kings or rebels almost invariably flee south to Nubia (cf. Török 1989: 70).

2   Discussions of the rise of the twenty-fifth Dynasty have often been from a very Egyptocentric viewpoint, with its origins in 19th century colonialism, as discussed at length by Morkot Chapter 11 and Wengrow Chapter 9, both this volume.

Acknowledgments

The author would like to thank David Edwards, David O'Connor, Andrew Reid and Peter Ucko for their useful comments on earlier drafts of this chapter.

References

Note: references to chapters and books in the *Encounters with Ancient Egypt* series are denoted in bold type.

Abungu, G. H. O. 1998, City States of the East African Coast and their Maritime Contacts, in G. E. Connah (ed.), *Transformations in Africa: Essays on Africa's Later Past*, 204–218. Leicester: Leicester UP

Adams, B. 1988, *Predynastic Egypt*. Princes Risborough: Shire

Adams, R. 1993, African-American Studies and the State of the Art, in M. Azevedo (ed.), *Africana Studies: A Survey of Africa and the African Diaspora*, 25–45. Durham, NC: Carolina Academic Press

Adams, W. Y. 1964, Post-Pharaonic Nubia in the Light of Archaeology, 1. *Journal of Egyptian Archaeology* 50, 102–120

Adams, W. Y. 1976, *Meroitic North and South. A Study in Cultural Contrasts*. Berlin: Akademie

Adams, W. Y. 1977, *Nubia Corridor to Africa*. London: Allen Lane

Adams, W. Y. 1981, Ecology and Economy in the Empire of Kush. *Zeitschrift für Ägyptische Sprache und Alterumskunde* 108, 1–11

Adams, W. Y. 1988, The Nile Trade in Post-Pharaonic Times. *Sahara* 1, 21–36

Adams, W. Y. 1994, The Invention of Nubia, in C. Berger, G. Clerc and N. Grimal (eds), *Hommages à Jean Leclant* 2, 17–22. Cairo: Institut Français d'Archéologie Orientale

Adams, W. Y. 1998, The Misappropriation of Nubia. *Sudan Studies* 21, 1–9

Addison, F. 1949, *Jebel Moya. Wellcome Excavations in the Sudan vol. I, 1910–1914*. Oxford: OUP

Akyeampong, E. 1996, *Drink, Power and Cultural Change*. London: James Currey

Al-Bataal, S. 1994, Agricultural Implements in the Northern Sudan, in M. M. M. Ahmed (ed.), *Indigenous Knowledge for Sustainable Development in the Sudan*, 233–309. Khartoum: Khartoum UP

Alexander, J. 1988, The Saharan Divide in the Nile Valley. *African Archaeological Review* 6, 73–90

Allen, J. 1988, *Genesis in Egypt: The Philosophy of Ancient Egyptian Creation Accounts*. New Haven: Yale UP

Amanze, J. J. N. 1994, *Botswana Handbook of Churches*. Gaborone: Pula

Andah, B. W. 1979, Iron Age Beginnings in West Africa: Reflections and Suggestions. *West African Journal of Archaeology* 9, 135–150

Andah, B. W. 1987, Agricultural Beginnings and Early Farming Communities in West and Central Africa. *West African Journal of Archaeology* 17 (Special Book Issue: B. W. Andah and A. I. Okpoko (eds), *Foundations of Civilization in Tropical Africa*), 171–204

Anderson, W. 1992, Badarian Burials: Evidence of Social Inequality in Middle Egypt during the Early Predynastic Era. *Journal of the Archaeological Research Center in Egypt* 29, 51–66

Appiah, K. A. 1993, Europe Upside Down: Fallacies of the New Afrocentrism. *Times Literary Supplement*, 12 February, 24–25

Arens, W. and I. Karp 1989, *Creativity of Power*. Washington, DC: Smithsonian Institution

Argenti, N. 1999, Ephemeral Monuments, Memory and Royal Sempiternity in a Grassfields Kingdom, in A. Forty and S. Küchler (eds), *The Art of Forgetting*, 21–52. Oxford: Berg

Arkell, A. J. 1953, *Shaheinab. An Account of the Excavation of a Neolithic Occupation Site Carried Out for the Sudan Antiquities Service in 1949–50*. Oxford: OUP

Arkell, A. J. 1955, *A History of the Sudan, from the Earliest Times to 1821*. London: Athlone

Arkell, A. J. and P. J. Ucko 1968, Review of Predynastic Development in the Nile Valley. *Current Anthropology* 6, 145–166

Asad, T. (ed.) 1973, *Anthropology and the Colonial Encounter*. London: Ithaca

Asad, T. 1979, Equality in Nomadic Systems? Notes Towards the Dissolution of an Anthropological Category, in *Pastoral Production and Society*. Cambridge: CUP

Asante, M. K. 1992, *Afrocentricity*. Trenton, NJ: Africa World Press

Assmann, J. 1989a, State and Religion in the New Kingdom, in W. K. Simpson (ed.), *Religion and Philosophy in Ancient Egypt*, 55–88. New Haven: Yale UP

Assmann, J. 1989b, *Mâat: L'Egypte pharaonique et l'idée de justice sociale*. Paris: Julliard

Aston, D. A. 1989, Takeloth II – a King of the 'Theban Twenty-third Dynasty'? *Journal of Egyptian Archaeology* 75, 139–153

Aston, D. A. and J. H. Taylor 1990, The Family of Takeloth III and the 'Theban' Twenty-Third Dynasty, in A. Leahy (ed.), *Libya and Egypt c 1300–7550 BC*, 131–154. London: Society for Libyan Studies

Astour, M. 1967, *Hellenosemitica: an Ethnic and Cultural Study in West Semitic Impact on Mycenaean Greece*. Leiden: Brill

Autuori, J. C. 1996, *Egipto y África. Origen de la civilización y la monarquía faraónicas en su contexto Africano*. Barcelona: Editorial Ausa

Autuori, J. C. 1998, Egypt, Africa and the Ancient World, in C. Eyre (ed.), *Proceedings of the Seventh International Congress of Egyptologists, Cambridge, 3–9 September 1995*, 261–272. Leuven: Peeters

Baines, J. 1991, Society, Morality and Religious Practice, in B. Shafer (ed.), *Religion in Ancient Egypt: Gods, Myths and Personal Practice*, 123–200. Ithaca: Cornell UP

Baines, J. 1995, Origins of Egyptian Kingship, in D. O'Connor and D. P. Silverman (eds), *Ancient Egyptian Kingship*, 95–148. Leiden: Brill

Baines, J. 1997, Kingship Before Literature: the World of the King in the Old Kingdom, in R. Gundlach and C. Raedler (eds), *Selbstverständnis und Realität: Akten des symposiums zur ägyptischen königsideologie, Mainz 15–17 Juni 1995*, 125–173. Wiesbaden: Harrassowitz

Baines, J. 1999, Forerunners of Narrative Biographies, in A. Leahy and J. Tait (eds), *Studies on Ancient Egypt in Honour of H. S. Smith*, 23–37. London: Egypt Exploration Society

Baines, J. and N. Yoffee 1998, Order, Legitimacy and Wealth in Ancient Egypt and Mesopotamia, in G. M. Feinman and J. Marcus (eds), *Archaic States*, 199–260. Santa Fe: School of American Research Press

Bard, K. 1987, The Geography of Excavated Predynastic Sites and the Rise of Complex Society. *Journal of the American Research Center in Egypt* 24, 81–93

Bard, K. 1994, *From Farmers to Pharaohs. Mortuary Evidence for the Rise of Complex Society in Egypt*. Sheffield: Sheffield Academic Press

Barndon, R. 1996, Fipa Ironworking and its Technological Style, in P. Schmidt (ed.), *The Culture of African Ironworking*, 58–73. Gainesville: University of Florida Press

Barndon, R. 2001, Masters of Metallurgy – Masters of Metaphor, unpublished PhD thesis, University of Bergen

Barrett, J. C. 1994, *Fragments from Antiquity*. Oxford: Blackwell

Barrow, J. [1801] 1975, *An Account of a Journey to the Booshuanas. A Journey to Cochinchina*. Kuala Lumpur: OUP

Barth, F. 1967, Economic Spheres in Darfur, in R. Firth (ed.), *Themes in Economic Anthropology*, 149–174. London: Tavistock

Barth, F. 1987, *Cosmologies in the Making: a Generative Approach to Cultural Variation in Inner New Guinea*. Cambridge: CUP

Barth, F. 1990, The Guru and the Conjurer: Transactions in Knowledge and Shaping of Culture in S. E. Asia and Melanesia. *Man* 25, 640–653

Barth, H. [1857–1858] 1965, *Travels and Discoveries in North and Central Africa*. London: Frank Cass

Bar-Yosef, O. and A. Khazanov (eds) 1992, *Pastoralism in the Levant. Archaeological Materials in Anthropological Perspectives*. Wisconsin: Prehistory Press

Bates, O. [1912] 1970, *The Eastern Libyans: An Essay*. London: Frank Cass

Battaglia, D. 1990, *On the Bones of the Serpent*. Chicago: University of Chicago Press

Baumann, H. 1955, *Das Doppelte geschlecht*. Berlin: Reimer

Baumgartel, E. 1960, *The Cultures of Prehistoric Egypt II*. Oxford: OUP

Bekaert, S. 1998, Multiple Levels of Meaning and Tension of Consciousness. *Archaeological Dialogues* 5, 6–29

Belier, W. W. 1991, *Decayed Gods: Origin and Development of Georges Dumézil's 'idéologie tripartite'*. Leiden: Brill

Benevensite, E. 1973, *Indo-European Language and Society*. London: Faber

Bennett, B. S. 1997, Suppose a Black Man Tells a Story: the Dialogues of John Mackenzie the Missionary and Sekgoma Kgari the King and Rainmaker, in K. Darkwah (ed.), *That Tremendous Voice: Essays in Honour of Leonard Diniso Ngcongco*, 43–54. Gabarone: University of Botswana

Bennett, B. S. 2001, The Contested History of *Modimo*, unpublished paper presented to the Botswana-Lesotho-Swaziland conference on Theology and Religious Studies, Gaborone

Berlinerblau, J. 1999, *Heresy in the University: The Black Athena Controversy and the Responsibilities of American Intellectuals*. New Brunswick, NJ: Rutgers UP

Bernal, M. 1985, Black Athena: The African and Levantine Roots of Greece. *Journal of African Civilizations* 7, 66–82

Bernal, M. 1987, *Black Athena: the Afroasiatic Roots of Classical Civilization, Volume I. The Fabrication of Ancient Greece, 1785–1985*. London: Free Association Press

Bernal, M. 1991, *Black Athena: the Afroasiatic Roots of Classical Civilization, Volume II. The Documentary and Archeological Evidence*. New Brunswick, NJ: Rutgers UP

Bernal, M. 2001, *Black Athena Writes Back: Martin Bernal Responds to his Critics*. Durham: Duke UP

Bietak, M. 1968, *Studien zur chronologie der Nubischen C-Gruppe*. Vienna: Böhalu in Kommission

Binsbergen, W. van (ed.) 1996/1997. Black Athena: Ten Years After. *Talanta* 38/9

Biobaku, S. O. 1971, *The Origin of the Yoruba*. Lagos: University of Lagos

Blench, R. M. 1993, Recent Developments in African Language Classification, in T. Shaw, P. J. J. Sinclair, B. Andah and A. Okpoko (eds), *The Archaeology of Africa: Food, Metals and Towns*, 126–138. London: Routledge

Blench, R. M. 1995, Is Niger-Congo Simply a Branch of Nilo-Saharan?, in R. Nicolai and F. Rottland (eds), 5th Nilo-Saharan Linguistics Colloquium, Proceedings, *Nilo-Saharan* 10, 83–130. Cologne: Köppe

Blench, R. M. 2000, African Minor Livestock Species, in R. M. Blench and K. C. MacDonald (eds), *The Origins and Domestication of African Livestock: Archaeology, Genetics, Linguistics and Ethnography*, 314–338. London: UCL Press

Bloch, M. 1992, *Prey into Hunter: the Politics of Religious Experience*. Cambridge: CUP

Bonhême, M-A. and A. Forgeau 1988, *Pharaon – les secrets du pouvoir*. Paris: Armand Colin

Bonnet, C. (ed.) 1990, *Kerma, Royaume de Nubie*. Geneva: Museé d'Art et d'Histoire

Bonnet, C. 1999, Les fouilles archéologiques de Kerma (Soudan). *Genava* 47, 47–86

Borchardt, L. 1913, *Das grabdenkmal des königs Sahu-re Band II Die Wandbilder*. Leipzig: J. C. Hinrichs

Boschman, D. R. 1994, *The Conflict between New Religious Movements and the State in the Bechuanaland Protectorate prior to 1949, Studies on the Church in Southern Africa, vol. 3*. Gaborone: University of Botswana

Bourdieu, P. 1977, *Outline of a Theory of Practice* (trans. R. Nice). Cambridge: CUP

Bradley, D. and R. Loftus 2000, Two Eves for Taurus? Bovine Mitochondrial DNA and African Cattle Domestication, in R. M. Blench and K. C. MacDonald (eds), *The Origins and Domestication of African Livestock: Archaeology, Genetics, Linguistics and Ethnography*, 244–250. London: UCL Press

Breasted, J. H. 1905, *A History of Egypt from the Earliest Times to the Persian Conquest*. London: Hodder and Stoughton

Breasted, J. H. 1906–1907, *Ancient Records of Egypt, Historical Documents from the Earliest Times to the Persian Conquest*. Chicago: University of Chicago Press

Breasted, J. H. 1924, *A History of Egypt from the Earliest Times to the Persian Conquest*. 2nd edition, London: Hodder and Stoughton

Breasted, J. H. 2001, *Ancient Records of Egypt, Volume 2, The Eighteenth Dynasty*. Urbana: University of Illinois Press

Bruce, J. 1790, *Travels to Discover the Source of the Nile in the Years 1768, 1769, 1770, 1771, 1772 and 1773*. Edinburgh: Ruthven

Brugsch, H. 1877, *Geschichte Ägypten's unter den Pharaonen: nach den Denkmälern*. Leipzig: J. C. Hinrichs

Brugsch, H. 1879, *A History of Egypt under the Pharaohs Derived Entirely from the Monuments* (trans. H. Danby Seymour, completed and edited by P. Smith). London: John Murray

Brugsch, H. 1891, *Egypt under the Pharaohs. A History Derived Entirely from the Monuments*. 2nd edition, condensed and revised by M. Brodrick, London: John Murray

Brugsch, H. 1902, *Egypt under the Pharaohs: A History Derived Entirely from the Monuments*. 3rd edition, London: John Murray

Brunton, G. 1937, *Mostagedda and the Tasian Culture. British Museum Expeditions to Middle Egypt 1928, 1929*. London: Quaritch

Brunton, G. 1948, *Matmar. British Museum Expeditions to Middle Egypt, 1929–31*. London: Quaritch

Brunton, G. and G. Caton-Thompson 1928, *The Badarian Civilization and Prehistoric Remains Near Badari*. London: Quaritch

Budge, E. A. W. 1907, *The Egyptian Sudan, its History and Monuments*. London: Kegan Paul

Budge, E. A. W. 1911, *Osiris and the Egyptian Resurrection*. London: Philip Lee Warner

Bullard, R. G. 2001, The Berbers of the Maghreb and Ancient Carthage, in E. M. Yamauchi (ed.), *Africa and Africans in Antiquity*, 180–209. East Lansing: Michigan State UP

Burckhardt, J. L. 1822, *Travels in Nubia*. London: J. Murray

Burkert, W. 1984, *Die Orientalisierende epoche in der Griechischen religion und literatur*. Heidelberg: Winter

Burnett, C. 2003, Images of Ancient Egypt in the Latin Middle Ages, in P. J. Ucko and T. C. Champion (eds), *The Wisdom of Ancient Egypt: changing visions through the ages*, 65–100. London: UCL Press

Burton, J. W. 1980, The Village and the Cattle Camp: Aspects of Atuot Religion, in I. Karp and C. S. Bird (eds), *Explorations in African Systems of Thought*, 268–297. Bloomington: Indiana UP

Butzer, K. 1976, *Early Hydraulic Civilization in Egypt: a Study in Cultural Ecology*. Chicago: University of Chicago Press

Cailliaud, F. 1826, *Voyage à Meroé, au fleuve blanc*. Paris: Imprimerie Royale

Campbell, A. 1998, Archaeology in Botswana: Origins and Growth, in P. J. Lane, A. Reid and A. K. Segobye (eds), *Ditswa Mmung: the Archaeology of Botswana*, 24–49. Gaborone: Pula

Caneva, I. 1988, *El Geili. The History of a Middle Nile Environment 7000 BC–AD 1500*, Oxford: British Archaeological Reports

Caneva, I. 1991, Prehistoric Hunters, Herders and Tradesmen in Central Sudan: Data from the Geili Region, in W. V. Davies (ed.), *Egypt and Africa. Nubia from Prehistory to Islam*, 6–15. London: British Museum Press

Caneva, I. and A. Marks. 1990, More on the Shaqadud Pottery: Evidence for Saharo-Nilotic Connections During the 6th–4th Millennium BC. *Archéologie du Nil Moyen* 4, 11–35

Carr, C. J. 1977, *Pastoralism in Crisis. The Dasanetch and their Ethiopian Lands*. Chicago: University of Chicago Press

Carsten, J. and S. Hugh-Jones 1995, *About the House. Lévi-Strauss and Beyond*. Cambridge: CUP

Casalis, E. [1859] 1997, *The Basutos*. Facsimile of London: James Nisbet

Castillos, J. J. 1982, *A Reappraisal of the Published Evidence on Egyptian Predynastic and Early Dynastic Cemeteries*. Toronto: Benben

Cauvin, J. 2000, *The Birth of the Gods and the Origins of Agriculture*. Cambridge: CUP

Celenko, T. (ed.) 1996, *Egypt in Africa*. Indianapolis: Indianapolis Museum of Art

Červíček, P. 1986, *Rock Pictures of Upper Egypt and Nubia*. Naples: Herder-Roma

Chaix, L. and A. Grant 1987, A Study of a Prehistoric Population of Sheep (*Ovis aries* L.) from Kerma (Sudan): Archaeozoological and Archaeological Implications. *Archaeozoologia* 1, 77–92

Chami, F. 1994, *The Tanzanian Coast in the First Millennium AD*. Uppsala: Uppsala University

Champion, T. C. 2003a, Egypt and the Diffusion of Culture, in D. Jeffreys (ed.), *Views of Ancient Egypt since Napoleon Bonaparte: imperialism, colonialism and modern appropriations*, 127–146. London: UCL Press

Champion, T. C. 2003b, Beyond Egyptology: Egypt in 19th and 20th Century Archaeology and Anthropology, in P. J. Ucko and T. C. Champion (eds), *The Wisdom of Egypt: changing visions through the ages*, 167–186. London: UCL Press

Chang, C. and H. A. Koster 1986, Beyond Bones: Towards an Archaeology of Pastoralism. *Advances in Archaeological Method and Theory* 9, 97–148

Chapman, J. 2000, Tension at Funerals: Social Practices and the Subversion of Community Structure in Later Hungarian Prehistory, in M-A. Dobres and J. Robb (eds), *Agency in Archaeology*, 169–195. London: Routledge

Chenal-Vélardé, I. 1997, Les Premiers traces de boeuf domestique en Afrique du Nord. *Archaeozoologia (Grenoble)* 9, 11–40

Chesterton, G. K. 1914, *The Flying Inn*. London: Methuen

Chidester, D. 1996, *Savage Systems: Colonialism and Comparative Religion in Southern Africa*. Charlottesville: University of Virginia Press

Childe, V. G. 1936, *Man Makes Himself*. London: Watts

Childs, S. T. 1991, Technology, Styles and Ironsmelting Furnaces in Bantu speaking Africa. *Journal of Anthropological Archaeology* 10, 332–359

Childs, S. T. and W. J. Dewey 1996, Forging Symbolic Meaning in Zaire and Zimbabwe, in P. Schmidt (ed.), *The Culture and Technology of African Iron Production*, 145–171. Gainesville: University of Florida Press

Chlodnicki, M. 1984, Pottery from the Neolithic Settlement at Kadero (Central Sudan), in L. Krzyzaniak and M. Kobusiewicz (eds), *Origin and Early Development of Food-Producing Cultures in North-Eastern Africa*, 337–343. Poznan: Archaeological Museum

Cialowicz, K. M. 1987, *Les Têtes massues des Périodes Prédynastique et Archaïque dans la Vallée du Nil*. Warsaw: Nakladem Uniwersytetu Jagiellonskiego

Clark, J. D. 1962, Africa, South of the Sahara, in R. Braidwood and G. Willey (eds), *Courses towards Urban Life*, 1–33. New York: Wenner Gren Foundation

Clark, J. D. 1971, A Re-examination of the Evidence for Agricultural Origins in the Nile Valley. *Proceedings of the Prehistoric Society* 37, 34–79

Clark, J. D. 1976, Prehistoric Populations and Pressures Favoring Plant Domestication in Africa, in J. R. Harlan, J. M. J. De Wet and A. B. L. Stemler (eds), *Origins of African Plant Domestication*, 67–105. The Hague: Mouton

Clegg, A. 1986, Some Aspects of Tswana Cosmology. *Botswana Notes and Records* 18, 33–37

Cline, E. H. and D. O'Connor 2003, The Mystery of the 'Sea Peoples', in D. O'Connor and S. Quirke (eds), *Mysterious Lands*, 107–138. London: UCL Press

Close, A. 1995, Few and Far Between: Early Ceramics in North Africa, in W. K. Barnett and J. W. Hoopes (eds), *The Emergence of Pottery: Technology and Innovation in Ancient Societies*, 23–37. Washington, DC: Smithsonian Institution

Cohen, D. W. and E. S. A. Odhiambo 1992, *Burying SM: the Politics of Knowledge and the Sociology of Power in Africa*. London: James Currey

Cole, S. 1964, *The Prehistory of East Africa*. London: Weidenfeld and Nicolson

Collett, D. 1993, Metaphors and Representation Associated with Precolonial Iron-Smelting in East and South Africa, in T. Shaw, P. J. J. Sinclair, B. Andah and A. Okpoko (eds), *The Archaeology of Africa: Food, Metals and Towns*, 499–511. London: Routledge

Collingwood, R. G. 1946, *The Idea of History*. Oxford: Clarendon

Collins, R. O. 2000, Malakal Revisited. Britain in the Southern Sudan After Fifty Years, paper given at the 5th Triennial Meeting of the International Sudan Studies Association, 30 August–1 September 2000, University of Durham

Comaroff, J. and J. Comaroff 1992, *Ethnography and the Historical Imagination*. Boulder: Westview

Connah, G. E. 1987, *African Civilizations: Precolonial Cities and States in Tropical Africa: an Archaeological Perspective*. Cambridge: CUP

Connah, G. E. (ed.) 1998, *Transformations in Africa*. Leicester: Leicester UP

Cornell, T. J. 1995, *The Beginnings of Rome: Italy and Rome from the Bronze Age to the Punic Wars (c.1000–264 BC)*. London: Routledge

Crabtree, W. A. 1921, Zulu Origins. *Bantu Studies* 1, 25–29

Crawford, O. G. S. 1948, People Without a History. *Antiquity* 22, 8–12

Cribb, R. 1991, *Nomads in Archaeology*. Cambridge: CUP

Crowder, M. 1973, *Revolt in Bussa: A Study of British 'Native Administration' in Nigerian Borgu, 1902–1935*. London: Faber and Faber

David, N, J. Sterner and K. Gavua 1988, Why Pots are Decorated. *Current Anthropology* 23, 365–389

Davidson, B. 1977, *A History of West Africa 1000–1800*, London: Longman

Davies, N. de G. 1926, *The Tomb of Huy*. London: Egypt Exploration Society

Davies, N. de G. 1943, *The Tomb of Rekh-mi-re at Thebes*. New York: Arno

Davies, W. V. (ed.) 1991, *Egypt and Africa: Nubia from Prehistory to Islam*. London: British Museum Press

de Heusch, L. 1980, Heat, Physiology and Cosmogony: *Rites de Passage* amongst the Tonga, in I. Karp and C. S. Bird (eds), *Explorations in African Systems of Thought*, 27–43. Washington, DC: Smithsonian Institution

de Heusch, L. 1982, *The Drunken King: or The Origin of the State* (trans. R. Willis). Bloomington: Indiana UP

de Heusch, L. 1985, *Sacrifice in Africa: A Structuralist Approach*. Manchester: Manchester UP

de Maret, P. and G. Thiry 1996, How Old is the Iron Age in Central Africa?, in P. R. Schmidt (ed.), *The Culture and Technology of African Iron Production*, 29–39. Gainesville: University of Florida Press

Delafosse, M. 1900, Sur les Traces probables de civilization Egyptienne et d'hommes de race blanche à la Cote d'Ivoire. *l'Anthropologie* 11, 431–451, 543–568, 677–690

Denham, D. and H. Clapperton 1826, *Narrative of Travels and Discoveries in Northern and Central Africa, in the Years 1822, 1823 and 1824*. London: John Murray

Derry, D. E. 1956, The Dynastic Race in Egypt. *Journal of Egyptian Archaeology* 42, 80–85

Desmedt, C. 1991, Poteries anciennes décorées à la roulette dans le région des Grands Lacs. *African Archaeological Review* 9, 161–196

Devisch, R. 1993, *Weaving the Threads of life: the Khita Gyn-eco-logical Healing Cult among the Yaka.* Chicago: University of Chicago Press

Devisse, J. 1981, Annex to Chapter 1: Report of the Symposium on 'The Peopling of Ancient Egypt and the Deciphering of the Meroitic Script', Cairo, 28 January–3 February 1974, in G. Mokhtar (ed.), *UNESCO General History of Africa Volume II*, 58–82. California: Heinemann

Diagne, P. 1981, History and Linguistics, in J. Ki-Zerbo (ed.), *UNESCO General History of Africa Volume 1*, 233–260. California: Heinemann

Dieterlen, G. and D. Sylla 1992, *L'Empire de Ghana: le Wagadou et les traditions de Yéréré.* Paris: Karthala

Dietler, M. 1990, Driven by Drink: the Role of Drinking in the Political Economy and the Case of Early Iron Age France. *Journal of Anthropological Archaeology* 9, 352–406

Dietler, M. 1996, Feasts and Commensal Politics in the Political Economy, in P. Wiessner and W. Schiefenhövel (eds), *Food and the Status Quest*, 87–125. Oxford: Berghahn

Dietler, M. and B. Hayden 2001, *Feasts: Archaeological and Ethnographic Perspectives on Food, Politics and Power.* Washington, DC: Smithsonian Institution

Diop, Cheikh A. 1955, *Nations nègres et culture.* Paris: Présence Africaine

Diop, Cheikh A. 1960, *l'Afrique noire précolonial.* Paris: Présence Africaine

Diop, Cheikh A. 1967, *Antériorité des civilisations nègres.* Paris: Présence Africaine

Diop, Cheikh A. 1974, *The African Origin of Civilization: Myth or Reality* (trans. Mercer Cook). Westport, CT: Lawrence Hill & Co

Diop, Cheikh A. 1981, Origin of the Ancient Egyptians, in G. Mokhtar (ed.), *UNESCO General History of Africa Volume II*, 27–57. California: Heinemann

Diop, Cheikh A. 1987, *Precolonial Black Africa* (trans. Harold Salemson). Brooklyn, NY: Lawrence Hill

Diop, Cheikh A. 1991, *Civilization or Barbarism: an Authentic Anthropology* (trans. Yaa-Lengi Meema Ngemi). Brooklyn, NY: Lawrence Hill

Dirar, H. A. 1993, *The Indigenous Fermented Foods of the Sudan: a Study in African Food and Nutrition.* Wallingford: CAB International

Dirar, H. A. 1994, Indigenous Fermented Foods and Beverages of Rural Areas of the Sudan, in M. M. M. Ahmed (ed.), *Indigenous Knowledge for Sustainable Development in the Sudan*, 43–80. Khartoum: Khartoum UP

Dixon, D. M. 1964, The Origin of the Kingdom of Kush (Napata-Meroe). *Journal of Egyptian Archaeology* 50, 121–132

Dobres, M-A. 2000, *Technology and Social Agency.* Oxford: Blackwell

Douglas, M. (ed.) 1987, *Constructive Drinking: Perspectives on Drink from Anthropology.* Cambridge: CUP

Douglas, M. and B. Isherwood 1979, *The World of Goods: Towards an Anthropology of Consumption.* London: Allen Lane

Drake, St C. 1987, *Black Folk Here and There: An Essay in History and Anthropology.* Los Angeles: University of California

Drioton, É. 1962, *Les Peuples de l'Orient Méditerranéen II. L'Égypte.* 4th edition, expanded and revised by J. Vandier. Paris: Presses Universitaires de France

Du Toit, A. 1983, No Chosen People: the Myth of the Calvinist Origins of Afrikaner Nationalism and Racial Ideology. *American Historical Review* 88, 920–952

Dubois, F. 1897, *Timbuctoo the Mysterious* (trans. D. White). London: Heinemann

Dubois, W. E. B. 1975, *The Negro.* New York: Kraus-Thompson

Dubois, W. E. B. 1976, *The World and Africa.* New York: Kraus-Thompson

Dumézil, G. 1941–1945. *Jupiter Mars Quirinus*. Turin: Einaudi

Dumézil, G. 1949, *L'Heritage Indo-Européen*. Paris: Gallimard

Dumézil, G. 1968, *Mythe et épopée*. Paris: Gallimard

Dunham, D. 1947, Outline of the Ancient History of the Sudan, Part V. *Sudan Notes and Records* 28, 1–10

Dunham, D. 1955, *Royal Cemeteries of Kush. Vol. I. El Kurru*. Cambridge, Mass: Museum of Fine Arts

Dupuis, C. F. [1795] 1822, *Origine de tous les cultes, ou la religion universelle*. Paris: Babeuf

Earle, T. (ed.) 1991, *Chiefdoms: Power, Economy, and Ideology*. Cambridge: CUP

Earle, T. 1994, Political Domination and Social Evolution, in T. Ingold (ed.), *Companion Encyclopedia of Anthropology. Humanity, Culture and Social Life*, 940–961. London: Routledge

Earle, T. 1997, *How Chiefs Come to Power*. Stanford: Stanford UP

Edwards, D. N. 1996a, Power and the State in the Middle Nile: An Example for the Study of State Development in Sudanic Africa. *Archaeological Review from Cambridge* 13, 5–20

Edwards, D. N. 1996b, *The Archaeology of the Meroitic State: New Perspectives on its Social and Political Organization*. Oxford: Tempus Repartum

Edwards, D. N. 1998a, Meroe and the Sudanic Kingdoms. *Journal of African History* 39, 175–193

Edwards, D. N. 1998b, *Gabati. A Meroitic, Post-Meroitic and Medieval Cemetery in Central Sudan, Volume I*. London: Sudan Archaeological Research Society

Edwards, D. N. 1999, *Musawwarat es Sufra III. A Meroitic Pottery Workshop at Musawwarat es Sufra*. Wiesbaden: Harrassowitz

Edwards, D. N. and D. Q. Fuller 2000, Notes on the Meroitic "Epistolary" Tradition: New Texts from Arminna West and Qasr Ibrim. *Meroitic Newsletter, Bulletin d'Informations Méroitiques* 27, 77–98

Edwards, I. E. S. 1961, *The Pyramids of Egypt*. London: Parrish

Ehret, C. 1982, Population Movement and Culture Contact in the Southern Sudan c. 3000 BC to AD 1000: a Preliminary Linguistic Overview, in J. Mack and P. Robertshaw (eds), *Culture History in the Sudan: Archaeology, Linguistics and Ethnohistory*, 19–48. Nairobi: British Institute in Eastern Africa

Eiselen, W. M. and I. Schapera 1937, Religious Beliefs and Practices, in I. Schapera (ed.), *The Bantu-Speaking Tribes of South Africa: an Ethnographical Survey*, 247–270. London: Routledge

Ellenberger, D. F. [1912] 1997, *History of the Basuto: Ancient and Modern*. Morija: Morija Museum and Archives

El-Medani, K. A. 1994, Some Aspects of Indigenous Farming Knowledge in the Blue Nile Area: the Case of Abu Gumi Village, in M. M. M. Ahmed (ed.), *Indigenous Farming Systems, Knowledge and Practices in the Sudan*, 95–135. Khartoum: Khartoum UP

Emery, W. B. 1965, *Egypt in Nubia*. London: Hutchinson

Evans-Pritchard, E. E. 1937, *Witchcraft, Oracles and Magic among the Azande*. Oxford: OUP

Evans-Pritchard, E. E. 1940, *The Nuer. A Description of Modes of Livelihood and Political Institutions of a Nilotic People*. Oxford: Clarendon

Evans-Pritchard, E. E. 1956, *Nuer Religion*. Oxford: OUP

Exchoffier, L., B. Fellegrini, A. Sanchez-Mazas, C. Simon and A. Langaney 1987, Genetics and History of Sub-Saharan Africa. *Yearbook of Physical Anthropology* 30, 151–194

Fairman, H. W. 1965, Ancient Egypt and Africa. *African Affairs* (Special Issue), 69–75

Fairservis, W. 1989, Cattle and Archaic Egypt. *The Review of Archaeology* 10, 5–9

Farb, P. and G. Armelagos 1980, *Consuming Passions: the Anthropology of Eating*. Boston, Mass: Houghton Mifflin

Fattovich, R. 1991, At the Periphery of the Empire: the Gash Delta (Eastern Sudan), in V. Davies (ed.), *Egypt and Africa: Nubia from Prehistory to Islam*. London: British Museum Press

Fauvelle-Aymar, F-X., J. P. Chrétien and C-H. Perrot 2000, *Afrocentrisme: l'histoire des Africains entre Egypte et Amérique*. Paris: Editions Karthala

Finkelstein, I. 1995, *Living on the Fringe: the Archaeology and History of the Negev, Sinai and Neighbouring Regions in the Bronze and Iron Ages*. Sheffield: Sheffield Academic Press

Fisher, C. 1917, The Eckley B. Coxe Jr. Expedition. *The Museum Journal* (Philadelphia) 8, 211–237

Frankfort, H. 1932, Modern Survivors from Punt, in S. R. Glanville (ed.), *Studies Presented to F. Ll. Griffith*, 445–453. London: Egypt Exploration Society

Frankfort, H. 1948, Mesopotamia, in H. Frankfort, *Kingship and the Gods: A Study of Ancient Near Eastern Religion as the Integration of Society and Nature, Book II*, 215–336. Chicago: University of Chicago Press

Frankfort, H. 1950, The African Foundation of Ancient Egyptian Civilization, in *Atti del 1 Congresso Internazionale di Preistoria e Protostoria Mediterranea*, 115–117. Florence: L. S. Olschki

Frankfort, H. 1951, *The Birth of Civilization in the Near East*. Bloomington: Indiana UP

Frazer, J. G. 1914, *The Golden Bough. Part IV. Adonis Attis Osiris*. London: Macmillan

Friedman, R. 2001, Excavating in the Nubian Cemeteries. *Nekhen News* 13, 22–26

Frobenius, L. 1898, *Der Ursprung der Afrikanischen kultur*. Berlin: Reimer

Frobenius, L. 1913, *The Voice of Africa vol. 1*. London: Hutchinson

Frobenius, L. 1931, *Erythraa: länder und zeiten des hiligen königsmordes*. Berlin: Atlantis

Fuller, D. Q. 1996, Chiefdom, State or Checklist? A Review Article. Review of O'Connor 1993, *Archaeological Review from Cambridge* 13, 113–122

Fuller, D. Q. 1997, The Confluence of History and Archaeology in Lower Nubia: Scales of Continuity and Change. *Archaeological Review from Cambridge* 14, 105–128

Fuller, D. Q. 1999, A Parochial Perspective on the End of Meroe: Changes in Cemetery and Settlement at Arminna West, in D. A. Welsby (ed.), *Recent Research in Kushite History and Archaeology. Proceedings of the 8th International Conference for Meroitic Studies*, 203–217. London: British Museum Press

Fuller, D. Q. forthcoming, *Arminna West: The Late Nubian Necropolis and Buildings Excavated 1963*, Philadelphia: University Museum

Galaty, J. G. and P. Bonte 1991, *Herders, Warriors, and Traders: Pastoralism in Africa*. Boulder: Westview

Galaty, J. G. and P. C. Salzmann (eds) 1981, *Change and Development in Nomadic and Pastoral Societies*. Leiden: Brill

Gardiner, A. H. 1957, *Egyptian Grammar: being an Introduction to the Study of Hieroglyphs*. 3rd edition, Oxford: Griffith Institute/Ashmolean Museum

Gardiner, A. H. 1961, *Egypt of the Pharaohs: An Introduction*. Oxford: Clarendon

Garlake, P. 1982, Prehistory and Ideology in Zimbabwe. *Africa* 52, 1–19

Gautier, A. 1987, Prehistoric Men and Cattle in North Africa: A Dearth of Data and a Surfeit of Models, in A. E. Close (ed.), *Prehistory of Arid North Africa: Essays in Honour of Fred Wendorf*, 163–187. Dallas: Southern Methodist UP

Gell, A. 1995, On Coote's "Marvels of Everyday Vision". *Social Analysis* 38, 18–31

Gerharz, R. 1994, *Jebel Moya*. Berlin: Akademie

Geus, F. 1984, *Rescuing Sudan Ancient Cultures*. Khartoum: National Museums of the Sudan

Geus, F. 1986, Des Tombes contemporaines du Néolithique de Khartoum à el Ghaba (Taragma), in M. Krause (ed.), *Nubische studien. Tagungsakten der 5. Internationalen Konferenz der International Society for Nubian Studies, Heidelberg*, 22–25, 67–70. Mainz am Rhein: von Zabern

Geus, F. 1991, Burial Customs in the Upper Main Nile: an Overview, in W. V. Davies (ed.), *Egypt and Africa: Nubia from Prehistory to Islam*, 57–73. London: British Museum Press

Gifford, D. 1978, Ethnoarchaeological Observations of Natural Processes Affecting Cultural Materials, in R. A. Gould (ed.), *Explorations in Ethnoarchaeology*, 77–102. Albuquerque: University of New Mexico Press

Gill, S. J. 1993, *A Short History of Lesotho: from the Late Stone Age until the 1993 Elections*. Morija: Morija Museum and Archives

Girard, R. 1977, *Sacred Violence*. Chicago: University of Chicago Press

Goody, J. 1971, *Technology, Tradition and the State in Africa*. Oxford: OUP

Goody, J. 1976, *Production and Reproduction*. Cambridge: CUP

Goody, J. 1982, *Cooking, Cuisine and Class: a Study in Comparative Sociology*. Cambridge: CUP

Gosden, C. and J. Hather (eds) 1999, *The Prehistory of Food: Appetites for Change*. London: Routledge

Grébenart, D. 1988, *Les Premiers métallurgistes en Afrique Occidentale*. Paris: Editions Errance

Greenberg, J. H. 1955, *Studies in African Linguistic Classification*. New Haven: Compass

Grégoire, H. B. [1810] 1997, *An Enquiry Concerning the Intellectual and Moral Faculties, and Literature of Negroes* (trans. D. B. Warden). New York: M. E. Sharpe

Gregory, C. A. 1982, *Gifts and Commodities*. London: Academic Press

Griffith, F. L. 1911, *Karanog: The Meroitic Inscriptions of Shablul and Karanog*. Philadelphia: University Museum

Griffith, F. L. 1912, *Meroitic Inscriptions II*. London: Egyptian Exploration Society

Grigson, C. 2000, *Bos Africanus* (Brehm)? Notes on the Archaeozoology of the Native Cattle of Africa, in R. M. Blench and K. C. MacDonald (eds), *The Origins and Development of African Livestock: Archaeology, Genetics, Linguistics and Ethnography*, 38–60. London: UCL Press

Grove, A. 1993, Africa's Climate in the Holocene, in T. Shaw, P. J. J. Sinclair, B. Andah and A. Okpoko (eds), *The Archaeology of Africa: Food, Metals and Towns*, 32–42. London: Routledge

Guyer, J. I. 1995, Wealth in People, Wealth in Things – Introduction. *Journal of African History* 36, 83–90

Guyer, J. I. and S. M. Eno Belinga 1995, Wealth in People as Wealth in Knowledge: Accumulation and Composition in Equatorial Africa. *Journal of African History* 36, 91–120

Haaland, G. 1998, Beer Blood and Mother's Milk: the Symbolic Context of Economic Behaviour in Fur Society. *Sudan Notes and Records* 2, 53–76

Haaland, R. 1987, *Socio-Economic Differentiation in the Neolithic Sudan*. Oxford: British Archaeological Reports

Haaland, R. 1995, Sedentism, Cultivation, and Plant Domestication in the Holocene Middle Nile Region. *Journal of Field Archaeology* 22, 157–173

Hall, H. R. 1925, The Ethiopians and Assyrians in Egypt. *Cambridge Ancient History* III, 270–288. Cambridge: CUP

Hall, M. 1990, 'Hidden History': Iron Age Archaeology in Southern Africa, in P. T. Robertshaw (ed.), *A History of African Archaeology*, 59–77. London: James Currey

Hall, M. 1995, Great Zimbabwe and the Lost City, in P. J. Ucko (ed.), *Theory in Archaeology: a World Perspective*, 167–182. London: Routledge

Hall, R. N. 1905, *Great Zimbabwe*. London: Methuen

Hamill, J. and P. Mollier 2003, Rebuilding the Sanctuaries of Memphis: Egypt in Masonic Iconography and Architecture, in J-M. Humbert and C. A. Price (eds), *Imhotep Today: Egyptianizing architecture*, 207–220. London: UCL Press

Harlan, J. R. 1989, Wild-Grass Seed Harvesting in the Sahara and Sub-Sahara of Africa, in D. R. Harris and G. C. Hillman (eds), *Foraging and Farming: the Evolution of Plant Exploitation*, 79–98. London: Unwin Hyman

Harlan, J. R. 1993, The Tropical African Cereals, in T. Shaw, P. J. J. Sinclair, B. Andah and A. Okpoko (eds), *The Archaeology of Africa: Food, Metals and Towns*, 53–60. London: Routledge

Harris, M. 1968, *The Rise of Anthropological Theory: a History of Theories of Culture*. New York: HarperCollins

Harrison, T. 2003, Upside Down and Back to Front: Herodotus and the Greek Encounter with Egypt, in R. Matthews and C. Roemer (eds), *Ancient Perspectives on Egypt*, 145–156. London: UCL Press

Hartog, F. 1988, *The Mirror of Herodotus. The Representation of the Other in the Writing of History* (trans. J. Lloyd). Berkeley: University of California Press

Hassan, F. A. 1981, Historical Nile Floods and their Implications for Climatic Change. *Science* 212, 1,142–1,145

Hassan, F. A. 1988, The Predynastic of Egypt. *Journal of World Prehistory* 2, 136–185

Hastings, A. 1979, *A History of African Christianity 1950–1975*. Cambridge: CUP

Hastings, A. 1996, *The Church in Africa, 1450–1950*. Oxford: Clarendon

Hastings, L. 1947, *Dragons are Extra*. Harmondsworth: Penguin

Hatch, J. 1970, *Nigeria: The Seeds of Disaster*. Chicago: Henry Regnery

Haycock, B. 1976, Comment, in W. Y. Adams, *Meroitic North and South: A Study in Cultural Contrasts*. Berlin: Akademie

Hayward, L. 1990, The Origin of the Raw Elephant Ivory Used in Greece and the Aegean During the Late Bronze Age. *Antiquity* 64, 103–109

Heidorn, L. 1994, Historical Implications of the Pottery from the Earliest Tombs at el Kurru. *Journal of the American Research Center in Egypt* 31, 115–131

Helck, W. 1954, *Untersuchungen zu den beamtentiteln des Ägyptischen alten reiches*. Glückstadt: Augustin

Hendrickx, S. and B. Midant-Reynes 1988, Preliminary Report on the Predynastic Living Site Maghara 2 (Upper Egypt). *Orientalia Lovaniensia Periodica* 19, 5–16

Hendrickx, S. and P. Vermeersch 2000, Prehistory: from the Palaeolithic to the Badarian Culture, in I. Shaw (ed.), *The Oxford History of Ancient Egypt*, 17–44. Oxford: OUP

Herbert, E. W. 1984, *Red Gold of Africa*. Madison: University of Wisconsin Press

Herbert, E. W. 1993, *Iron, Gender and Power: Rituals of Transformation in African Societies*. Bloomington: Indiana UP

Heritier, F. 1981, *L'Exercice de la parenté*. Paris: Gallimard

Herskovits, M. 1926, The Cattle Complex in East Africa. *American Anthropologist* 28, 230–272

Hintze, H. (ed.) 1978, *Africa in Antiquity, I. The Essays*. New York: Brooklyn Museum

Hochschild, A. 1998, *King Leopold's Ghost*. Boston, Mass: Houghton Mifflin

Hodder, I. 1982, *Symbols in Action*. Cambridge: CUP

Hodder, I. 1990, *The Domestication of Europe*. Oxford: Blackwell

Hodges, G. R. 1997, Introduction, in H. B. Grégoire, *An Enquiry Concerning the Intellectual and Moral Faculties, and Literature of Negroes* (trans. D. B. Warden (1810)), ix–xxii. New York: M. E. Sharpe

Hoffman, M. A. 1979, *Egypt before the Pharaohs. The Prehistoric Foundations of Egyptian Civilization*. New York: Knopf

Hölbl, G. 2001, *A History of the Ptolemaic Empire* (trans. T. Saavedra). London: Routledge

Hole, F. 1978, Pastoral Nomadism in Western Iran, in R. A. Gould (ed.), *Explorations in Ethnoarchaeology,* 127–168. Albuquerque: University of New Mexico Press

Holmes, D. and R. Friedman 1994, Survey and Test Excavations in the Badari Region, Egypt. *Proceedings of the Prehistoric Society* 60, 105–142

Holmes, G. 1914, Areas of American Indian Culture Characterisation. *American Anthropologist* 16, 413–416

Hölscher, W. 1937, *Libyer und Ägypter: beiträge zur ethnologie und geschicte libyscher völkerschaften nach den altägyptischen quellen.* Glückstadt: Augustin

Holy, L. 1974, *Neighbours and Kinsmen: A Study of the Berti People of Darfur.* London: C. Hurst

Horowitz, M. 1967, A Reconsideration of the Eastern Sudan. *Cahiers d'Études* 7, 381–398

Hoskins G. A. 1835, *Travels in Ethiopia: Above the Second Cataract of the Nile.* London: Longman

Howe, S. 1998, *Afrocentrism: Mythical Past and Imagined Homes.* London: Verso

Huard, P. and L. Allard-Huard. 1980, Limite Occidentale des influences culturelles transmises au Sahara Nigéro-Tchadien par le groupe C de Nubie. *Bulletin de l'Institut Français d'Archéologie Orientale du Caire,* 671–692

Hurreiz, S. H. and H. Bell 1975, *Directions in Sudanese Linguistics and Folklore.* Khartoum: Khartoum UP

Iliffe, J. 1995, *Africans: the History of a Continent.* Cambridge: CUP

Insoll, T. 1996, *Islam, Archaeology and History: Gao Region (Mali) ca. AD 900–1250.* Oxford: British Archaeological Reports

Iten, O. 1979, *Economic Pressures on Traditional Society.* Bern: Peter Lang

Jackson, A. 1999, *Botswana 1939–1945: an African Country at War.* Oxford: Clarendon

James, P. J., I. J. Thorpe, N. Kokkinos, R. Morkot and J. Frankish 1991a, *Centuries of Darkness.* London: Jonathan Cape

James, P. J., I. J. Thorpe, N. Kokkinos, R. Morkot and J. Frankish 1991b, Review Feature: Centuries of Darkness. *Cambridge Archaeological Journal* 1, 227–253

James, P. J., I. J. Thorpe, N. Kokkinos, R. Morkot and J. Frankish 1992, Centuries of Darkness: a Reply to Critics. *Cambridge Archaeological Journal* 2, 127–144

James, W. 1971, Beer, Morality and Social Relations Among the Uduk. *Sudan Society* 5, 17–27

James, W. and N. J. Allen (eds) 1998, *Marcel Mauss. A Centenary Tribute.* New York: Berghahn

Jeal, T. 1985, *Livingstone.* London: Pimlico

Jedrej, M. C. 1995, *Ingessana. The Religious Institutions of a People of the Sudan Ethiopian Borderland.* Leiden: Brill

Jeffreys, D. (ed.) 2003a, *Views of Ancient Egypt since Napoleon Bonaparte: imperialism, colonialism and modern appropriations.* London: UCL Press

Jeffreys, D. 2003b, Introduction – Two Hundred Years of Ancient Egypt: Modern History and Ancient Archaeology, in D. Jeffreys (ed.), *Views of Ancient Egypt since Napoleon Bonaparte: imperialism, colonialism and modern appropriations,* 1–18. London: UCL Press

Johnson, D. 1990, Fixed Shrines and Spiritual Centres in the Upper Nile. *Azania* 25, 41–58

Johnson, D. 1994, *Nuer Prophets: A History of Prophecy from the Upper Nile in the 19th and 20th Centuries.* Oxford: Clarendon

Johnson, S. 1921, *The History of the Yorubas.* Lagos: Christian Missionary Society (Nigeria) Bookshops

Johnston, H. H. 1902, *The Uganda Protectorate.* London: Hutchinson

Jones, R. 1998, The Ethnic Groups of Present Day Borgu, in E. Bossen, C. Hardung and R. Kuba (eds), *Regards sur le Borgou: pouvoir et altérité dans une région Ouest-Africaine*, 71–89. Paris: L'Harmattan

Junker, H. 1920, *Bericht über die grabungen der Akademie der Wissenschaften in Wien auf den Friedhöfeu von El Kubanieh, Winter 1910–1911.* Vienna: Holder-Pickler-Tempsley

Keenan, G. H. 2002, The Lesser Gods of the Sahara. *Public Archaeology* 2, 131–150

Kees, H. 1953, *Das Priestertum im Ägyptischen staat vom neuen reich bis zur spätzeit.* Leiden: Brill

Kemp, B. J. 1977, The Early Development of Towns in Egypt. *Antiquity* 51, 185–200

Kemp, B. J. 1983, Old Kingdom, Middle Kingdom and Second Intermediate Period c. 2686–1552 BC, in B. Trigger, B. Kemp, D. O'Connor and A. Lloyd, *Ancient Egypt: A Social History*, 71–182. Cambridge: CUP

Kemp, B. J. 1989, *Ancient Egypt. Anatomy of a Civilization.* London: Routledge

Kendall, T. 1982, *Kush: Lost Kingdom of the Nile.* Brockton, Mass: Fuller Museum

Kendall, T. 1989, Ethnoarchaeology in Meroitic Studies, in S. Donadoni and S. Wenig (eds), *Studia Meroitica 1984*, 625–745. Berlin: Akademie

Kendall, T. 1999, The Origin of the Napatan State: El Kurru and the Evidence for the Royal Ancestors, in S. Wenig (ed.), *Studien zum antiken Sudan Meroitica*, 3–117. Berlin: Harrassowitz

Khazanov, A. 1984, *Nomads and the Outside World.* Cambridge: CUP

King, M. and E. King 1992, *The Story of Medicine and Diseases in Malawi: the 130 Years since Livingstone.* Blantyre: Montfort

Kirwan, L. P. 1960, The Decline and Fall of Meroe. *Kush* 8, 163–173

Kitchen, K. A. 1971, Punt and How to Get There. *Orientalia* 40, 184–207

Kitchen, K. A. 1973, *The Third Intermediate Period in Egypt (1100–650 BC).* Warminster: Aris and Phillips

Kitchen, K. A. 1993, The Land of Punt, in T. Shaw, P. J. J. Sinclair, B. Andah and A. Okpoko (eds), *The Archaeology of Africa: Food, Metals and Towns*, 587–607. London: Routledge

Kleppe, E. J. 1982, The Debbas on the White Nile, Southern Sudan, in J. Mack and P. Robertshaw (eds), *Culture History in the Southern Sudan: Archaeology, Linguistics and Ethnohistory*, 59–70. Nairobi: British Institute in Eastern Africa

Kleppe, E. J. 1986, The Prehistory of Southern Sudan. Approaches made before 1950, in M. Krause (ed.), *Nubische Studien*, 113–121. Mainz am Rhein: von Zabern

Kluckhohn, C. 1936, Some Reflections on the Method and Theory of the Kulturkreislehre. *American Anthropologist* 38, 157–196

Klumpp, D. and C. Kratz 1993, Aesthetics, Expertise, and Ethnicity: Okiek and Maasai Perspectives on Personal Ornament, in T. Spear and R. Waller (eds), *Being Maasai: Ethnicity and Identity*, 195–222. London: James Currey

Kollmann, P. 1899, *The Victoria Nyanza.* London: Swan Sonnenschein

Koponen, J. 1988, *People and Production in Late Precolonial Tanzania.* Uppsala: Scandinavian Institute of African Studies

Kopytoff, I. (ed.) 1987, *The African Frontier: the Reproduction of Traditional African Societies.* Bloomington: Indiana UP

Kronenberg, A. 1959, Some Notes on the Religion of the Nyimang. *Kush* 7, 197–213

Krzyzaniak, L. 1977, *Early Farming Cultures on the Lower Nile. The Predynastic Period in Egypt.* Warsaw: Centre d'Archéologie Méditerranéenne de l'Académie Polanaise des Sciences

Krzyzaniak, L. 1991, Early Farming in the Middle Nile Basin: Recent Discoveries at Kadero (Central Sudan). *Antiquity* 65, 515–532

Kuper, A. 1979, Regional Comparison in African Anthropology. *African Affairs* 78, 103–113

Kuper, A. 1982, *Wives for Cattle: Bridewealth and Marriage in Southern Africa*. London: Routledge

Kusimba, C. M. 1999, *The Rise and Fall of Swahili States*. Walnut Creek: AltaMira

Leach, E. 1990, Aryan Invasions over Four Millennia, in E. Ohnuki-Tierney (ed.), *Culture Through Time*, 227–245. Stanford: Stanford UP

Leahy, A. 1985, The Libyan Period in Egypt: An Essay in Interpretation. *Libyan Studies* 16, 51–65

Leahy, A. (ed.) 1990, *Libya and Egypt c. 1300–750 BC*. London: Society for Libyan Studies

Lecointe, Y. 1987, Le Site Néolithique d'El Ghaba: deux années d'activité (1985–86). *Archéologie du Nile Moyen* 2, 69–87

Lefkowitz, M. 1997, *Not out of Africa: How Afrocentrism became an Excuse to Teach Myth as History*. New York: New Republic and Basic Books

Lefkowitz, M. and G. Rogers (eds) 1996, *Black Athena Revisited*. Chapel Hill: University of North Carolina Press

Lenoble, P. 1992, Cônes de déjections archéologiques dans les djebels à cimitières tumulaires proches de Méroé. *Beiträge zur Sudanforschung* 5, 73–91

Lenoble, P. 1999, The Division of the Meroitic Empire and the End of Pyramid Building in the 4th Century AD: an Introduction to Further Excavations of Imperial Mounds in the Sudan, in D. A. Welsby (ed.), *Recent Research in Kushite History and Archaeology. Proceedings of the 8th International Conference for Meroitic Studies*, 157–198. London: British Museum

Lenoble, P. and N. e M. Sharif 1992, Barbarians at the Gates? The Royal Mounds of El Hobagi and the End of Meroë. *Antiquity* 66, 626–635

Lévi-Strauss, C. 1970, *The Raw and the Cooked. Introduction to Science and Mythology* (trans. J. and D. Weightman). London: Jonathan Cape

Lévi-Strauss, C. 1983, *The Way of the Masks*. London: Jonathan Cape

Lévi-Strauss, C. 1987, *Anthropology and Myth. Lectures 1951–1982*. Oxford: Blackwell

Lewicki, T. 1974, *West African Food in the Middle Ages*. Cambridge: CUP

Lhote, H. 1959, *The Search for the Tassili Frescoes: the Rock Paintings of the Sahara* (trans. A. H. Brodrick). London: Hutchinson

Lhote, H. 1973, *A la Découverte des fresques du Tassili*. Paris: Arthaud

Lienhardt, G. 1961, *Divinity and Experience. The Religion of the Dinka*. Oxford: Clarendon

Livingstone, D. 1857, *Missionary Travels and Researches in South Africa*. London: Murray

Livingstone, D. and C. Livingstone [1865] 1971, *Narrative of an Expedition to the Zambesi and its Tributaries; and of the Discovery of Lakes Shirwa and Nyassa, 1858–1864*. New York: Johnson

Lloyd, A. 2000, The Late Period (664–332 BC), in I. Shaw (ed.), *The Oxford History of Ancient Egypt*, 364–394. Oxford: OUP

Lodge, D. 1983, *The British Museum is Falling Down*. Harmondsworth: Penguin

Lorton, D. 1976, The Treatment of Criminals in Ancient Egypt Through the New Kingdom. *Journal of the Economic and Social History of the Orient* 20, 2–64

Lucas, J. O. 1970, *Religions in West Africa and Ancient Egypt*. Apapa: Nigerian National Press

Macadam, M. F. L. 1955, *The Temples of Kawa, Vol. II*. Oxford: OUP

MacDonald, K. C. 1997, Korounkorokalé Revisited: the Pays Mande and the West African Microlithic Technocomplex. *African Archaeological Review* 14, 161–200

MacDonald, K. C. 1998a, Archaeology, Language, and the Peopling of West Africa: a consideration of the evidence, in R. Blench and M. Spriggs (eds), *Archaeology and Language II: Archaeological Data and Linguistic Hypotheses*, 33–66. London: Routledge

MacDonald, K. C. 1998b, Before the Empire of Ghana: Cattle and the Origins of Cultural Complexity in the Sahel, in G. Connah (ed.), *Transformations in Africa: Essays on Africa's Later Past*, 71–103. Leicester: Leicester UP

MacDonald, K. C. 2000, The Origins of African Livestock: Indigenous or Imported?, in R. Blench and K. C. MacDonald (eds), *The Origins and Development of African Livestock: Archaeology, Genetics, Linguistics and Ethnography*, 2–17. London: UCL Press

MacDonald, K. C., H. Crawford and F. Y. C. Hung 1995, Prehistory as Propaganda. *Papers from the Institute of Archaeology* 6, 1–10

MacGaffey, W. 1966, Concepts of Race in the Historiography of Northeast Africa. *Journal of African History* 7, 1–17

MacGaffey, W. 1980, African Religions: Types and Generalisations, in I. Karp (ed.), *Explorations in African Systems of Thought*, 301–328. Washington, DC: Smithsonian Institution

Mackay, A. M. 1890, *Alexander Mackay*. London: Hodder and Stoughton

Mackenzie, J. [1871] 1971, *Ten Years North of the Orange River: a Story of Everyday Life and Work among the South African Tribes from 1859–69*. London: Frank Cass

MacMichael, H. 1922, *A History of the Arabs in the Sudan; and some Account of the People who Preceded them and of the Tribes Inhabiting Dárfur*. Cambridge: CUP

Mahachi, G. and W. Ndoro 1997, The Socio-Political Context of Southern African Iron Age Studies with Special Reference to Great Zimbabwe, in G. Pwiti (ed.), *Caves, Monuments and Texts: Zimbabwean Archaeology Today*, 89–108. Uppsala: Uppsala University

Majer, J. 1992, The Eastern Desert and Egyptian Prehistory, in R. Friedman and B. Adams (eds), *The Followers of Horus: Studies Dedicated to Michael Allen Hoffman*, 227–234. Oxford: Oxbow

Mallory, J. P. and D. Q. Adams (eds) 1997, *Encyclopaedia of Indo-European Culture*. Chicago: Fitzroy Dearborn

Mamdani, M. 1996, *Citizen and Subject*. London: James Currey

Mandelbaum, D. 1965, Alcohol and Culture. *Current Anthropology* 6, 281–293

Mann, M. 1986, *The Sources of Social Power, Volume 1. A History of Power from the Beginning to AD 1760*, Cambridge: CUP

Mann, M. 1988, *States, War and Capitalism*. Oxford: Blackwell

Maquet, J. 1975, *Africanity: the Cultural Unity of Black Africa*. Oxford: OUP

Marcus, J. and G. M. Feinman 1998, Introduction, in G. M. Feinman and J. Marcus (eds), *Archaic States*, 3–14. Santa Fe: School of American Research

Maseia, J. R. 1985, Tswana Literature, in B. W. Andrzejewski, S. Pilaszewicz and W. Tyloch (eds), *Literature in African Languages: Theoretical Issues and Sample Survey*, 635–649. Cambridge: CUP

Masonen, P. 2000, *The Negroland Revisited: Discovery and Invention of the Sudanese Middle Ages*. Helsinki: Finnish Academy of Science and Letters

Mauss, M. [1950] 1990, *The Gift* (trans. W. D. Halls). New York: Norton

Mawson, A. N. M. 1991, Bringing What People Want: Shrine Politics among the Agar Dinka. *Africa* 61, 354–369

Mazrui, A. A. 1986, *The Africans: a Triple Heritage*. London: BBC

Mbeki, T. 1998, Inaugural Speech to the South African Parliament, in T. Mbeki, *The Writings of Th. Mbeki*. Capetown: University of Capetown Press

McIntosh, R. J. 1999, Western Representations of Urbanism and Invisible African Towns, in S. K. McIntosh (ed.), *Beyond Chiefdoms: Pathways to Complexity in Africa*, 56–65. Cambridge: CUP

McIntosh, S. K. (ed.) 1999a, *Beyond Chiefdoms: Pathways to Complexity in Africa*. Cambridge: CUP

McIntosh, S. K. 1999b, Pathways to Complexity: an African Perspective, in S. K. McIntosh (ed.), *Beyond Chiefdoms: Pathways to Complexity in Africa*, 1–30. Cambridge: CUP

McIntosh, S. K. and R. J. McIntosh 1980, *Prehistoric Investigations in the Region of Jenné, Mali*. Oxford: British Archaeological Reports

McIntosh, S. K. and R. J. McIntosh 1988, From Stone to Metal: New Perspectives on the Later Prehistory of West Africa. *Journal of World Prehistory* 2, 89–133

McIntosh, S. K. and R. J. McIntosh 1993, Cities without Citadels: Understanding Urban Origins along the Middle Niger, in T. Shaw, P. J. J. Sinclair, B. Andah and A. Okpoko (eds), *The Archaeology of Africa: Food, Metals and Towns*, 622–641. London: Routledge

Meeks, D. 2003, Locating Punt, in D. O'Connor and S. Quirke (eds), *Mysterious Lands*, 53–80. London: UCL Press

Meyerowitz, E. L. A. 1960, *The Divine Kingship in Ghana and Ancient Egypt*. London: Faber and Faber

Miaffo, D. 1977, *Role social de l'autopsie traditionelle chez les Bamileke*. Yaounde: University of Yaounde

Midant-Reynes, B. 2000, *The Prehistory of Egypt. From the First Egyptians to the First Pharaohs* (trans. I. Shaw). Oxford: Blackwell

Mill, J. S. 1850, On the Negro Question. *Fraser's Magazine,* January, 29–30

Miller, C. L. 1985, *Blank Darkness. Africanist Discourse in French*. Chicago: University of Chicago Press

Millet, N. B. 1968, Meroitic Nubia, unpublished PhD thesis, Yale University

Millet, N. B. 1981, Social and Political Organization in Meroe. *Zeitschrift für Ägyptische Sprache und Altertumskunde* 108, 124–141

Mohammed-Ali, A. S. A. 1982, *The Neolithic Period in Sudan, c. 6000–2500 BC*. Oxford: British Archaeological Reports

Momigliano, A. D. 1984, Georges Dumézil and the Trifunctional Approach to Roman Civilization. *History and Theory* 23, 312–330

Moodie, T. D. 1975, *The Rise of Afrikanerdom: Power, Apartheid and the Afrikaner Civic Religion*. Berkeley: University of Los Angeles Press

Moraes Farias, P. F. de 1998, For a Non-Culturalist Historiography of Béninois Borgu, in E. Bossen, C. Hardung and R. Kuba (eds), *Regards sur le Borgou: pouvoir et altérité dans une région Ouest-Africaine*, 39–69. Paris: L'Harmattan

Morkot, R. G. 1994a, Economic and Cultural Exchange between Kush and Egypt, unpublished PhD thesis, University of London

Morkot, R. G. 1994b, The Nubian Dark Age. *Études Nubiennes. Conférence de Genève. Actes du VIIᵉ Congrès International d'Études Nubiennes, 3–8 Septembre 1990*, 45–47

Morkot, R. G. 1995, The Foundations of the Kushite State. A Response to the Paper of László Török, *Actes de la VIIIe Conférence Internationale des Études Nubiennes* 1, 229–242

Morkot, R. G. 1999a, The Origin of the 'Napatan' State. A contribution to T. Kendall's main paper, in *Studien zum Antiken Sudan. Akten der 7. Internationalen Tagung für Meroitistische Forschungen vom 14 bis 19 September 1992 in Gosen/bei Berlin*, 139–148. Berlin: Akademie

Morkot, R. G. 1999b, Kingship and Kinship in the Empire of Kush, in *Studien zum Antiken Sudan. Akten der 7. Internationalen Tagung für Meroitistische Forschungen vom 14 bis 19 September 1992 in Gosen/bei Berlin*, 179–229. Berlin: Akademie

Morkot, R. G. 2000, *The Black Pharaohs. Egypt's Nubian Rulers*. London: Rubicon

Morkot, R. G. 2001, Egypt and Nubia, in S. E. Alcock, T. N. D'Altroy, K. D. Morrison and C. M. Sinopoli (eds), *Empires. Perspectives from Archaeology and History*, 227–251. Cambridge: CUP

Morkot, R. G. and S. Quirke 2001, Inventing the 25th Dynasty: Turin Stela 1467 and the Construction of History, in C. B. Arnst, I. Hafemann and A. Lohwasser (eds), *Begegnungen. Antike kulturen im Niltal. Festgabe für Erika Endesfelder, Karl-Heinz Priese, Walter Friedrich Reineke, Steffen Wenig von Schülern und Mitarbeiten*, 349–363. Leipzig: Helmar Wodtke und Katharina Stegbauer

Mudimbe, V. Y. 1988, *The Invention of Africa: Gnosis, Philosophy and the Order of Knowledge*. London: James Currey

Müller, K. O. 1820–1824, *Geschichten hellenischer stämme und städte*. Breslau: Orchomenos die Minyer

Murdock, G. P. 1959, *Africa: its Peoples and their Cultural History*. New York: McGraw-Hill

Murnane, W. J. 1987, The Gebel Sheikh Suleiman Monument: Epigraphic Remarks. *Journal of Near Eastern Studies* 46, 282–285

Murray, O. 1980, *Early Greece*. Cambridge, Mass: Harvard UP

Muzzolini, A. 1995, *Les Images rupestres du Sahara*. Toulouse: Alfred Muzzolini

Naville, E. n. d., *The Temple of Deir el-Bahari III*. London: Kegan Paul

Neumann, K. 1999, Early Plant Food Production in the West African Sahel: New Evidence, in M. Van der Veen (ed.), *The Exploitation of Plant Resources in Ancient Africa*, 73–80. New York: Kluwer

Nicholson S. E. 1998, Historical Fluctuations of Lake Victoria and other Lakes in the Northern Rift Valley of East Africa, in J. T. Lehman (ed.), *Environmental Change and Response in East African Lakes*, 7–36. London: Kluwer

Nyerere, J. K. 1973, *Freedom and Development*. Oxford: OUP

O'Connor, D. 1982, Appendix: the Toponyms of Nubia and of Contiguous Regions in the New Kingdom, in J. Clark (ed.), *The Cambridge History of Africa Vol. 1: From the Earliest Times to c. 500 BC*, 925–940. Cambridge: CUP

O'Connor, D. 1983, New Kingdom and Third Intermediate Period, 1552–664 BC, in B. Trigger, B. Kemp, D. O'Connor and A. Lloyd, *Ancient Egypt: A Social History*, 183–278. Cambridge: CUP

O'Connor, D. 1986, The Locations of Yam and Kush and their Historical Implications. *Journal of the American Research Center in Egypt* 23, 27–50

O'Connor, D. 1987, The Location of Irem. *Journal of Egyptian Archaeology* 73, 99–136

O'Connor, D. 1989, City and Palace in New Kingdom Egypt. *Cahier de recherches de l'Institut de Papyrologie et d'Egyptologie de Lille, Sociétés Urbaines en Égypte et au Soudan* 11, 73–87

O'Connor, D. 1990, The Nature of Tjemhu: (Libyan) Society in the Later New Kingdom, in A. Leahy (ed.), *Libya and Egypt c. 1300–750 BC*. London: Society for Libyan Studies

O'Connor, D. 1991a, Early States Along the Nubian Nile, in W. K. Davies (ed.), *Egypt and Nubia: From Prehistory to Islam*, 145–165. London: British Museum Press

O'Connor, D. 1991b, Mirror of the Cosmos: The Palace of Merenptah, in E. Bleiberg and R. Freed (eds), *Fragments of a Shattered Visage: The Proceedings of the International Symposium on Ramesses the Great*, 167–198. Memphis: Memphis State University

O'Connor, D. 1993, *Ancient Nubia: Egypt's Rival in Africa*. Philadelphia: University of Pennsylvania Press

O'Connor, D. 1995, Beloved of Maat, the Horizon of Re: The Royal Palace in New Kingdom Egypt, in D. O'Connor and D. Silverman (eds), *Ancient Egyptian Kingship*, 263–300. Leiden: Brill

O'Connor, D. 2003, Egypt's Views of 'Others', in J. Tait (ed.), *'Never had the like occurred': Egypt's view of its past*, 155–186. London: UCL Press

O'Connor, D. forthcoming, The Eastern High Gate: Sexualized Architecture at Medinet Habu?, in *Festschrift for Dieter Arnold*

O'Connor, D. and S. Quirke 2003a, Introduction: Mapping the Unknown in Ancient Egypt, in D. O'Connor and S. Quirke (eds), *Mysterious Lands*, 1–22. London: UCL Press

O'Connor, D. and S. Quirke (eds) 2003b, *Mysterious Lands*. London: UCL Press

O'Connor, D. and A. Reid (eds) 2003, *Ancient Egypt in Africa*. London: UCL Press

O'Connor, D. and D. P. Silverman (eds) 1995, *Ancient Egyptian Kingship*. Leiden: Brill

Obayemi, A. 1985, The Yoruba and Edo-Speaking Peoples and their Neighbors before 1600 AD, in J. F. A. Ajayi and M. Crowder (eds), *History of West Africa*, 255–322. London: Longman

Obenga, T. 1981, Sources and Specific Techniques used in African History: General Outline, in J. Ki-Zerbo (ed.), *UNESCO General History of Africa Volume I*, 72–86. California: Heinemann

Obenga, T. 2001, *Le Sens de la lutte contre l'Africanisme eurocentriste*. Paris: L'Harmattan

Oliver, R. and B. M. Fagan 1975, *Africa in the Iron Age*. Cambridge: CUP

Oliver, R. and J. D. Fage 1962, *A Short History of Africa*. Harmondsworth: Penguin

Oliver, R. and J. D. Fage 1988, *A Short History of Africa*. 6th edition, Harmondsworth: Penguin

Oyelaran, P. 1998, Early Settlement and Archaeological Sequence of the Northeast Yorubaland. *African Archaeological Review* 15, 65–80

Parfitt, T. 1997, *Journey to the Vanished City: the Search for a Lost Tribe of Israel*. London: Phoenix

Patterson, T. C. 1997, *Inventing Western Civilization*. New York: Monthly Review

Perry, W. J. 1923, *The Children of the Sun: a Study in the Early History of Civilization*. London: Methuen

Person, A, M. Dembélé and M. Raimbault 1991, Les Mégalithes de la zone lacustre, in M. Raimbault and K. Sanogo (eds), *Recherches archéologiques au Mali*, 473–510. Paris: Karthala

Petrie, W. M. F. 1905, *A History of Egypt from the XIXth to the XXXth Dynasties*. London: Methuen

Phillipson, D. W. 1993, *African Archaeology*. 2nd edition, Cambridge: CUP

Pikirayi, I. 1993, *The Archaeological Identity of the Mutapa State*. Uppsala: Uppsala University

Polanyi, K. 1968, *Primitive, Archaic and Modern Economies. Essays of Karl Polanyi*. New York: Doubleday

Posener, G. 1960, *De la divinité du pharaon*. Paris: Imprimerie Nationale

Postgate, N. 1995, Royal Ideology and State Administration in Sumer and Akkad, in J. M. Sasson (ed.), *Civilizations of the Ancient Near East, vol. I*, 395–412. New York: Scribner

Pradelles de Latour, C-H. 1991, *Ethnopsychanalyse en pays Bamileke*. Paris: École Lacanienne de Psychanalyse

Prakash, G. (ed.) 1995, *After Colonialism. Imperial Histories and Postcolonial Displacements*. Princeton: Princeton UP

Pwiti, G. 1996, *Continuity and Change, An Archaeological Study of Farming Communities in Northern Zimbabwe AD 500–1700*. Uppsala: Uppsala University

Rashidi, R. 1992, *Introduction to the Study of African Classical Civilizations*. London: Karnak

Rawlinson, G. 1881, *History of Ancient Egypt*. London: Longmans, Green and Co

Ray, B. C. 1991, *Myth, Ritual and Kingship in Buganda*. Oxford: OUP

Redfield, R. 1956, *Peasant Society and Culture*. Chicago: University of Chicago Press

Redford, D. B. 1982, A Bronze Age Itinerary in Trans Jordan. *Journal of the Society for the Study of Egyptian Antiquities* 12, 55–74

Reid, A. 1997, Lacustrine States, in J. O. Vogel (ed.), *The Encyclopedia of Precolonial Africa*, 501–507. Walnut Creek: AltaMira

Reid, A. 2001, Cattle, Identity and Genocide in the African Great Lakes Region. *Archaeology International* 4, 35–38

Reinold, J. 1991, Néolithique Soudanais: les coutumes funéraires, in W. V. Davies (ed.), *Egypt and Africa. Nubia from Prehistory to Islam*, 16–29. London: British Museum Press

Reinold, J. 2000, *Archéologie au Soudan. Les Civilisations de Nubie*. Paris: Editions Errance

Reisner, G. A. 1917, Excavations at Napata, the Capital of Ethiopia. *Museum of Fine Arts Bulletin* 15, 25–34

Reisner, G. A. 1918a, Outline of the Ancient History of the Sudan. Part One. *Sudan Notes and Records* 1, 3–15

Reisner, G. A. 1918b, Known and Unknown Kings of Ethiopia. *Museum of Fine Arts Bulletin* 16, 67–82

Reisner, G. A. 1919, Outline of the Ancient History of the Sudan. *Sudan Notes and Records* 2, 35–80

Reisner, G. A. 1921, The Royal Family of Ethiopia. *Museum of Fine Arts Bulletin* 19, 21–38

Reisner, G. A. 1923, *Excavations at Kerma I.* Cambridge, Mass: Harvard UP

Renfrew, C. 1990, *Archaeology and Language: the Puzzle of Indo-European Origins.* Cambridge: CUP

Rilly, C. 2000, Deux examples de décrets oraculaires amelétiques en Méroïtique: les ostraca REM 1317/1168 et REM 1319 de Shokan. *Meroitic Newsletter* 27, 99–118

Roberts, N. 1915, The Bagananoa of MaLaboch: Notes on their Early History, Customs and Creed. *South African Journal of Science* 13, 241–256

Robertshaw, P. T. 1990, The Development of Archaeology in East Africa, in P. T. Robertshaw (ed.), *A History of African Archaeology*, 78–94. London: James Currey

Robertshaw, P. T. 1999, Seeking and Keeping Power in Bunyoro-Kitara, Uganda, in S. K. McIntosh (ed.), *Beyond Chiefdoms: Pathways to Complexity in Africa*, 124–125. Cambridge: CUP

Robertshaw, P. T. and D. Taylor 2000, Climatic Change and the Rise of Political Complexity in Western Uganda. *Journal of African History* 38, 393–421

Roscoe, J. 1923, *The Bakitara.* Cambridge: CUP

Rosellini, I. 1833, *I Monumenti dell'Egitto e della Nubia ... Monumenti storici. Vol. II.* Pisa: Niccolo Capurro

Rosellini, I. 1841, *I Monumenti dell'Egitto e della Nubia ... Monumenti storici. Vol. IV.* Pisa: Niccolo Capurro

Roset, J-P. 1987, Paleoclimatic and Cultural Conditions of Neolithic Development in the Early Holocene of Northern Niger, in A. Close (ed.), *Prehistory of Arid North Africa: Essays in Honor of Fred Wendorf*, 211–234. Dallas: Southern Methodist UP

Roth, A. M. 1991, *Egyptian Phyles in the Old Kingdom: the Evolution of a System of Social Organization.* Chicago: University of Chicago Press

Roth, A. M. 2001, Afrocentrism, in D. B. Redford (ed.), *The Oxford Encyclopedia of Ancient Egypt vol. 1*, 29–32. Oxford: OUP

Rowlands, M. 1994, The Politics of Identity in Archaeology, in G. C. Bond and A. Gilliam (eds), *Social Construction of the Past: Representation as Power*, 129–143. London: Routledge

Rowlands, M. 1998a, The Archaeology of Colonialism, in K. Kristiansen and M. Rowlands (eds), *Social Transformations in Archaeology: Global and Local Perspectives*, 327–333. London: Routledge

Rowlands, M. 1998b, The Embodiment of Sacred Power in the Cameroon Grassfields, in K. Kristiansen and M. Rowlands (eds), *Social Transformations in Archaeology: Global and Local Perspectives*, 410–428. London: Routledge

Rowlands, M. 1999, The Cultural Economy of Sacred Power, in P. Ruby (ed.), *Les Princes de la Protohistoire et l'Émergence de l'État*, 165–172. Rome: École Française de Rome

Rowlands, M. and J. P. Warnier 1993, The Magical Production of Iron in the Cameroon Grassfields, in T. Shaw, P. J. J. Sinclair, B. Andah and A. Okpoko (eds), *The Archaeology of Africa: Food, Metals and Towns*, 512–550. London: Routledge

Rowley-Conwy, P. 1989, Nubia AD 0–550 and the 'Islamic' Agricultural Revolution: Preliminary Botanical Evidence from Qasr Ibrim, Egyptian Nubia. *Archéologie du Nil Moyen* 3, 131–138

Rowley-Conwy, P., W. Deakin and C. H. Shaw 1999, Ancient DNA from Sorghum: the Evidence from Qasr Ibrim, Egyptian Nubia, in M. van der Veen (ed.), *The Exploitation of Plant Resources in Ancient Africa*, 55–62. London: Kluwer

Sadr, K. 1991, *The Development of Nomadism in Ancient Northeast Africa.* Philadelphia: University of Pennsylvania Press

Sahlins, M. 1985, *Islands of History.* Chicago: University of Chicago Press

Said, E. W. 1978, *Orientalism.* London: Routledge and Kegan Paul

Samuel, D. 1996, Archaeology of Ancient Egyptian Beer. *Journal of American Society of Brewing Chemists* 54, 3–12

Samuel, D. 2000, Brewing – Baking, in P. Nicholson and I. Shaw (eds), *Ancient Egyptian Materials and Technology,* 537–576. Cambridge: CUP

Sanders, E. R. 1969, The Hamitic Hypothesis: its Origin and Functions in Time Perspective. *Journal of African History* 10, 521–532

Sanderson, G. N. 1964, Sudan Notes and Records as a Vehicle of Research on the Sudan. *Sudan Notes and Records,* 164–170

Säve-Söderbergh, T. 1946, *The Navy of the Eighteenth Egyptian Dynasty.* Uppsala: Uppsala University

Säve-Söderbergh, T. and L. Troy 1991, *New Kingdom Pharaonic Sites. The Finds and the Sites.* Uppsala: Almsqvist and Wiksell

Scham, S. A. 2003, Ancient Egypt and the Archaeology of the Disenfranchised, in D. Jeffreys (ed.), *Views of Ancient Egypt since Napoleon Bonaparte: imperialism, colonialism and modern appropriations,* 171–178. London: UCL Press

Scheid, J. 1983, G. Dumézil et la méthode experimentale. *Opus* 2, 343–354

Schiffer, M. B. and A. R. Miller 1999, *The Material Life of Human Beings. Artifacts, Behavior, and Communication.* London: Routledge

Schmidt, P. R. 1981, *The Origins of Iron Smelting in Africa: a Complex Technology in Tanzania.* Providence, RI: Brown University

Schmidt, W. 1935, The Oldest Culture-Circles in Asia. *Monumenta Serica* 1, 1–16

Schoenbrun, D. L. 1998, *A Green Place, A Good Place.* Oxford: James Currey

Seligman, C. G. 1913, Some Aspects of the Hamitic Problem in the Anglo-Egyptian Sudan. *Journal of the Royal Anthropological Institute of Great Britain and Ireland* 43, 593–705

Seligman, C. G. 1930, *The Races of Africa.* Oxford: OUP

Seligman, C. G. 1934, *Egypt and Negro Africa: a Study of Divine Kingship.* London: Routledge

Seligman, C. G. and B. Z. Seligman 1932, *Pagan Tribes of the Nilotic Sudan.* London: Routledge and Kegan Paul

Shaw, F. L. S. 1905, *A Tropical Dependency.* London: James Nisbet

Shaw, T. 1971, The Prehistory of West Africa, in J. F. A. Ajayi and M. Crowder (eds), *History of West Africa,* 33–77. London: Longman

Shaw, T. 1977, *Unearthing Igbo-Ukwu.* Ibadan: OUP

Shaw, T. 1981, The Prehistory of West Africa, in J. Ki-Zerbo (ed.), *General History of Africa vol. I,* 611–633. California: Heinemann

Shaw, T. 1985, The Prehistory of West Africa, in J. F. A. Ajayi and M. Crowder (eds), *History of West Africa,* 48–86. 3rd edition, London: Longman

Shaw, T., P. J. J. Sinclair, B. Andah and A. Okpoko (eds), 1993, *The Archaeology of Africa: Food, Metals and Towns.* London: Routledge

Sherratt, A. G. 1986, Cups that Cheered, in W. Waldren and R. Kennard (eds), *Bell Beakers of the Western Mediterranean,* 81–106. Oxford: British Archaeological Reports

Sherratt, A. G. 1997, *Economy and Society in Prehistoric Europe. Changing Perspectives.* Edinburgh: Edinburgh UP

Sherratt, A. G. 1999, Cash-Crops before Cash: Organic Consumables and Trade, in C. Gosden and J. Hather (eds), *The Prehistory of Food,* 13–34. London: Routledge

Shinnie, P. L. 1967, *Meroe: A Civilisation of the Sudan.* London: Thames and Hudson

Shinnie, P. L. 1996, *Ancient Nubia.* London: Kegan Paul

Sinclair, P. J. J., T. Shaw and B. Andah 1993, Introduction, in T. Shaw, P. J. J. Sinclair, B. Andah and A. Okpoko (eds), *The Archaeology of Africa: Food, Metals and Towns*, 1–31. London: Routledge

Smith, A. B. 1986, Cattle Domestication in North Africa. *African Archaeological Review* 4, 197–203

Smith, A. B. 1992, *Pastoralism in Africa: Origins and Development Ecology*. London: Hurst

Smith, G. E. 1923, *The Ancient Egyptians and the Origins of Civilization*. London: Harper

Smith, G. E. 1933, *The Diffusion of Culture*. London: Watts

Smith, G. E. and F. W. Jones 1910, *The Archaeological Survey of Nubia, Report for 1907–1908, vol. II*. Cairo: Government Printing Department

Smith, R. S. 1976, *Kingdoms of the Yoruba*. London: Methuen

Smith, W. S. 1998, *The Art and Architecture of Ancient Egypt*. Revised by W. K. Simpson, New Haven: Yale UP

Smith, W. S. and W. K. Simpson 1981, *The Art and Architecture of Ancient Egypt*. Harmondsworth: Penguin

Snape, S. 2003, The Emergence of Libya on the Horizon of Egypt, in D. O'Connor and S. Quirke (eds), *Mysterious Lands*, 93–106. London: UCL Press

Snowden, F. 1983, *Before Color Prejudice. The Ancient View of Blacks*. Cambridge, Mass: Harvard UP

Sommer, G. 1992, A Survey of Language Death in Africa, in M. Brenzinger (ed.), *Language Death: Factual and Theoretical Explanations with Special Reference to East Africa*, 301–417. Berlin: Mouton de Gruyter

Southall, A. 1956, *Alur Society*. Cambridge: CUP

Southall, A. 1988, The Segmentary State in Africa and Asia. *Comparative Studies in Society and History* 30, 52–82

Southall, A. 1999, The Segmentary State and the Ritual Phase in Political Economy, in S. K. McIntosh (ed.), *Beyond Chiefdoms: Pathways to Complexity in Africa*, 31–38. Cambridge: CUP

Spaulding, J. 1979, Farmers, Herdsman and the State in Rainland Sennar. *Journal of African History* 20, 329–347

Spaulding, J. 1985, *The Heroic Age in Sennar*. East Lansing: Michigan State University

Spaulding, J. and L. Kapteijns 1991, The Orientalist Paradigm in the Historiography of the Late Precolonial Sudan, in J. O'Brien and W. Roseberry (eds), *Golden Ages, Dark Ages*, 139–151. California: University of California Press

Speke, J. H. 1863, *Journal of the Discovery of the Source of the Nile*. Edinburgh: Blackwood

Spencer, A. J. 1993, *Early Egypt. The Rise of Civilization in the Nile Valley*. London: British Museum Press

Spencer, P. 1998, *The Pastoral Continuum. The Marginalization of Tradition in East Africa*. Oxford: Clarendon

St John, R. B. 2000, Libya in Africa: Looking Back, Moving Forward. *Journal of Libyan Studies* 1, 18–32

Stanley, H. M. 1878, *Through the Dark Continent*. London: Sampson Low, Marston and Co

Stanley, H. M. 1890, *In Darkest Africa*. London: Sampson Low, Marston, Searle and Rivington

Stanley, H. M. 1899, *Through the Dark Continent*. London: George Newnes

Stein, B. 1998, *A History of India*. Oxford: Blackwell

Sterner, J. 1992, Sacred Pots and Symbolic Reservoirs, in J. Sterner and N. David, *The African Commitment*, 171–80. Calgary: University of Calgary Press

Sutton, J. E. G. 1974, The Aquatic Civilization of Middle Africa. *Journal of African History* 15, 527–546

Sutton, J. E. G. 1977, The African Aqualithic. *Antiquity* 51, 25–34

Sutton, J. E. G. and A. Reid forthcoming, *Ntusi: a Pastoral and Agricultural Center of the Mid-Iron Age in Western Uganda*. Nairobi: British Institute in Eastern Africa

Tait, J. 2003, The Wisdom of Egypt: Classical Views, in P. J. Ucko and T. C. Champion (eds), *The Wisdom of Egypt: changing visions through the ages*, 23–38. London: UCL Press

Tambiah, S. J. 1990, *Magic, Science and Religion and the Scope of Rationality.* Cambridge: CUP

Tanner, J. 2003, Finding the Egyptian in Early Greek Art, in R. Matthews and C. Roemer (eds), *Ancient Perspectives on Egypt*, 115–144. London: UCL Press

Tantala, R. L. 1989, The Early History of Kitara in Western Uganda: Process Models of Religious and Political Change, unpublished PhD thesis, University of Wisconsin at Madison

Taylor, G. 1927, *Environment and Race: a Study of the Evolution, Migration, Settlement, and Status of the Races of Man.* Oxford: OUP

Thabit, T. H. 1959, International Relations of the Sudan in Napatan Times. *Sudan Notes and Records* 40, 19–22

Thirlwall, C. 1835, *A History of Greece. Vol. I.* London: Longman

Togola, T. 1996, Iron Age Occupation in the Mema Region, Mali. *African Archaeological Review* 13, 91–110

Topozada, Z. 1988, Les Deux campagnes d'Amenhotep III en Nubie. *Bulletin de l'Institut Français d'Archéologie Orientale du Caire* 88, 153–165

Török, L. 1976, Comment to Adams, in W. Y. Adams, *Meroitic North and South. A Study in Cultural Contrasts*, 95–102. Berlin: Akademie

Török, L. 1978, Two Meroitic Studies: The Meroitic Chamber in Philae and the Administration of Nubia in the 1st to 3rd Centuries. *Oikumene* 2, 217–237

Török, L. 1979, *Economic Offices and Officials in Meroitic Nubia.* Budapest: Schiff-Giorgini

Török, L. 1980, To the History of the Dodekaschoenos between 250 BC and 298 AD. *Zeitschrift fur Ägyptische Sprache und Altertumskunde* 107, 76–86

Török, L. 1984, Economy and Empire in Kush: A Review of the Written Evidence. *Zeitschrift fur Ägyptische Sprache und Altertumskunde* 111, 45–69

Török, L. 1987, The Historical Background: Meroe, North and South, in F. Hintze (ed.), *Meroitische Forschungen 1980*, 139–229. Berlin: Akademie

Török, L. 1988, *Late Antique Nubia.* Budapest: Archaeological Institute of the Hungarian Academy of Sciences

Török, L. 1989, Kush and the External World, in S. Donadoni and S. Wenig (eds), *Studia Meroitica 1984*, 49–215. Berlin: Akademie

Török, L. 1992, Ambulatory Kingship and Settlement History: A Study on the Contribution of Archaeology to History. *Cahier de recherches de l'Institut de Papyrologie et d'Egyptologie de Lille* 17, 111–126

Török, L. 1995a, The Emergence of the Kingdom of Kush and her Myth of the State in the First Millennium BC. *Cahier de recherches de l'Institut de Papyrologie et d'Égyptologie de Lille* 17, 203–228

Török, L. 1995b, The Birth of an Ancient African Kingdom. Kush and her Myth of the State in the First Millennium BC. *Cahier de recherches de l'Institut de Papyrologie et d'Egyptologie de Lille*, supplement 4

Török, L. 1997a, *Meroe City. An Ancient African Capital.* London: Egypt Exploration Society

Török, L. 1997b, *The Kingdom of Kush. Handbook of the Napatan-Meroitic Civilization.* Leiden: Brill

Török, L. 1999a, The Origin of the Napatan State. The Long Chronology of el Kurru. *Studien zum Antiken Sudan*, 149–159. Berlin: Harrassowitz

Török, L. 1999b, On the Foundations of Kingship Ideology in the Empire of Kush. *Studien zum Antiken Sudan*, 273–287. Berlin: Harrassowitz

Toynbee, A. 1934–1961. *A Study of History.* Oxford: OUP

Treinen-Claustre, F. 1982, *Sahara et Sahel à l'age du fer, Borkou, Tchad.* Paris: Société des Africanistes

Trevor-Roper, H. 1963, The Rise of Christian Europe: the Great Recovery. *The Listener and BBC Television Review* vol. lxx, no. 1809 (Thursday 28 November), 871–875

Trigger, B. G. 1965, *History and Settlement in Lower Nubia*. New Haven: Yale UP

Trigger, B. G. 1976a, *Nubia under the Pharaohs*. London: Thames and Hudson

Trigger, B. G. 1976b, Comment, in W. Y. Adams, *Meroitic North and South. A Study in Cultural Contrasts*. Berlin: Akademie

Trigger, B. G. 1978a, The Inter-Societal Transfer of Institutions, in *Time and Traditions. Essays in Archaeological Interpretation*, 216–228. New York: Columbia UP

Trigger, B. G. 1978b, The Concept of Community, in *Time and Traditions. Essays in Archaeological Interpretation*, 115–121. New York: Columbia UP

Trigger, B. G. 1982, Reisner to Adams: Paradigms in Nubian Cultural History, in J. M. Plumley (ed.), *Nubian Studies*, 223–226. Warminster: Aris and Phillips

Trigger, B. G. 1983, The Rise of Egyptian Civilization, in B. G. Trigger, B. J. Kemp, D. O'Connor and A. B. Lloyd, *Ancient Egypt: A Social History*, 1–70. Cambridge: CUP

Trigger, B. G. 1993, *Early Civilizations. Ancient Egypt in Context*. Cairo: American University in Cairo Press

Trigger, B. G. and A. Heyler 1970, *The Meroitic Funerary Inscriptions from Arminna West*. New Haven and Philadelphia: Peabody Museum and University Museum

Trowell, M. and K. P. Wachsmann 1953, *Tribal Crafts of Uganda*. Oxford: OUP

Tucker, A. R. 1908, *Eighteen Years in Uganda and East Africa*. London: Edward Arnold

Tutundzic, S. P. 1989, The Problem of Foreign North-Eastern Relations of Upper Egypt, Particularly in Badarian Period: an Aspect, in L. Krzyzaniak and M. Kobusiewicz (eds), *Late Prehistory of the Nile Basin and the Sahara*, 255–260. Poznan: Archaeological Museum

Tyler, J. 1891, *Forty Years Among the Zulus*. Boston and Chicago: Congregational Sunday-School and Publishing Society

Ucko, P. J. 1969, Penis Sheaths: a Comparative Study. *Proceedings of the Royal Anthropological Institute of Great Britain and Ireland*, 27–67

Ucko, P. J. and T. C. Champion (eds) 2003, *The Wisdom of Egypt: changing visions through the ages*. London: UCL Press

Valeri, V. 1994, *Kingship and Sacrifice*. Chicago: University of Chicago Press

Van Sertima, I. 1985, *African Presence in Early Europe*. New Brunswick, NJ: Transaction

Van Sertima, I. 1987, *African Presence in Early America*. New Brunswick, NJ: Transaction

Van Sertima, I. 1995, *Egypt: Child of Africa*. New Brunswick, NJ: Transaction

Van Sertima, I. and L. Williams (eds) 1989, *Great African Thinkers, Volume I, Cheikh Anta Diop*. New Brunswick, NJ: Transaction

Vansina, J. 1984, Western Bantu Expansion. *Journal of African History* 25, 129–145

Vansina, J. 1990, *Paths in the Rainforest: Toward a History of Political Tradition in Equatorial Africa*. Madison: University of Wisconsin Press

Vansina, J. 1994–1995, A Slow Revolution: Farming in Subequatorial Africa. *Azania* 29–30, 15–26

Vansina, J. 1995, New Linguistic Evidence and 'the Bantu Expansion'. *Journal of African History* 36, 173–195

Vantini, G. 1975, *Oriental Sources Concerning Nubia*. Warsaw: Polish Academy of Sciences

Vernet, R. and J. Onrubia-Pintado 1994, La Place des ancêtres des Berbères dans le Sahara Néolithique, in G. Aumassip, N. Ferhat and A. Heddouche (eds), *Milieux, hommes et techniques du Sahara préhistorique*, 53–67. Paris: L'Harmattan

Vine Branch Ministries 2000, *Precious Seeds, a Morning and Evening Christian Devotional*. July–December 2000, Ibadan: Vine Branch Ministries Inc

Vine Branch Ministries 2001, *Precious Seeds, a Morning and Evening Christian Devotional*. July–December 2001, Ibadan: Vine Branch Ministries Inc

Volney, F. C. [1804] 1991, *The Ruins of Empires*. Baltimore: Black Classic

Walker, D. [1829] 1993, *David Walker's Appeal to the Coloured Citizens of the World, but in Particular and very Expressly, to those of the United States of America*. Baltimore: Black Classic

Walker, N. 1997, In the Footsteps of the Ancestors: the Matsieng Creation Site in Botswana. *South African Archaeological Bulletin* 52, 95–104

Ward, J. 1905, *Our Sudan. Its Pyramids and Progress*. London: J. Murray

Warnier, J-P. 1993, *L'Esprit d'entreprise au Cameroun*. Paris: Karthala

Watkins, T. 1990, The Origins of House and Home? *World Archaeology* 21, 336–347

Wayland, E. J. 1934, Notes on the Biggo bya Mugenyi: Some Ancient Earthworks in Northern Buddu. *Uganda Journal* 2, 21–32

Weissleder, W. 1978, Aristotle's Concept of Political Structure and the State, in R. Cohen and E. R. Service (eds), *Origins of the State: the Anthropology of Political Evolution*, 187–203. Philadelphia: Institute for the Study of Human Issues

Welsby, D. A. 1996, *The Kingdom of Kush. The Napatan and Meroitic Empires*. London: British Museum Press

Wendorf, F. and R. Schild 1980, *Prehistory of the Eastern Sahara*. New York: Academic Press

Wendorf, F. and R. Schild 1998, Nabta Playa and its Role in Northeastern African Prehistory. *Journal of Anthropological Archaeology* 17, 97–123

Wengrow, D. 1999, The Intellectual Adventure of Henri Frankfort: a Missing Chapter in the History of Archaeological Thought. *American Journal of Archaeology* 103, 597–613

Wengrow, D. 2001, Rethinking 'Cattle Cults' in Early Egypt: Towards a Prehistoric Perspective on the Narmer Palette. *Cambridge Archaeological Journal* 11, 91–104

Wengrow, D. forthcoming, Comparative Animal Art of the Neolithic Fertile Crescent and Nile Valley: a Long-Term Perspective on Early State Formation, unpublished D Phil thesis, University of Oxford

West, M. L. 1997, *The East Face of Helicon: West Asiatic Elements in Greek Poetry and Myth*. Oxford: OUP

Wetterstrom, W. 1993, Foraging and Farming in Egypt: the Transition from Hunting and Gathering to Horticulture in the Nile Valley, in T. Shaw, P. J. J. Sinclair, B. Andah and A. Okpoko (eds), *The Archaeology of Africa: Food, Metals and Towns*, 165–226. London: Routledge

Wicker, F. D. P. 1990, *Egypt and the Mountains of the Moon*. Braunton, Devon: Merlin

Wiedemann, A. 1884, *Ägyptische Geschichte. 2. Teil: von dem Tode Tutmes' III. bis auf Alexander den Grossen. Handbücher der Alten Geschichte*. Gotha: Friedrich Andreas Perthes

Wilkinson, J. G. 1854, *A Popular Account of the Ancient Egyptians*. New York: Harper

Wilkinson, T. A. H. 1999, *Early Dynastic Egypt*. London: Routledge

Williams, B. B. 1991, *Noubadian X-Group Remains from Royal Complexes in Cemeteries Q and 219 and from Private Cemeteries q, r, v, w, b, j, and m at Qustul and Ballana*. Chicago: Oriental Institute

Willis, R. 1967, The Head and the Loins, Lévi-Strauss and Beyond. *Man* 2, 510–534

Wilson, J. A. 1956, *The Culture of Ancient Egypt*. Chicago: University of Chicago Press

Wilson, J. A. 1960, Egypt through the New Kingdom. Civilization without Cities, in C. H. Kraeling and R. M. Adams (eds), *City Invincible*, 124–164. Chicago: University of Chicago Press

Wilson, P. 1996, Foot Outlines and Inscriptions, in P. Rose (ed.), *Qasr Ibrim. The Hinterland Survey*, 102–110. London: Egypt Exploration Society

Wingate, F. R. 1918, Foreword. *Sudan Notes and Records* 1, 1–2

Wissler, C. 1917, *The American Indian, An Introduction to the Anthropology of the New World.* New York: Douglas C. McMurtie

Wolf, E. 1982, *Europe and the People without History.* Berkeley, Los Angeles: University of California Press

Woodhouse, J. 1998, Iron in Africa: Metal from Nowhere, in G. Connah (ed.), *Transformations in Africa: Essays on Africa's Later Past*, 160–185. Leicester: Leicester UP

Woolley, C. L. and D. Randall-MacIver 1910, *Karanog. The Romano-Nubian Cemetery.* Philadelphia: University of Pennsylvania Press

Wright, K. I. 2000, The Social Origins of Cooking and Dining in early Villages of Western Asia. *Proceedings of the Prehistoric Society* 66, 1–33

Wrigley, C. C. 1996, *Kingship and State.* Cambridge: CUP

Young, R. A. [1829] 1972, The Ethiopian Manifesto, Issued in Defense of the Black Man's Rights in the Scale of Universal Human Freedom, in S. Stuckey (ed.), *The Ideological Origins of Black Nationalism*, 37–38. Boston: Beacon

Yurco, F. J. 1996, Black Athena: An Egyptological Review, in M. Lefkowitz and G. Rogers (eds), *Black Athena Revisited*, 62–102. Chapel Hill: University of North Carolina Press

Yurco, F. J. 2001, Egypt and Nubia: Old, Middle, and New Kingdom Eras, in E. M. Yamauchi (ed.), *Africa and Africans in Antiquity*, 28–112. East Lansing: Michigan State UP

Zachernuk, P. S. 1994, Of Origins and Colonial Order: Southern Nigerian Historians and the 'Hamitic Hypothesis' c. 1870–1970. *Journal of African History* 35, 427–455

Zauzich, K-Th. 1999, Zwei orakelbitten aus Qasr Ibrim. *Enchoria* 25, 178–182

Zeissl, H. von. 1944, *Äthioper und Assyrer in Ägypten. Beiträge zur geschichte der Ägyptischen "Spätzeit".* Hamburg: Augustin

Zeuner, F. E. 1954, Domestication of Animals; Cultivation of Plants, in C. Singer, E. J. Holmyard, A. R. Hall and T. I. Williams (eds), *A History of Technology*, 327–375. Oxford: OUP

Index

Libyan elements in its cultural
development 156, 158–159; milk diet **10:4**,
149; noble savage histories 160; Nuri royal
cemetery 156; racist interpretations of 156;
royal burials **11:2**, **11:3**, 151, 153, 156, 157;
royal succession 163–164, 168; royal
women, portrayals of **10:3**, 149; state
origins 151, 153, 155, 158–159, 160–161, 172;
textual sources 153; *see also* Meroitic
Kingdom, Nubia

Naqada: cereal production, introduction of
129

Ndebele: *see* Nguni

Necho II: circumnavigation of Africa 17

Nigeria: Christian teaching's hostility to
Ancient Egypt 90–91; Hamitic Hypothesis
87; *see also* Yoruba

Nile: minima **5:9**, 56, 57, 58, 75; source of,
search for 56, 110

Nimrod: myth of 84, 85

Nkrumah, K. 39

North, J.: Ancient Egyptians, colour of 11

Nubia: Africa, relationship with 169, 172;
agricultural origins 143, 147; alcohol, ritual
uses of 146; amphorae 146; Ancient Egypt,
contacts with 12, 14, 15, 41, 101, 103, 104,
141, 146, 151; Ancient Egyptian cultural
forms, adoption of 170–171, 178, 179, 183;
Arabicization and the rejection of alcohol
147; artistic portrayals of **1:2**, 13; beer and
work 144–145; beer consumption 143–144;
bread consumption 147; cattle herds 148–
149; cereal production, origins 143; copper,
cultural value of 147; culinary traditions
143–144, 145, 146, 147, 183; cultural
distinctiveness of 16, 17, 141, 142, 147–148,
150; drinking, material culture of 146;
drinking, social roles of 144–145, 146;
eating, social roles of 146; Egyptian
domination 151; Egyptianization 16, 17;
elite culture 146; imported wine 146;
libations 146; marginalization of 168;
merissa beer 143, 145; metal drinking
vessels 146; millet production 145; Napatan
Meroitic Kingdom 15, 16, 17; Nubian
archaeology 138, 139, 140; pastoralism 148–
149; sacrifice 149; sorghum cultivation 142,
143, 145; state formation 128; wheat,
adoption of 147; wine, import of 146; *see
also* Kush, Meroitic Kingdom, Sudan

Nubian Museum 140

Nubian Studies: Egyptological bias 138–140,
152, 172

Nuer: drinking, social role of 145; millet,
social role of 145; residential mobility 131;
sacrifice 42

Nuri: Napatan royal cemetery 156

Nyerere, Julius 39; Ancient Egypt, negative
view of 10; *Ujamaa* policy 10

Ogolian hyper-arid 96, 97

Ophir 115

Orientalism 122, 140

Osorkon: Theban rebellions 164, 165

palaces: cosmological references of 20–21

pastoralism: Badarian 129; colonialism,
impact of 131; Great Lakes 66, 67, 73;
marginalization of in archaeological
thought 130–131; Middle Nile 148–149;
neolithic 129–130; Nubia 148–149;
residential mobility 130–131; shrines of 132;
Sudan 129–130, 148–149; Trans-Saharan
Pastoral Complex 104

Perry, W. J. 41

Peul: Ancient Egyptian origins 95

pharaohs 124–125; African chieftainship,
relationship to 19, 53–54, 87–89; divine
containment in royal ceremony 20; divine
kingship 20; kingship as the embodiment
of sacred power 125; palaces, cosmological
references of 20–21; potency, symbolism of
53; sexuality, symbolism of 53

Philae: Meroitic inscriptions 176, 177

Phoenicians: Ancient Greece, cultural
influence on 31; denial of their cultural
achievements 26, 27

Piankh 154, 156

Piye 160; burial of **11:2**, **11:3**, 151, 157;
conquest of Egypt 159, 169, 172; Libya,
conflict with 153

post-processualism: autochthonism of 39

prestige goods economy: Meroitic Kingdom
174, 178, 183

primary horticultural community 133–134

processualism: autochthonism of 39

Pselchis: temple inscriptions 176

Ptolemy IV 176, 177

Punt: artistic portrayals of **1:3**, **10:3**, 13, 149;
Egyptian contacts 12, 15, 101; location of
12–13; Queen of Punt, portrayal of **10:3**, 149

pygmies: Harkhuf's acquisition of 101